For

☞ Ethnography

$\bigcirc$SAGE | **50** YEARS

SAGE was founded in 1965 by Sara Miller McCune to support the dissemination of usable knowledge by publishing innovative and high-quality research and teaching content. Today, we publish more than 750 journals, including those of more than 300 learned societies, more than 800 new books per year, and a growing range of library products including archives, data, case studies, reports, conference highlights, and video. SAGE remains majority-owned by our founder, and on her passing will become owned by a charitable trust that secures our continued independence.

Los Angeles | London | Washington DC | New Delhi | Singapore

For Ethnography

Paul Atkinson

$SAGE

Los Angeles | London | New Delhi
Singapore | Washington DC

⑤SAGE

Los Angeles | London | New Delhi
Singapore | Washington DC

SAGE Publications Ltd
1 Oliver's Yard
55 City Road
London EC1Y 1SP

SAGE Publications Inc.
2455 Teller Road
Thousand Oaks, California 91320

SAGE Publications India Pvt Ltd
B 1/I 1 Mohan Cooperative Industrial Area
Mathura Road
New Delhi 110 044

SAGE Publications Asia-Pacific Pte Ltd
3 Church Street
#10-04 Samsung Hub
Singapore 049483

Editor: Chris Rojek
Production editor: Sushant Nailwal
Copyeditor: Elaine Leek
Proofreader: Anna Gilding
Indexer: Avril Ehrlich
Marketing manager: Michael Ainsley
Cover design: Lisa Harper-Wells
Typeset by C&M Digitals (P) Ltd, Chennai, India
Printed in Great Britain by
CPI Group (UK) Ltd, Croydon, CR0 4YY

© Paul Atkinson 2015

First published 2015

Apart from any fair dealing for the purposes of research or private study, or criticism or review, as permitted under the Copyright, Designs and Patents Act, 1988, this publication may be reproduced, stored or transmitted in any form, or by any means, only with the prior permission in writing of the publishers, or in the case of reprographic reproduction, in accordance with the terms of licences issued by the Copyright Licensing Agency. Enquiries concerning reproduction outside those terms should be sent to the publishers.

Library of Congress Control Number: 2014948953

British Library Cataloguing in Publication data

A catalogue record for this book is available from the British Library

ISBN 978-1-84920-607-5
ISBN 978-1-84920-608-2 (pbk)

At SAGE we take sustainability seriously. Most of our products are printed in the UK using FSC papers and boards. When we print overseas we ensure sustainable papers are used as measured by the Egmont grading system. We undertake an annual audit to monitor our sustainability.

Contents

About the Author   vi
Acknowledgements   vii

1 Introduction   1

2 The Perspectives of Ethnography   9

3 Fieldwork Commitments   34

4 Analytic Perspectives   55

5 Interaction and the Ceremonial Order   73

6 Accounts and Narratives   92

7 Aesthetics, Artefacts and Techniques   109

8 Structuring Forms   129

9 Representations   153

10 The Ethics of Ethnography   172

11 Conclusions   189

References   197
Index   209

About the Author

Paul Atkinson is Distinguished Research Professor of Sociology at Cardiff University. He is an Academician of the Academy of Social Sciences, a Fellow of the Learned Society of Wales, and a Fellow of the Institute of Welsh Affairs. His books include *Creating Conditions* (with Katie Featherstone), *Everyday Arias: An Operatic Ethnography*, *Contours of Culture* (with Sara Delamont and William Housley), *Interactionism* (with William Housley), *Risky Relations* (with Katie Featherstone, Aditya Bharadwaj and Angus Clarke), *Key Themes in Qualitative Research* (with Sara Delamont and Amanda Coffey).

Acknowledgements

This book reflects the experience of teaching and writing about ethnography over a period of forty years. Along the way I have benefited from the colleagueship of many students and colleagues, at Cardiff and elsewhere. They include Martyn Hammersley, Amanda Coffey, William Housley, Rob Smith, Bella Dicks, Katie Featherstone, Maggie Gregory, Odette Parry, Rachel Hurdley, Corinne Funnell and all the participants in the Cardiff Ethnography Group. I have learned from them all, and indeed from many others. I am especially grateful to Sam Hillyard for her critical and constructive reading of this book in draft. As ever, my greatest debt is to Sara Delamont, the perfect academic and life companion, whose intellectual and personal qualities are a constant inspiration. The shortcomings of the book are, of course, mine alone. As this is something of a personal manifesto, that last statement is especially true. I am also grateful to colleagues at SAGE, for their trust and patience.

1
Introduction

Part of the inspiration for writing this book – or at least for writing in the way I have – was my reading of a volume on the conduct of ethnography by Marcel Mauss, one of the founders of modern anthropology (Mauss 2007). It was never written as a book by Mauss himself: like a number of classics (George Herbert Mead, de Saussure), it is based on a series of lecture courses. Mauss's lectures were delivered at the Institute of Ethnology at the University of Paris. Shorthand lecture notes were taken by Denise Paulme, apparently over several academic years. Although Mauss apparently claimed to have been 'tidying up' the typescript, he did not in fact edit the materials for publication. The published volume therefore bears all the hallmarks of its origins, and is in no sense a finished work. Indeed, Mauss appears not even to have completed the planned series of lectures, as topics identified as coming later in the course never actually appear.

Mauss's lectures have very little in common with anything we would expect today from a textbook on ethnographic research methods, in anthropology or any other discipline. They were in fact created for a very particular kind of audience: 'The instructions in the present book are intended for administrators or colonists who lack professional training' (p. 11). The chapters (lectures) provide systematic, structured guidance, therefore, for the collection of ethnographic facts and artefacts: there is a strong emphasis on assembling the 'archives' of what are referred to as archaic societies. It is a sign of the book's vintage that Mauss is, of course, quite comfortable with the notion that his focus is on 'archaic' societies that fall within the French colonial ambit. (He thus excludes what he refers to as genuinely 'primitive' peoples, who are presumed to lack much of the cultural inventory that provides his stock-in-trade.) The lectures seem like rather dry lists of categories about which the ethnographer ought to collect evidence.

Mauss would certainly not prove a vade mecum for the discerning ethnographer in today's academic world. But embedded within it, and informing it, are two of Mauss's abiding preoccupations: systems of classification, and systems of technique. The typologies of artefacts and events reflect more than simply a 'butterfly collecting' mentality. It reflects one of Mauss's most significant contributions to anthropological and sociological thought. His work on classification, co-authored with Emile Durkheim in *Primitive Classification*, is one of the most significant works to emerge from that tradition. It established a style of thought that permeated various forms of French anthropology and sociology, through Claude Lévi-Strauss to Pierre Bourdieu. Amongst Mauss's other works, it is to be found in his discussion of Eskimo culture and its temporal cycles. Likewise, his interest in *techniques* – which is embedded in the *Manual of Ethnography*. Mauss's analysis of technique became well known through the translation of his essay 'Les techniques du corps' and its incorporation into recent work on the sociology of the body. This was not a one-off interest in the body alone, even though in his *Manual*, you will glimpse his fascination with the management of the body. The ethnographic observer is enjoined to record the body at rest, asleep, at work, at play and so on. But the notion of technique is a generic one: it refers to the use of material resources (the body, tools, materials) to accomplish culturally defined tasks: see also Mauss (2006) on the significance of technique. I have tried to take general inspiration from Mauss, while applying it to the proliferation of research methods that have emerged in the years since his Paris lectures.

In essence, my argument is as follows. There has been an explosion of research methods texts. Many of them deal with qualitative research methods. Many of those deal with ethnographic fieldwork. I have contributed to that methodological literature myself. The student or novice researcher cannot want for general advice about how to conduct her or his research project. Texts will take the student reader through all the steps of a normal project, from negotiating access to the field, through the management of social relations in the field, the methods and procedures of data collection, to the methods of data analysis and the conventions of ethnographic reportage. More detailed and specific methods of data collection may also be dealt with, and the latter are also the subject-matter of individual methods books. On the other hand, it is far from clear to me that the standard methods books give the novice (or indeed the more experienced fieldworker) much clue as to what to look at and what to look for.

It is my contention that we can readily identify some general phenomena, some generic social processes, that repay close and systematic attention in the conduct of ethnographic field research, in the same spirit as Mauss's identification of broad ethnographic themes. Of course, Mauss was not the first or the only anthropologist to suggest what anthropologists ought to look for or look at, what they ought to explore with informants, or to collect by way of materials culture. But he was certainly one of the most imaginative and gifted in his own analyses of culture and social process. In the course of this book – which is by no means comprehensive I freely admit – I want to follow the precepts of Marcel Mauss, suggesting some of the most fruitful ways of looking at and thinking about any given social world.

Before we embark on more technical matters, let us start this book on a thoroughly positive note. Ethnographic fieldwork is not just *a* way to conduct social research. It is a very special way. It is, if not *the* way, a distinctive way of knowing and being as a social scientist (Halstead et al. 2008). It is immensely satisfying personally and intellectually. It provides uniquely privileged opportunities to enter into and to share the everyday lives of other people. It provides us with the challenge of transforming that social world into texts and other forms of representation that analyse and reconstruct those distinctive lives and actions. Methodological and epistemological niceties aside, and quite apart from the principles outlined later in this book, the conduct of ethnographic fieldwork is the most rewarding and most faithful way of understanding the social world. It is an approach to research that deserves to be accorded a special place. It is worth stressing these things, because when we start to get into methodological and other issues, it is all too easy to get bogged down in arcane disputes and to lose sight of the intrinsic curiosity that drives us all to conduct first-hand, field research.

In the current climate, that may sound like a superfluous assertion. Surely, qualitative research methods have never been so popular and widespread. Surely, such research methods are now widely endorsed. But therein lies a problem. While 'qualitative research' is hugely fashionable and popular in many disciplines, that is not to be equated with ethnography. Now I do not want to attach a quasi-religious or mystical value to ethnographic research. But I do want to remind us that there is a world of difference between a commitment to long-term field research – spending time in one or more social settings, with a number of people as they go about their everyday lives – and the conduct of a few interviews or focus groups. The latter are 'qualitative' but they are certainly not ethnographic.

It has become increasingly apparent that the term 'ethnography' is appropriated by and for research that is nothing of the kind. So while I do not want to fetishise such things, I do insist on ethnographic fieldwork that involves some degree of direct participation and observation, and that it constitutes a radically distinctive way of understanding social activity *in situ*. Hence my repeated use of old-fashioned terms like *fieldwork*. In doing so I do not make the assumption that 'fields' are simple things, or that they exist unproblematically as bounded entities. Nor do I suggest that they cannot be distributed across multiple physical sites, nor indeed that they may in today's world be virtual rather than material. What I do insist on is that we ought always to conduct fieldwork in settings wherever and however they are brought into being by social actors who collectively engage in their production. Equally, I am not so naïve as to overlook the extent to which fields are also produced by our own activities of fieldwork. Indeed, the reasons I like the old-fashioned term are twofold: first, it reminds us that it *is* work, and not a reflection of personal virtue or innate quality; secondly, it also reminds us that the 'fields' of fieldwork are themselves worked at, and are produced through such work. In turn, we are also reminded that work in this context involves mental work, but it also calls for physical and emotional work too. We have to work at our engagement and our participation, as well as working with the social actors whose lives we want to share and understand.

Hence, for all the merits of interviews, documentary analysis and the like, and for all the rich variety of qualitative research that is currently being conducted, and all the methodological innovations that are being explored, an old-fashioned approach to ethnographic fieldwork lies at the heart of this book. This is not an old-fogey nostalgia for an invented tradition, or a rejection of current methods and approaches. Indeed I want to stress the many and varied ways in which ethnography can be done, the extraordinary variety of data that can be generated, and to celebrate some of the technologies available to do so. So the book looks back, in asserting some of the abiding virtues of ethnographic research. But it also pays due regard to contemporary issues of data collection, analysis and representation. My approach, however, is predicated on the view that the contemporary appeal of ethnographic research needs to be grounded firmly in its traditional values. We overlook our origins at our peril, and too many contemporary commentators find novelty where there is none, revealing nothing new but a collective ignorance of the past.

Ethnography shares a distinctive way of knowing that aligns it with contemporary cultural sensitivities more widely. The visual arts, cultural studies, sociology and anthropology all share an ethnographic focus on local sites of social relations and cultural forms (Foster 1995). They include: a close attention to the particularities of social life; an equally close attention to the forms of their representation; the reflexive attention to the productive work of the artist, writer and ethnographer; an awareness of the work of biographical and autobiographical construction. The ethnographic gaze captures and calls into question the tensions between the self and the other, between the near and the distant, between the familiar and the strange. It is not new. It is as old, in general terms, as human curiosity and the encounter between the writer and an 'other'. While having somewhat different connotations, we can detect the ethnographic imagination at work from Antiquity onwards (Evans 2005; Woolf 2011).

There is, therefore, nothing merely fashionable about the conduct of ethnographic research, in the sense of it being of recent origin. It is an approach to professional social research that dates back to the beginning of the last century. Of course, as a distinctively human response to encounters with new peoples, places and situations, it is as old as human society itself. It is too often overlaid with all sorts of epistemological and theoretical 'positions' and disputes. To some degree, of course, academic debate and intellectual justifications are unavoidable, but too much is made of them. In the course of this book I want to stress the positive aspects of ethnographic research, offering the reader a wide array of published sources to draw on, and encouraging the pursuit of many topics.

I hope, therefore, that readers will not lose sight of some of the most fundamental issues in ethnographic research. It is far more than a dry methodological topic, or the battleground for competing definitions of research excellence. It is – in anthropology, sociology and other disciplines – born of a thoroughgoing commitment to understanding other people's social worlds. It is a profoundly ethical form of enterprise, based as it is on a commitment to other people's everyday lives. It does not seek to manipulate others for 'scientific' ends. It is a deeply humane undertaking, precisely because it is predicated on the ethnographer's personal commitment, and on the common humanity shared by the researcher and by the researched. It is also a profoundly *social* form of research, in that the researcher is committed to sharing the everyday life of the people with whom she or he does the fieldwork.

In that sense, too, ethnographic field research is – above all other ways of conducting research – faithful to the social world under investigation and the people who make it. It is coterminous with it. Conducted and analysed adequately, it preserves the essential complexity of that world and those lives. It follows the contours of culture and the lines of social organisation. It captures the patterns of significance that make the world comprehensible and meaningful. It follows the dimensions of the everyday – spatial, temporal, interpersonal. It traces the dimensions of culture – material, aesthetic, semiotic. It analyses the language and communication of everyday actors – accounts, memories and interactions.

It is not easy. The methodical exploration, analysis and re-construction of a given social world is a demanding task. It calls for an intellectual discipline to complement those personal commitments already alluded to. It is one of the several aims of this book to engender a disciplined approach to ethnographic fieldwork. We all need prompts and reminders of where to look, what to look at and how to do so. (And by 'looking' I really mean all the senses and modalities of comprehension.) The goal of ethnographic fieldwork is not to amass an inchoate array of personalised impressions and experiences (however illuminating they might be), but to collect and analyse data in the interests of developing systematic conceptual frameworks.

So this book is devoted to fieldwork – in some ways a pleasingly old-fashioned term that evokes the long history of sociological and anthropological work. In the chapters that follow, therefore, I outline some of the basic commitments of ethnographic research. I try to cut through the many different 'ologies' and 'isms' that plague our disciplines, in order to identify common themes, and guiding principles that I believe we might all endorse. It needs emphasis here: I am not endorsing a vague array of 'qualitative' methods. In doing so I deliberately resist many of the recent claims for novelty – especially associated with the claims for postmodernism – that I believe have undermined much of the great ethnographic tradition (Atkinson and Delamont 2004). In the same vein I outline some issues in the conduct of ethnographic field research. For some readers this may be recapitulation of truisms, but for others this re-statement of ethnographic practice may need reaffirmation. A third chapter then discusses the analytic strategies of ethnography, before I devote four major chapters to some of the key issues that ethnographers ought to pay attention to. In other words, these chapters are about key issues that ethnographers need to concentrate on in the development of a sustained and systematic analysis of any social world. In the first of those chapters I focus on the analysis of social encounters. I suggest that we need to be reminded of the centrality of social interaction and the interaction order. This may seem odd, given that social encounters might seem a central concern – notably in interactionist sociology. But there has been so much emphasis on the presentation of individual informants' accounts that we need to remind ourselves that participating in and observing social activities, including interactions, ought to be a central preoccupation. Here I locate one of my main reservations about a great deal of contemporary qualitative research – an emphasis on the interview and a failure to observe forms of interaction. The key analytic point here is that encounters have their own intrinsic order, and that ethnographic analysis must pay full attention to such formal properties. The next three chapters address further formal properties of social life: accounts and narratives; time and space; aesthetics and artefacts. Here the main theme is continued. While by no means a comprehensive listing of analytic issues, together these chapters exemplify the extent to which we need to respect the intrinsic organisation of social phenomena. Hence they carry my fundamental argument: ethnography is not about creating evocative descriptions of personal experience (one's own or others'). It is about the analysis of social action and social organisation.

The book is concluded with two further chapters that deal with contemporary issues of some import for the present and future of ethnography. The first concerns the writing and representation of ethnographic texts. Here I argue that the various over-heated debates concerning the textual representation of ethnography and the identification of successive crises of representation have had a disproportionate effect, while recent excursions into alternative literary forms have displayed a strange paradox. This is a paradox that runs through a great deal of contemporary debate and practice: while there are intellectual appeals to poststructuralism and postmodernism, in effect the proponents of apparently avant-garde literary styles actually reinstate a Romantic subject. Moreover, this subject seems to inhabit a world that is devoid of social and cultural organisation. Finally, I address current debates and vexations concerning the management of research ethics. Here I reaffirm some of the central values of ethnographic fieldwork, while suggesting that a lot of contemporary ethical regulation is sociologically or anthropologically illiterate.

This, then, is not yet another methods book on how to do ethnographic fieldwork. It is, on the other hand, a book on how to think about it. Equally, it is not intended to be a comprehensive introduction to ethnographic methods. It is selective in its themes and their treatment. The introductory chapters outline what might (pompously) be described as a manifesto – hence the title of the book – and they have a polemical aspect to them. They are certainly not intended to be reviews of the literature. Indeed, the reader will find them lightly referenced. The student in search of an elementary guide to the research-methods literature will find such texts elsewhere. I have tried not to hold up the flow of the text with undue numbers of citations. The rest of the chapters draw on a variety of illustrative examples: some come from very recent work, some from more classic studies. The breadth of coverage is deliberate, as I want to emphasise the ethnographic tradition as well as current issues. Also, I have tried to cull illustrative materials from a diverse range of research fields. Too often, it seems to me, authors develop their methodological arguments exclusively from their own field of specialisation, without regard for disciplinary diversity or variation in subject-matter. But if we do that as authors, how are we ever going to encourage our students to think comparatively and to generate ideas that transcend their own narrow field of specialisation?

This book is not a comprehensive guide to the conduct of field research, and it is certainly not intended to be a comprehensive review of all the potentially relevant literature – methodological and substantive. It is highly selective in its coverage, dealing as it does with topics that seem to me to be of particular importance, and selectively illustrated. The attentive reader will notice that there is a degree of repetition here and there. This is not a reflection of careless drafting. Rather, I recognise that books like this are not necessarily read from cover to cover, from start to finish. Readers are likely to read individual chapters, especially if student readers are prescribed particular sections by their instructors. Consequently, there are a few themes that need occasional reiteration in order to maintain the overall tenor of my arguments.

2
The Perspectives of Ethnography

There are many books on the conduct of ethnography, and there are even more on qualitative research in general. In recent years the tag 'qualitative research' seems to have acquired a particular set of connotations, and to have achieved a very special currency, while 'qualitative inquiry' has taken on an even more fashionable set of connotations. Neither is endorsed in this book. One needs a decent justification for adding to that pile of texts. The rationale for this particular book is as follows. There are indeed many methods textbooks. They nearly all try to tell student readers 'how to do it' in terms of the steps and procedures to be gone through in terms of research design, data collection, analysis and writing. Experience suggests, however, that students – and indeed more advanced researchers – can read all the available textbooks, not least those that offer recipes for action in the field, but still be left with little idea of how to proceed. The reason is that there is a huge absence – presumably normally taken for granted by authors and their readers – at the heart of too much of the methodological literature.

In essence, novice ethnographers can spend time 'in the field' but have singularly little idea about what to look for, how to organise their thoughts and reflections and how to structure their ethnographic work. This book aims to provide its readers with precisely that – a strong sense of how to proceed intellectually while engaging in ethnographic fieldwork. To a considerable extent, of course, this means that there is a degree of overlap between the contents of this book and methodological advice about 'analysis'. But we cannot leave a proper understanding of the purpose and content of ethnographic work until a phase of the work called 'analysis'. In ways I shall elaborate on, we need to be engaged in analytic work from the very outset, and in order to do so, we need some general guiding precepts and 'directions along which to look', as Herbert Blumer (1954) called his 'sensitizing ideas'. It is a truism of ethnographic fieldwork that data collection and analysis proceed *pari passu*. In other words, the collection of data is informed by the emergence of potentially rewarding analytic concepts, and in turn fieldwork helps us to extend, develop and refine those concepts. Therefore, one cannot really divorce analytic frameworks from the research process more generally. Equally, one cannot undertake meaningful ethnographic work without a strong sense of the sort of social science one intends to produce. In other words, one needs some robust analytic ideas to guide ethnographic fieldwork. My purpose in writing this book, therefore, is to provide the would-be fieldworker with an array of potentially fruitful ideas and perspectives.

Although this book is not intended to be a practical manual on how to do it (as opposed to how to think about it) I realise that some outline of ethnography's methods is necessary. In introducing the subject-matter of the book, therefore, I shall also introduce some of ethnography's practical requirements. In terms of the day-to-day conduct of ethnographic fieldwork, however, this book should be read alongside my previous contributions to the field (e.g. Hammersley and Atkinson 2007) and equivalent texts (e.g. Delamont 2002, 2014). Likewise, my text with Coffey (Coffey and Atkinson 1996) covers many of the basic issues I would always wish to emphasise on matters of data analysis, as does the later volume on analysis (Atkinson et al. 2008). As I have already suggested, there are many textbooks that outline the general principles and procedures for the practical conduct of ethnographic fieldwork. Others offer a variety of epistemological rationales for such research. Others still advocate particular strategies of data collection or data analysis. The would-be fieldworker is spoiled for choice when it comes to textbook, vade mecum advice. On the other hand, my own experience as a teacher, mentor and editor suggests that this textbook knowledge is deficient. In one sense, of course, it must always be imperfect as a guide to conduct. Ethnographic fieldwork has a number of characteristics that are more or less independent of any particular research site or setting. It is intensely practical, and it is often unpredictable. It is as much a matter of 'craft' knowledge as it is a matter of epistemology or scientific method. (This is not to imply, incidentally, that there are any research strategies that are free of craft practicalities: fieldwork is especially craft-like, however.) On the other hand, it is the case that there are clear problems for novice – and indeed experienced – researchers that escape most of the published manuals of advice and reflection.

The most important thing – and it provides the rationale for the rest of this book – is that many would-be fieldworkers seem to have little sense of what to look for. I do not mean that they just do not know what to 'observe' in any given setting, on any given day of being in the field. I mean that there is a huge gap in our collective literature. We wax lyrical about how to gain access to a given setting, how to establish social relationships with our hosts, how to behave in ethically approved ways and so on. But as to what this 'field' actually consists of, or what the substance of fieldwork might be – these are almost always implicit. Consequently, one modest aim of this book is to provide ethnographers with a sense of content or substance: the sort of social and cultural phenomena they might usefully think about before, during and after fieldwork. Here I have not attempted to review all of the other texts of methodological guidance, preferring to concentrate on outlining my own perspectives and precepts.

These themes will not simply be check-lists of cultural inventories. They will be essentially *analytic* themes, bearing directly on contemporary approaches to ethnographic practice. The latter are, after all, not to be wheeled out only when the fieldwork is over and 'the data' are transformed from an inert heap of notes, transcripts, documents, photographs, maps, sketches, or artefacts. We know that successful and productive fieldwork proceeds not on a linear model of research design, but in a cyclical fashion. The development of analytic themes and ideas is an emergent property of our engagement with the field, and of our systematic reflections on the data. These emergent ideas can then guide further, more focused and directed fieldwork, in turn yielding more detailed or finely tuned analytic ideas. But these analytic ideas do not leap out of the data, they do not hatch out of notebooks, without considerable input from the analyst. Data, irrespective of their physical form, are something to think with and think through. We interact with the data. In doing so, we need to bring ideas *to* the data as well as trying to derive ideas *from* them. But since these ideas are part of the cyclical process of field research it follows that we need to bring ideas to the field. We need, as a minimum, a framework for understanding social worlds, cultural systems and social processes. This might, ultimately, mean that we need a vast amount of education in the social sciences before we embark on any particular ethnographic enterprise. In the ideal world, perhaps, that might be so. But in the real world, practitioners need at least a framework of ideas and perspectives. We all need exemplars to point us in profitable and fruitful directions.

I am motivated by something a bit more thoroughgoing than the need simply to give readers some useful analytic pointers, based on a reaction to contemporary fashions in social research. I am not alone in thinking that there are some profound and widespread problems in contemporary methodological thought and research practice. That can be summed up as a loss of social-scientific imagination, and a divorce of ethnographic research from its disciplinary roots. As a consequence, key features of ethnographic research are being lost to view and need to be re-stated and re-emphasised. There is absolutely no doubt that varieties of 'qualitative' research have become prominent in recent decades. The sheer volume of published research and of methodological texts is remarkable. Although it has become commonplace to complain about the embattlement of qualitative research and the apparent preference for numerical analysis on the part of influentials (such as funding bodies or appointing committees), qualitative research projects – ethnographies among them – are in the ascendant in some of our disciplines, and they have well-established footholds in others. Obviously, social and cultural anthropology remains almost synonymous with ethnographic practice, and 'the ethnography' (such as the resulting published monograph) is the mainstay of the discipline. Indeed, many anthropologists speak and write as if they and they alone undertook such fieldwork. Elsewhere, the emphasis has often been on 'qualitative' research, or 'qualitative inquiry' as it is also becoming known (with connotations that rather take us beyond the scope of this present book). Such research strategies have become widespread in sociology, cultural studies, human geography, education, nursing and healthcare studies, social psychology and indeed the entire spectrum of human, social disciplines.

Unfortunately, in the process, the original inspiration and thrust of ethnographic field research has become diluted. We have lost a number of things. First, we seem to have lost the understanding that the conduct of ethnography involves an intensive period of engagement ('participant observation') in a given social milieu. Too often we discover the studies that have been called 'ethnographic' are nothing of the kind, but are based entirely on interviews, and contain absolutely no engagement with a 'field' of social activity. This is not just a matter of personal commitment or faith. My implied criticism here is not simply that interviews alone represent the easy way out, and are essentially a lazy way of undertaking social research. (As a matter of fact, I do feel that, and I also believe that the increasing use of strategies like focus groups is an even more lazy and superficial way of conducting research.) Rather, the fundamental problem is this: ethnographic fieldwork – in a variety of forms – is essential if we are to grasp a number of basic issues in everyday social life and its routine conduct. These are not matters of choice or style, therefore. I remain committed to the view, as I have been for over forty years, that the conduct of ethnographic work is predicated on a number of key issues. I shall outline them in the following paragraphs.

Before I do so, however, I want to flag what I understand to be the recurrent limitation of too much contemporary qualitative inquiry, enshrined in a number of influential methods textbooks and handbooks, and reflected in many published studies. Because there is an unwarranted emphasis on the collection of personal accounts through interviews, there is far too much emphasis on the collection and interpretation of individual informants' personal experiences, recollections and the like. Indeed, it is too often asserted that the goal of qualitative research is to understand informants' social world from their point of view, or to make sense of their experiences. We may wish to do so, we may even have to do so. But it is not the whole story. This treats the field of research as composed of individuals, and their personal, even private, realms of recollected experience and feeling. Now it is undeniable that phenomena that we can call 'experiences' are a part of everyday social life, and their narrative expression is an important feature of normal social conduct. It is equally the case that 'subjective' states like feelings are also important in the conduct of social life. But they are not the be-all and end-all of social life, nor do they exhaust the phenomena that qualitative research of any stripe might concern itself with. They are certainly not the stuff of ethnography.

In exploring what that social stuff might be, and how we might best study it, I am going to affirm some distinctly old-fashioned precepts. My main goal is to help reverse some of the most recent and fashionable trends in social research, to assert some older and – in my view – more profitable lines of inquiry. In doing so I know that I lay myself open to misinterpretation and even misrepresentation. But I think that it is important to try to redress the balance in favour of some longer-standing commitments and priorities. In general terms, my argument is that we risk losing sight of some elementary concerns in sociology, anthropology and cognate fields. In the fashionable excitement of postmodernism and other 'posts', we have lost sight of the recurrent and elementary issues of social organisation and social order. We have lost sight of the multiple ways in which social conduct is patterned through routine and ritualised methods of conduct. We forget that cultural domains display codes of organisation and of signification. We overlook the many ways in which experience itself is constructed by and through socially shared, culturally prescribed forms.

In other words, we readily lose sight of the principles that are used to organise everyday social life as relatively predictable, stable and comprehensible. The lure of postmodernism too readily leads practitioners to abandon all grasp of the truly *social*. That is, the socially shared practices that make everyday life possible, the shared conventions that render culture comprehensible and the socially distributed competences that enable actors to create everyday life. We lose all sense, if we are not careful, of the regularities and patterns of mundane social activity, of the routines, recipes and rules that help constitute collective action.

Social organisation and social action are at the heart of the ethnographic enterprise, just as they are at the enduring heart of any social science. As I shall make clear, this does not mean a call for completely outmoded accounts of 'structure and function' as generic explanatory schemes. Equally, attention to socially shared competence, practices and conventions does not spell a return to appeals to internalised norms and values in accounting for collective behaviour. We do not have to be unreconstructed structuralists in order to recognise that there are patterns and orders to language and other semiotic modes of communication. There is a degree of stability and predictability in everyday social life that rests on shared conventions and prescriptions, shared systems of significance and collective action.

In other words, I want to direct attention to some of the enduring features of social analysis. I want to insist that an ethnographic stance and a methodical analysis of ethnographic data can still generate insights into a given social world. We can go well beyond the analytic reconstruction of a local social world, in generating generic concepts and formal analyses that transcend the local and the particular. For this is yet another danger that assails qualitative research. There is no doubt that intensive fieldwork can illuminate a social setting, a group, a culture or a milieu in a way that few other approaches can. (Fictional works are often persuasive but lacking in concrete specificity, while journalists' accounts are too often superficial, however engaging.) Ethnographies undoubtedly display the significance of the *local*, the *concrete* and the *practical*; they display the multiple means whereby everyday life is enacted and brought into being in specific settings. But ethnographic analysis need not and should not remain fixed at that local level. We can and should move *between* different versions of local reality, in order to move our analysis to the *generic* level, developing concepts – even models – that capture recurrent features of social life across a range of social situations or cultural domains. This, after all, is the legacy of some of the most influential of writers whose ideas inhabit contemporary ethnographic practice – Erving Goffman, Harvey Sacks, Clifford Geertz, Dorothy Smith – to name but four from very different backgrounds, but who shared a rare ability to move from the small, local, or apparently insignificant to describe social phenomena of widespread relevance. I shall return from time to time to these and other social analysts with a similar ethnographic vision.

Now I realise – as I have acknowledged already – that the perspectives I have just alluded to and that I shall develop as this book proceeds, can be represented as deeply unfashionable. Although one or two authors have claimed to find some of my contributions unhelpfully 'postmodern', I am more likely to be accused of celebrating a view of ethnography that invokes a 'scientific' or even 'positivist' approach that does violence to its essentially interpretative spirit, harking back to a modernist phase of research practice that has been swept away in a tide of postmodernism, postfeminism and postcolonialism. Little could be further from my actual intentions, or even my own research interests and practices. I do not give any credence to the view that prior to a very, very recent collective change of heart and habit, ethnographers were all committed to a view of their enterprise that precisely paralleled the procedures of an experimental science devoted to the production of predictive theories and law-like generalisations. The notion that successive generations of social anthropologists, urban sociologists and criminologists, or cultural analysts were entirely ignorant or insouciant as to the long-standing distinctions between natural-science and the cultural disciplines is risible. It is equally bizarre – and insulting to them – to imply that postwar field researchers like Howard Becker, Blanche Geer or Anselm Strauss were wedded to inappropriately positivist understandings of the sociological enterprise. The problem is that too many contemporary commentators cannot tell the difference between a *methodical* approach to the conduct of fieldwork and data collection, or a *systematic* approach to the analysis of data, and a rigid epistemology that assumes that the natural sciences provide a single model of inquiry. I insist on the difference. In the rush towards various 'post' positions, there has been a harmful rejection of elementary approaches to social research. Unfortunately, the accusation of positivism has become a kind of ritual insult that is applied without due regard for its meaning, or for the actual practices of those it is flung against.

One of the other issues that seems to me to have plagued ethnography and qualitative research more generally in recent years is the search for paradigms or their equivalent. For understandable pedagogical reasons, some authors have been keen to construct typologies of epistemological and theoretical positions to differentiate between varieties of research, research traditions, theoretical schools and the like. In the course of my discussions I shall not be trying to engage with such exercises. This is not because I am incapable of recognising the significance of intellectual traditions, nor because I think that theories are of no importance. I do, however, have a more positive reason for my attitude, as expressed here. I believe that the search for theoretical paradigms by way of justifications for ethnographic research is unhelpful for the most part. By that I do not mean that sociological, anthropological or other *ideas* are unimportant. The themes of this manifesto suggest quite the reverse. But ethnographic research methods – indeed, any social research methods – are not tied inevitably with any particular theoretical perspective. Ethnographic research is far from lacking in theory – either theoretical input or theoretical output. In fact, the generation of ideas is the main goal of ethnographic research, which goes well beyond the mere reconstruction of a single social setting.

But the endless typologising that seeks to separate out symbolic interactionist, ethnomethodological, phenomenological, or similar forms of 'theory' and link them to highly specific forms of inquiry seems spurious in most cases. Rather, I think we should base our research on a broad set of assumptions and findings about the social world, and recognise that the areas of overlap and consensus are much more important and much more prevalent than doctrinal differences that are used to create pettifogging distinctions. Many of the theoretical or epistemological 'positions' that are canvassed are essentially teachers' concepts: devices used to create curricula, methodological training activities and assessment tasks for students. Practical research, which undoubtedly needs to be guided by practical methodological advice, is rarely enhanced by such theoretical niceties. Productive ethnographic research is enhanced by an explicit recognition of a small number of key issues that virtually all field researchers ought to be able to endorse, and that ought to inform their research practice. In the following paragraphs I shall outline what I take to be these primary intellectual commitments. They derive from a variety of perspectives that reflect research perspectives in sociology, anthropology and other cultural disciplines. They are far from random, but they are not presented as components of a variety of 'unified theory'. No particular order or hierarchy of concepts is therefore implied in the following discussion. It will be seen that these ideas reflect an intellectual stance that is sometimes referred to as an 'interpretative' one. And interpretivism is often contrasted with positivism in the standardised textbooks. But I want to avoid using it as an over-arching justification here. These dualisms are often far too crudely drawn, and they become excuses for intellectual laziness. Also, appeals to interpretivism too often rely on rather vague notions of 'meaning'. While there is no doubt that ethnography is concerned with meaningful social action, it is also concerned with more than just what things or events mean to social actors. As I repeatedly emphasise, we are, or should be, preoccupied with forms of social organisation and routines of social action.

Everyday life is skilful

It is one of our fundamental precepts that social actors are *knowledgeable*. This is not an assumption that everybody is well-educated, or that people are equally adept at specialised, esoteric skills. Rather, what this assumes is that all social actors, by virtue of being members of a given cultural community, have a detailed and thorough grasp of the knowledge, rules, conventions and practices that constitute that way of life. People also develop more specialist abilities, on the basis of processes of socialisation and enculturation. We can think of these competences as *techniques*, practical and skilfully deployed.

Everyday life is physical

Social actors have bodies, and their physical presence in the world is an embodied one. Bodies are not only natural but are thoroughly socialised. The body is a means of carrying out the techniques and practices of competent everyday conduct. It is a means of expression. It is also a resource through which ordinary activities get done. Embodied work is one of the means whereby practical activity is accomplished and through which co-ordinated activity is managed. Even the most mundane of physical actions reflects its social basis.

Everyday life is symbolic

Social life is intensely symbolic in that it is rendered meaningful by its social actors. It is enacted through language acts. Social actors use language, in the form of speech acts, accounts, narratives and other spoken performances to conduct social interaction, and to enact rituals and routines of everyday activities. Language is not the only symbolic system. Cultural systems provide social actors with densely coded and richly nuanced systems of semiotics. Meanings are not fixed, in that they are always – in principle – available for redefinition. The fact that meanings are relatively fluid does not mean that language and other symbolic systems are without structure or system themselves, however. Spoken action displays high levels of organisation and structure.

Everyday life is enacted locally

Social order and meaning are produced locally. That does not mean 'local' in a simply geographical or spatial sense, although a strong sense of place is a key element in the construction of everyday social reality. It means, more fundamentally, that social action and social order have to be produced, or improvised in real time, from available cultural resources, collaboratively by social actors. It happens *in situ* and is not simply a reflection of pre-existing social norms and values. The improvisatory nature of social life means that social order is always an emergent property of collaboration and conflict. It is a matter of negotiation: social order is a property of negotiated outcomes.

Everyday life is performed

Social life does not 'just happen', it is *made to happen*. Language acts and practical activities are always enacted or performed. Social actors have a degree of self-consciousness in enacting their social identities. The 'self' is always social, in that it is a property of social encounters and engagements. Equally, phenomena like memories and emotions are enacted. They too are social, based on shared cultural resources; they are not simply private mental states.

Everyday life unfolds over time

Social action and social meanings evolve and develop over time. Such temporal unfolding is more than the simple lapse of chronological time. Social life has its own rhythms, its cycles, its distinctive tempi. These temporal flows are themselves patterned and ordered, therefore: they have intrinsic forms that impinge on as well as are shaped by social actions and encounters.

Everyday life takes place in specific locations

It is obvious that social life does not take place in a vacuum. Social actors have a clear and profound sense of place. Places and spaces are themselves socially marked: some are treated as mundane, others as special and even sacred. The physical arrangements of location are themselves an aspect of the orderliness of social life. Locations impose their own constraints on, as well as furnishing resources for, social action.

Everyday life is conducted through material artefacts

The physicality of places and spaces, and of bodies, extends to material things, goods and artefacts. The world of things has its own forms of organisation and significance. Material goods are endowed with meaning, through acts of making, through acts of exchange or gift-giving. They can embody memories and be sources of personal identity. They can be forms of display and performance, through which personal identities are fashioned.

As I acknowledged at the outset, this is not an exhaustive list, and its presentation here is necessarily schematic. No doubt readers can find areas in which it is deficient or incoherent. I have quite consciously ridden roughshod over several niceties, believing that a robust sense of the social is more productive than theoretical nit-picking. Nonetheless, I offer it here as one preliminary way of thinking about some of the key features of everyday life that necessarily and quite properly shape the conduct of ethnographic exploration. Several things follow from these elementary, if important, observations. The social worlds we engage with as researchers and the people that produce them are complex. The nature of this complexity is what gives rise to the main themes of this book, and needs to be outlined by way of introduction here. Complexity is not just about things being 'a bit complicated'. Complexity here means that everyday life comprises a number of principles of orderliness. In that sense, while social order may be fluid, improvised and even fragile, it is also robustly present in any and every manifestation of social life (Atkinson et al. 2008). Orderliness manifests itself in a number of ways. They include the following orders.

The interaction order

Erving Goffman (1983) famously suggested that we can identify an interaction order that has a degree of analytic autonomy analogous to an economic or political order. Social encounters have their own 'grammar', their own formal properties. The interaction order includes the widespread conventions of turn-taking and similar interactional devices that make social encounters possible, and create the conditions for them as going concerns.

The semiotic order

There are systems of signs that have an intrinsic order to them. It is not necessary to assume that there are fixed deep structures to cultural systems to recognise that any given culture or sub-culture has its own systems of signification – linguistic and otherwise. There are repertoires of language and gesture that social actors use to undertake social encounters and to get things done. There are codes of visual signs that are meaningful and create the possibility of symbolic displays. They help to create hierarchies of value.

The spatio-temporal order

Time and space are structured, or at least patterned. Places and spaces have boundaries, symbolic and material, that demarcate domains of activity, and zones of special significance. Time is structured in a multiplicity of ways, from long cycles of seasons and annual rounds of calendar rituals, to shorter periods of work or celebration, to the timetable of the daily round of mundane tasks. Temporal and spatial systems interact in framing social events. They are not, however, themselves independent of social action: time and space are themselves socially constructed, conventional systems.

The material order

The world of material goods and things itself is structured and patterned. Again, those systems are culturally defined, and are not independent of cultural convention. But shapes, materials, surfaces and colours all constitute cultural codes of material goods. Material artefacts are elements in systems of use and meaning. The materials themselves are worked on and transformed by social actors, who create goods endowed with meaning. The material order provides semiotic resources.

The aesthetic order

The patterns of culture are, in part, predicated on local definitions and assumptions about aesthetic value. They include judgements about personal appearance and attractiveness of persons, and by extension, of more general character. (The aesthetic and the moral merge into one another.) Aesthetic judgements apply equally to matters of material culture, as well as performative arts such as music and dance. There are, moreover, aesthetic values that apply to more mundane everyday practices, insofar as they are evaluated as being done with felicity, elegance, *savoir-faire* and the like. Aesthetic judgements are based on culturally shaped canons of value. They inform hierarchies of value and are in turn used to express social hierarchies and distinctions.

From some of the things I have already outlined, a number of issues also emerge. They need to be sketched in. Again, they reflect a generalised stance towards the analysis of social life, and are drawn from a variety of theoretical or epistemological perspectives. They constitute common ground, however, between a wide range of disciplinary traditions.

Everyday life is dialectical

Social forms, social institutions and social identities are produced through the everyday work of individual actors, and through their encounters. In turn, however, conventions, institutions and habituated forms of action exert a degree of constraint over social action. This is not a deterministic relationship. Rather, social conventions furnish resources through which actors produce their actions and interactions. There is, therefore, a reciprocal relationship between everyday actions and institutionalised orders of culture.

Everyday reality is socially constructed

The social construction of reality does not mean, and has never meant, that there is no material reality, or that phenomena are conjured up out of thin air, by whimsical acts of will or imagination. The fact that reality is socially constructed does not make it any less real. If a motor car is produced out of the real, practical labour of social actors, whose activities are co-ordinated, then that does not make the car any less real. If the everyday reality of a social situation like a school classroom or a hospital clinic is socially produced, then that does not make it any less real. Situations are real insofar as they are defined as real and are real in their consequences. Those consequences themselves are certainly real for the actors concerned, and many definitions (medical diagnoses, criminal convictions) can have profound consequences.

Now all of the issues so far sketched in suggest a number of very general principles, and they constitute the premises on which this book is based. My references to 'orders', 'codes' and the like are not accidental. I want to emphasise, as expressed already elsewhere (Atkinson et al. 2008), that social life displays multiple forms of orderliness. Social action is patterned. It involves routines, techniques, rituals. It follows temporal rhythms. It inhabits physical and symbolic spaces that are themselves ordered and patterned. The cultural resources that social actors use are themselves forms of order, being part of systems of signification and evaluation. Let me repeat, this is not an argument for a simple structuralism, or indeed a call for a return to a structural–functional model of social explanation. It *is*, however, a call for a re-specification of the basic aims of social research, and of course of ethnographic research in particular. It is important to insist that the main thrust of good ethnographic research is to understand how social action is accomplished, how orderly, co-ordinated activity is undertaken, how knowledgeable and skilful techniques are employed, how material goods and artefacts are made, used and circulated.

In other words, ethnographic research needs to engage with a social world that is itself highly ordered and patterned. In many ways social life is over-determined, in that various modes of social organisation are in play simultaneously – interactional, material, aesthetic and spatio-temporal. Any given social domain will be characterised by multiple layers of significance. It therefore is incumbent on the field researcher to be faithful to the intrinsic complexity of a social world. Moreover, it is important not to lose sight of the extent to which social life is itself intrinsically ordered and structured. Of course, it has to be made to display order: order is a practical accomplishment of social actors. But they can produce orderly activity because they draw on and use methods and resources that accomplish predictable, orderly activity. The fact that social order is a negotiated outcome does not mean that such negotiation takes place in a cultural vacuum. Social actors *share* cultural forms and resources. They generate orderly social encounters and they align their actions on the basis of shared resources.

These cultural forms and resources are not distributed randomly or equally. Knowledge and skills are differentially distributed. While we acknowledge that all social actors are enculturated and have a degree of cultural competence, we also acknowledge that there is esoteric knowledge that is not universally shared, or that is differentially valued. Also, we recognise that skills, knowledge and techniques are actively transmitted, acquired, as well as being contested and debated. In other words, there are social contours that reflect the distribution of cultural resources, and cultural contours that shape social differences.

These observations about social organisation, cultural codes and social action are, in some ways, the basic stuff of the social sciences. To that extent I find them unremarkable. But my comments run counter to several tendencies in contemporary methodological commentary on ethnographic methods and qualitative social research more generally. For a number of reasons, recent years have witnessed some justifications and applications of ethnographic and similar research strategies that are pale reflections of the ethnographic tradition. One clue to the contemporary malaise in the field is given by the repeated assertion by influential authors that it is the goal of research to understand the informant's point of view. In one, weak sense, this is incontrovertible. All of our ethnographic work is predicated on a methodological relativism that requires us to understand cultures and meanings from within the relevant cultural frames. But, as I have emphasised hitherto, an empathetic alignment with our research hosts is not the be-all and end-all of social research. By the same token, the focus of research is not exhausted by a stress on 'experience'. Recent versions of qualitative research have placed too much emphasis on the experiences of social actors, and indeed on the experiences of ethnographers themselves.

These tendencies reflect an inappropriately Romantic view of people as social beings, and of the research process itself. Ethnographic work does indeed allow us – require us even – to spend time *with* our hosts or informants. Sometimes – though by no means always – we establish close working relations with them. We sometimes do experience what they do, either directly or vicariously by virtue of our close engagement with them. It is at one level a requirement of ethnographic fieldwork that we can – as George Herbert Mead put it – 'take the role of the other', and engage in an empathic reconstruction of what our fellow men and women might comprehend of the world about them and of each other. The essential dialogue that lies at the heart of ethnography depends upon this pervasive human capacity. It means that we can also imaginatively grasp how our research hosts see us in the course of our fieldwork.

However, the goal of social research is not just an emotion-filled response to experiences. We do not study complex social relationships and equally complex cultural systems in order to gain material for an essentially emotional and personal response. Obviously there *are* genres of work and writing that approximate to that sort of experience-based understanding: forms of (auto)biography, essays and memoirs would be included in that category, where impressionistic evocations of people and places are accorded high value, and where the criteria of evaluation are themselves aesthetic and affective. It remains my contention, however, that this is not the primary goal of sociological or anthropological field research. Fieldwork represents a very considerable *personal* commitment, there is no doubt. We give up periods of our personal and working lives to spend time, often quite intensively and intimately, with people whose social worlds we want to understand. We certainly get involved in the actions, the talk, of other people. We can get to feel for them and about them. We can often use our personal response to situations – whether it be one of pleasure, boredom or aversion – as a touchstone in starting to make sense of them. But, to repeat myself, this is not the sole aim of research and it is not the main criterion of success. Consequently, we need a much more disciplined approach to investigating others and their lives than is furnished by the Romantic, experiential perspective. We need systematic, methodical investigations of what people *do*, as well as what they say or feel. We need to subject what they tell us and tell each other to systematic scrutiny. We need to make coherent sense of the material and symbolic resources they use and share. We need to pay close attention to the methods they use to make collective action possible, and to render it intelligible to one another. In other words, if they prefer a Formalist perspective over a Romantic one.

I shall, of course, develop some of these arguments in more detail, in less dry terms, in some of the chapters that follow. It is, however, important to try to establish quite what this book is about. In pursuing the themes of this book I am not advocating any single orthodoxy when it comes to social theory or meta-theory. In my own understanding of the overall enterprise I draw eclectically on the disciplinary traditions of social (mainly British) and cultural (mainly American) anthropology, in which I was originally trained, and sociology, which I have professed for many years. In terms of theoretical 'schools' I draw on aspects of symbolic interactionism, phenomenology, ethnomethodology, semiotics, discursive psychology, anthropological ideas of various traditions and cultural studies. In doing so I do not intend to dwell on theoretical niceties, or doctrinal disputes between their practitioners. I do believe, on the contrary, that – in the spirit outlined earlier in this chapter – it is possible to draw out from those intellectual traditions, a collection of ideas that share a broad set of family resemblances, and that together provide a productive framework for a distinctive understanding of social life.

I continue to advocate an approach to social understanding that emphasises the extent to which everyday life is an accomplishment that is inextricably dependent on meanings and interpretations. Any given social world is a domain of mutual interpretation on the part of its members. In doing so they draw on multiple methods of sense-making. They marshal and use culturally available resources. The rationality of their actions is dependent on cultural frames of reference, and is not based on a universal and context-free criterion of reason or logic. Again, this is a profoundly humanistic approach to social research. Equally, it does not preclude disciplined, close attention to what people actually do, how they do it and what the consequences are.

I am affirming that there are long-standing commitments that ethnographers can subscribe to. I am reacting quite explicitly against the sort of accounts offered by authors like Denzin and Lincoln in a series of influential statements (e.g. Denzin and Lincoln 1994, 2000, 2005). They have described transformations in qualitative research – in a model of increasingly rapid transformation – that implies that sociological work (oddly, they do not really impinge on anthropology) has progressed through a series of profound evolutionary – and indeed revolutionary – changes. Now I am far from convinced by this argument. Apart from anything else, I find no need to accuse previous generations of field researchers – cultural anthropologists and symbolic interactionists among them – as purblind positivists. Equally, phenomenological perspectives on everyday social life have been available for many decades before any 'post' transformations took place. For instance, Alfred Schütz's insights marrying German sociology in the tradition of Max Weber and Husserl's phenomenological philosophy can never have been plausibly linked with a positivist frame of mind. Berger and Luckman's English-language version of that phenomenological tradition is equally far removed from any adherence to a natural-science model of inquiry (Berger and Luckman 1967). Equally, many of the novel perspectives canvassed by contemporary authors inspired by Denzin and Lincoln, or indeed Denzin and Lincoln themselves (e.g. Denzin and Lincoln 2000, 2005) are not all that novel in reality. There have long been scholars working across the boundaries of social science and literature, or developing multiple modes of representation for their work, or exploring artistic movements such as surrealism alongside their social reportage (Atkinson 2013a).

While this is not intended to be a comprehensive handbook of how to conduct ethnographic fieldwork, it is nonetheless necessary to outline what I take to be its key and abiding features. This is especially true given that the term itself is widely misused and ethnographic research all too readily misrepresented. Ethnography has a particular meaning – which is narrower than the widely used 'qualitative research' or 'qualitative inquiry'. The conduct of ethnographic research is not based on a single method of data collection or analysis. It refers to a collection of possible methods, used singly or in combination. At its heart, however, is some form of participation in the everyday life of the social world under investigation. It is supremely a mode of understanding a setting or activity that is investigated in its complexity. What is conventionally referred to as 'participant observation' is at the heart of the ethnographic tradition and at the heart of ethnographic research. In the course of this book I am deliberately using the rather old-fashioned term of 'fieldwork' to capture that abiding sense of engagement and commitment. I know that the term itself can be heard in problematic ways. It does harken back to the image of the anthropologist or sociologist going into strange, possible foreign locations, dealing with exotic peoples (whether of distant, non-Western societies, peripheral rural communities, or urban ghettos in Western cities). Of course, I do not mean to repeat that. I use the term, however, in order to recapitulate the more fundamental sense of intensive and extensive engagement with a given social domain.

Equally, I recognise that 'fieldwork' implies a 'field'. I understand that 'fields' are not naturally given, bounded entities. Classic rationales and accounts of ethnography might seem to imply that the subject-matter of investigation consists of relatively autonomous and bounded entities – whether they be defined in geographical or cultural terms – often of relatively small size and associated with notions like 'community'. In the contemporary world, neither anthropologists nor sociologists would readily confine their research to such social worlds, or indeed assume that they exist in that form. In ways that I shall illustrate from time to time in this book, 'fields' can take on many different forms. They are certainly not self-contained entities, and they are not necessarily local, small-scale or defined by face-to-face social relations. 'Fields' are not bounded entities. They are not simply found objects. We create the fields we study, in collaboration with hosts and informants, through the research acts we enact.

Therefore, while I appear to endorse some 'traditional' values of ethnographic research, I do not do so in a totally unreconstructed manner. Indeed, everything contained in this book is predicated on the principle of reflexivity, enunciated with Martyn Hammersley (Hammersley and Atkinson 1983) and affirmed ever since. The principle of reflexivity, as articulated there and in this book, is *not* an exhortation to researchers to be 'reflective' practitioners, and capable of understanding their own actions as social researchers. The fundamental principle of reflexivity is an essential part of social research. It is an unavoidable feature of it. It is not an optional, if admirable, adjunct. Reflexivity is the condition whereby any social research inevitably helps to constitute the phenomenon under investigation. Social research is, therefore, necessarily reactive. Because our research topics consist of human conduct, and because those phenomena are produced by social actors, we are inevitably and inextricably implicated in what we study. We inevitably use natural language to study and to reconstruct everyday social life. We use the methods of everyday inquiry to conduct our research and to make sense of its findings. In that inevitability is to be found the principle of reflexivity and its consequences.

This is not a recipe for total relativism, and it does not mean that we cannot ever arrive at an understanding of the social world, and it is not in itself a recipe for solipsism. This is not an excuse for studying only ourselves, or translating an ostensible ethnography into an exercise in autobiography. It *does* imply a recognition of the essential character of social research in general, and ethnographic research in particular. It means that we actively engage with and explore the social world, and that in doing so we – to some extent – co-construct it in collaboration with the people we observe, talk to, listen to and otherwise engage with. That does not mean, I repeat, that the social world in question is transformed out of all knowledge and recognition. It does not mean that fieldwork is intellectually impossible. Indeed, there is no essential difference here between ethnography and any form of investigation – in the natural or the social sciences. Any system or organism that we investigate directly is potentially affected by that inquiry. Modern natural science, since the quantum mechanics revolution, is not predicated on the assumption that the observer can have no effect, and that the natural world can be studied independently of the acts of observation and measurement. In precisely the same way, social scientists have long accepted that the way we study and report the social world is profoundly implicated in how that world is constructed as an object of investigation.

The ethnographer, then, is committed to a reflexive enterprise. That implies several things. First, it obviates the patent falsehood of claiming that social research has no interactive effect. There is no need to wish away the manifest truth that as the fieldworker works with her or his hosts, while she or he is conversing with them, while she or he explores a given 'field', then that work is *active* in constituting social phenomena. The consequences of reflexivity imply what I prefer to call *reflective practice*. We cannot eliminate reactivity, but we can be conscious, self-aware of what we are doing. We cannot wish away or control out of existence the effects of reactivity. What we can do is to acknowledge, as far as we can, the essential character of social research *as* a series of social, interpersonal events. As such they are inevitably subject to interpretation: we interpret, make sense of, the social events and actions we witness and participate in, so do our hosts and informants. Moreover, they are actively engaged in making sense of us, as ethnographers. Fieldwork takes place within a mesh of social relations, and in a web of interpretations.

This is the strength of social research. It is the special strength of ethnographic research. Unlike many other approaches to inquiry, ethnographers explicitly recognise their own reactivity. They recognise the reflexive principle. Equally, ethnography can reasonably lay claim to being especially faithful to the social world. In that respect it differs from all other modes of social research. There is a direct homology between the procedures and processes of everyday life and the principles of ethnographic research. Both are predicated on interpersonal negotiation and both are grounded in temporal processes. Both are grounded in methods of interpretation and sense-making. The competence of the ethnographer, as a social actor who participates in ordinary social life, parallels exactly the competence of her or his fellow men and women. We use our human capacities of social action and interpretation to make sense of those self-same capacities in others. This is no difference in principle from everyday processes and procedures of mundane social life.

Now this is not, in itself, either a modernist nor a postmodernist perspective. In many important ways, indeed, it matters little what label is applied to it, as I do not regard it as a matter of choice or theoretical predilection. As I have emphasised, reflexivity and its consequences are necessary and unavoidable features of social research. Equally, it is not an excuse for shirking the serious and demanding work of carefully exploring and documenting a social world. Moreover, as I have indicated already, the social world exhibits patterns, principles of orderliness, cultural codes and conventions. The fact that we cannot have perfect knowledge of it, or that we cannot place ourselves outside of the social worlds we study, is absolutely no excuse for failing to study them as methodically and carefully as we possibly can. A proper concern for the cultural forms and social patterns of everyday life leads us to the subject-matter of sociology or anthropology, to the stuff of ethnographic research itself. This is not the impressionistic study of individual experiences, nor yet the empathetic reconstruction of individual social actors.

It is not enough simply to understand the social world 'from the point of view' of the social actor, though an ability to do so will certainly be a crucial part of the ethnographic enterprise. The ability to 'take the role of the other' and to enter into some sort of interpretative comprehension of others is a significant human characteristic, and it is one of the competences that ethnographers must draw on. It is, however, by no means the only way of conceptualising the research enterprise, and it is not the only competence that ethnographers should draw on. It is at best a partial goal. In fact it confuses the issue, because it imposes an essentially personal and experiential gloss on a research strategy that ought to include a concern with forms of social relations, forms of social order, rituals and routines of everyday performance, patterns of culture and the like.

Some of the problems stem not just from a misunderstanding of the goals of ethnography, but also from a debased coinage of research method. Far too much of what passes for 'ethnography' (or similar designations of sustained fieldwork) are nothing of the kind. There is, especially in that hinterland of research and publication that escapes the disciplinary confines of anthropology or sociology and that appeals to vague notions of 'qualitative inquiry', an over-reliance on talk with individual subjects. There is correspondingly little attention to the *social*. We find far too much research that is focused on a small number of individuals and their spoken accounts (in individual interviews or focus groups) that does nothing to address the practical actions and interactions that constitute everyday social life.

In the ensuing chapters I shall follow the logic of what I have outlined. I shall provide a structure of topics that guide the potential researcher and the fieldworker in identifying the forms and types of information, and hence of analysis that are possible and commendable in the course of fieldwork. In pursuing this agenda, I want to insist throughout that everyday social life is constructed through 'thick' media. The full meaning of this assertion will emerge in the course of the following chapters. Here a brief justification is offered. I mean that phenomena and features of everyday social settings that are often treated as background features, or as transparent mediums of communication, are themselves constitutive of social life, and have their own intrinsic properties. To take just one obvious example, language is clearly not a transparent medium. Language-use is one of the ways in which social life is accomplished. That includes the use of narratives, accounts, speeches, presentations, performances and other kinds of enactment. Narratives and performances have their own structures. Discursive resources are used to perform a wide variety of social actions. Language-use constructs a wide range of cultural forms. We cannot, therefore, treat narratives and accounts as transparent representations of actions and experiences. They clearly reflect culturally shared resources, formats and the like.

While this applies exceptionally clearly to language-use, it applies also to many other phenomena that are too readily treated as background features. For instance, it is clear that notwithstanding their strong local emphasis, many ethnographies seem to take place in a material vacuum. Disembodied social actors act and interact, but the material circumstances of their everyday lives are often annoyingly absent. For instance, the cultural arrangements of place and space are not mere background or 'context' features. They should not be taken as given. They simultaneously constrain and make possible social action. Places and spaces are themselves culturally shaped, reflecting social conventions, and impinging directly on socially organised activity. The materiality of place furnishes recourses that are used by social actors, and they are endowed with significance. They inscribe boundaries that are simultaneously material and symbolic.

The same general observation applies to material goods and objects. What is conveniently glossed as material culture should not be relegated to an esoteric and specialised field of studies. Objects have intrinsic properties: material substance, shape, colour. They have value: use value, exchange value, symbolic value. They can be tokens in the production and maintenance of social relations: economic goods, gifts. They can be the main focus of work and action itself: scientific outputs, craft objects, artistic achievements.

In other words, these kinds of phenomena and things are not mere adjuncts to social life. They are themselves culturally patterned, and they are intrinsically implicated in the conduct of social life. Moreover, they display regularities, insofar as they embody cultural conventions and codes. They display ordering in their own right, and those orderings are in turn the fabric of social life in all its manifestations. As argued elsewhere, the goal of 'thick description' should not, therefore, be thought of in terms of descriptive 'detail' in a diffuse sense. The thickness of ethnographic work rests on systematic attention to the 'thickness' of the multiple modes of order and action. So I believe that social life is constructed, in much the same way that we might think of the construction of a Japanese tea-bowl. Each tea-bowl is unique; each conforms to a generic, recognisable type. Each is the outcome of highly disciplined and predictable methods; each is the outcome of chance. Each reflects its unique cultural location, and the hand of the master-potter; each reflects a cultural tradition that is inscribed in the tea-bowl. While the making of a tea-bowl is closely tied to local traditions and aesthetic criteria, those can be learned and translated across national boundaries, and transmitted from generation to generation. The fact that everyday life is a process of becoming does not mean that it has no organisation, no structure and no methods for its making. It is the task of the ethnographer to make sense of these structuring principles, the methods that social actors employ, and the cultural categories that they collectively generate and sustain.

Each of the main chapters that follow suggests and exemplifies ways of looking at such phenomena. Each chapter makes some practical suggestions as to how the practising ethnographer in the field might pay due attention to them. Let us be clear that this is not really intended to be a check-list of 'notes and queries' that are to be followed slavishly and mechanistically. The idea is not simply to make ethnographic research projects 'more complete' by adding dimensions of complexity. The purpose of these chapters is to outline some of the underlying principles of social organisation that are to be found in the various modalities. My argument is a simple one. Ethnographers need to be attentive to these multiple forms of reality-production and embodiment. It is in that spirit, then, that I have invoked the precedent set by Marcel Mauss. Anthropology itself has not been notable for its methodological literature. Traditionally, it has treated the conduct of ethnography as a matter of personal qualities rather than methodological precepts. It is, therefore, remarkable that Mauss should have promoted a recognisably methodological slant on the conduct of ethnography. (It is, of course, no accident that his remarks were aimed primarily at non-anthropologists; research methods have always had rather artisanal connotations for elite anthropologists.) But Mauss offers sound advice, coupled with a thorough sense of how everyday life is pervaded by cultural forms that are amenable to systematic data collection.

I also want to make it clear that I do not equate the collection of data about these orders with separate technologies of data capture. Of course, there are affinities between types of social phenomena and ways of recording them. But these are not one-to-one relationships. In other words, when I write about the observation of visual topics, that does not mean that they can *only* become 'data' if they are captured by photography or video-recording. Attention to material culture does not equate to the physical collection of material specimens, or even photographic representations of them. Multi-modal ethnography can certainly be based on data collected and analysed in different media. Indeed, it is an integral part of my argument to suggest that, in many cases, it not only can but should. But that is not the same as a crude correspondence between the modalities of organisation and culture and the media of their investigation and reconstruction.

Consequently, I shall not be basing these discussions primarily on technological developments. Equally, I shall not be discussing issues of analysis and representation in terms of computational and other digital resources. I do not intend this to be a practical manual of digital photography and computer-aided analysis of field data. Equally, I do not wish to provide instruction in how to take fieldnotes. My interest is at a more generic level than that. I want to encourage ethnographic researchers to develop a particular kind of ethnographic sensibility that is attentive to the various *forms* of social life. I therefore want to insist on the significance of *disciplined* inquiry, and to *systematic* analysis of data derived from fieldwork. This is in opposition to approaches to 'qualitative' research that pay insufficient attention to the fundamental issues of social and cultural order, and that celebrate a diffuse form of experiential and celebratory form of exploration, with little or no grounding in the goals of principled social-scientific research.

In recent years social scientists have become wary of 'othering' people about whom they write, and with whom they undertake fieldwork. Othering has a number of connotations. Derived primarily from critiques of the anthropological tradition, it implies the creation of unwarranted distance between the self of the ethnographer and the other of the researched. It carries connotations over from versions of ethnography and ethnology that construct radical differences between the cosmopolitan observer and the local participants. Such differences can – for instance – include the portrayal of the 'others' as existing out of time, suspended in the eternity of the ethnographic present, leaving historical processes all but invisible. It can also carry notions of undue emphasis on the exoticism of other cultures or other actors. In this sense, othering can seem to exaggerate cultural differences, to the detriment of other cultures and actors. It smacks of the sort of intellectual failing known as *orientalism*. Deriving from Said's controversial commentary on Western representations of the East (that is, the Near East), orientalism refers to a gestalt of presuppositions that construct accounts of the other in terms of key differences – including images of an effete, soft, over-sexualised East, a cruel East and so on (Said 1978). It is not hard to find examples of this sort of othering whenever there are suggestions of exotic cultural phenomena. It is, after all, too easy to focus on the most glamorous, or repellent, or simply the most different aspects of a given social world that are the most noticeable, the most readily reported and the most newsworthy. It is an easy trap to fall into, if indeed a trap it be. There is a parallel process identified as Balkanism (Todorova 2009), for instance, that marginalises the Balkans from a Western European perspective.

Nowhere would othering seem more controversial than in the treatment of belief systems and practices derived from beliefs that are markedly different from the taken-for-granted cultural categories of the ethnographer's home culture. It is therefore all too easy to demonstrate a degree of apparent prejudice if the other is implicitly represented as irrational, or deficient in other ways. This is a recurrent criticism of the entire anthropological tradition – although it seems almost entirely misplaced to me. Anthropology has been the discipline most consistently committed to analyses that reject the spirit of orientalism, that avoids the denigration of other cultures, and celebrates cultural relativism as an analytic necessity. In the desire not to essentialise social worlds as exotic and alien, in recent years there have been a number of voices that have argued vociferously against othering social worlds, cultures and actors. Indeed, in some quarters the view of anthropology has swung round to the extent that 'anthropologising' people is taken to mean symbolic abuse. Now there can be no dispute about the fundamental analytic and ethical issues here. On the other hand, I want here to remind us that there is a proper way to approach 'the other', and that 'otherings' can be productive ways of approaching the task of social research. Indeed, I would be prepared to argue that some degree of 'othering' is a methodological prerequisite to productive ethnographic analysis. If we do not or cannot recognise some degree of difference between ourselves and significant others, then it remains stubbornly unclear how we can ever approach them as interlocutors from whom we might learn something new, or how we might closely observe their everyday doings, and from them learn to reconstruct their works and lives. If there is no difference, then there will be no learning, no dialogue, no social science. This relates directly to the recurrent issues of familiarity and strangeness that Sara Delamont and I explored some years ago (Delamont and Atkinson 1995) and have continued to explore since. One of the greatest problems confronting ethnographers, and indeed any sensible social researcher, is: how do I make a given social world or social process sufficiently familiar so as to render it accessible, while rendering it sufficiently strange as to gain analytic purchase on it? To put it another way, in the absence of any sense of strangeness, researchers are doomed to recapitulate their existing ideas, or to fail to generate any ideas at all.

In this context, strangeness is not a randomly chosen word, and it does not mean something like 'odd' or 'weird'. It derives its force from phenomenological-informed social science. Estrangement means finding ways of suspending or challenging one's own taken-for-granted categories of thought and action, in order to make the practices of others and oneself available for inspection. To render a social world or a social phenomenon strange, then, is to recognise it for what it is: conventional and culturally shaped, socially shared, skilfully accomplished, and semiotically complex. In other words, we have to recognise our universal human capacity to *learn* from and about our fellow women and men. We do not have to seek out only people who resemble us in order to understand them. On the contrary, encounters with strangers – of all sorts – provides us with the intellectual discipline on which any social science must be based. We have the capacity to take the role of the other. As intellectuals we are able to transcend our here-and-now circumstances. We can, as historians, interrogate the others of the past; as anthropologists and sociologists, the others of the present. We learn through encounters with others. It is our duty to seek out such encounters.

3
Fieldwork Commitments

Before we consider more concrete themes and topics, in this chapter I want to outline some basic issues in the conduct of fieldwork. As I have already made clear, this book is not intended to duplicate those many introductory texts that take the student or more experienced researcher through the key steps and stages of an ethnographic project. Yet I realise that stripped of any such methodological advice, the book will seem oddly incomplete. I therefore outline what I take to be the key methodological and practical components of ethnography. This is by way of introduction to the more significant and – I hope – original contributions that form the major chapters in the rest of this book. The elementary principles of ethnographic field research are simply stated. Their consequences are more complex. They are predicated on the extent to which the ethnographer devotes time and attention to one or more social domains.

Fieldwork is participatory

Ethnographic fieldwork always involves a degree of participation in the chosen field. To put it negatively, it is *not* the enactment of a series of interviews, however 'active' or exploratory they may be. Ethnographic fieldwork may involve many conversations, some of which may be in the form of interviews, but they alone do not constitute an adequate ethnography, worthy of the name (whatever other benefits there may prove to be). Now the degree and nature of that participation can (and should) vary considerably. I am not referring here simply to the spectrum from 'complete observer' to 'complete participant'. Rather, I want to emphasise the extent to which the conduct of ethnography necessarily and profoundly depends on the direct engagement (sensory and interactional) with a distinctive form of life. This aspect of 'participation' does not depend on the adoption of that way of life. One does not need to spend one's time as a school student, as a street person, as an employee in a complex organisation. Indeed, to equate ethnographic participation with such role-adoption is, at root, to trivialise it.

To participate is, in other words, to make a certain personal as well as intellectual commitment. It is also to exploit (in the best sense) one's full range of human capacities in order to make sense of a given social world. Such capacities include the ability to be observant, to take the role of the other, to listen, to learn and to imitate, indeed to do all of the things that everyday social actors do in order to make sense of themselves, others and the world about them. In order to do so we employ specialised methods of recording and thinking that transform participant observation from mundane activity, and that make it a form of theorised – rather than purely practical – activity.

Fieldwork is pragmatic

Ethnographic fieldwork is rarely based on predetermined research designs or tightly formulated research hypotheses. It is rarely conducted in the manner of hypothesis-testing, deductive research. Its guiding spirit has always been an exploratory one. That does not mean that the ethnographer approaches a given social setting with absolutely no ideas. It is a complete misperception to assume that the fundamental open-mindedness of the fieldworker is equivalent to an empty mind. Flexible fieldwork means that we are open to the multiple forms and dimensions that make up our research site(s). We follow the phenomena. We allow ourselves to suspend our taken-for-granted categories and presuppositions in order to explore them in a local setting. We seek to document how social settings are produced and sustained by their members. Our flexibility therefore mirrors the extent to which social situations are defined by social actors themselves.

Flexible fieldwork also means that our research is a developmental, interactive process. It does not and cannot proceed in a linear fashion – from research question to hypothesis, to data collection and so on – but is cyclical. In practice, we make a preliminary assessment of a given field and spend an initial period of time there. On the basis of those initial observations, we derive some preliminary working ideas. From those preliminary ideas we start to identify more cases and possibilities in the developing data, and our data collection is guided by those developing ideas. And so on. The process is rarely, if ever, perfectly complete, but we go on developing, extending and refining our ideas.

Throughout the process, our recurrent question is – or ought to be – 'What might this be a case of?' In other words, we repeatedly ask ourselves whether the actions we are observing, or perhaps participating in, might represent examples of a more general pattern, or a more general class of phenomena. We do not simply do fieldwork in order to collect together a mass of impressions. We certainly do not develop our sociological or anthropological understanding solely on the basis of accumulated cases and examples. We are constantly consciously reflecting on what they might prove to be examples *of*.

Fieldwork is comparative

Our understanding of a given field is always informed through a comparison with other settings and worlds. This does not mean, of course, that we have to research multiple sites all the time. But it does mean that the developmental logic – what is this a case of? – is always (in principle) pursued in relation to other studies and other research settings. We are constantly aware of the range of other, comparable studies, through which we can use our field data to develop ideas of adequate generality. This means that any general analytic question can be extended to encompass entire studies, not just single events and exemplars in the field. We ask ourselves repeatedly, and on an interactive, cyclical basis, what our own research site might be an example of. In this way, our ideas are constantly moving between the local, specific features of our research setting, and broader, trans-situational ideas. Most truly productive research in the ethnographic tradition has been generated on that basis.

Ethnography is generalisable

This sounds counter-intuitive. It is sometimes argued that ethnographic research necessarily and deliberately generates research that is *idiographic* – that is, that documents the particularities of a social domain but that does not lead to generalisable research findings. Idiographic research has conventionally been contrasted with research aims that are *nomothetic*. The latter refers to the aim of generating law-like generalities. However, it is perfectly possible for research to be generalisable without it being tied to law-like regularities. Indeed, the outcomes of ethnographic research are precisely of that sort, by virtue of their comparative nature. Scholars who are adequately acquainted with their own field(s) of specialisation will know that they are characterised by a corpus of ethnographic monographs and papers that constitute a cumulative and comparative research literature. This reflects the extent to which ethnographic fieldwork does not merely generate descriptions of local settings, but also aims to the development of generic concepts that transcend the local and that can be applied across a range of social situations. The latter often take the form of *ideal-types*. (This is so even when that particular designation is not used explicitly.) Those types are sometimes couched in terms of metaphors or other summary representations that are, in effect, *models*.

If one takes any major domain of empirical inquiry, it is clear that the relevant ethnographic monographs demonstrably document similar or equivalent social situations, and robust repertoires of concepts are mobilised to account for them. One can, for instance, point to many collections of ethnographic work, and identify major continuities and commonalities across them. Not only is there a recognisable genre of 'laboratory ethnography', but the laboratory life and work they describe are recognisably, and robustly, equivalent. The sociology and anthropology of medical institutions clearly explore comparable social settings, and do so in comparative ways. The ethnographic study of schools and classrooms is a coherent and indeed cumulative genre of studies. In other words, ethnographic fieldwork does not merely generate a series of isolated, incommensurable case studies. There is no reason to think that 'generalisation' is not relevant to ethnographic (or indeed any qualitative) research. These forms of generalisability are not dependent on simple notions of representation. The social sites that are studied are not 'sampled' so that they can stand for some presumed population of sites. Our sense of ethnographic generalisation is not, therefore, of the same form as that applied to inference from a sample to a population. It is different, but equally informative. As I have suggested, the ethnographic mode of generalisation is based in part on the derivation of ideal-types and patterns that can be found across a variety of research settings, and that can in turn inform further empirical studies. We can think of the relations between ethnographic works as forming a network of cross-references, of inter-textual relations and of a common conceptual apparatus.

Fieldwork is multi-modal

The conduct of fieldwork is not dependent on any one, single strategy of data collection. It is one of the strengths of ethnographic fieldwork, indeed, that it is not tied to any one method of research or one form of data. One reason for this re-statement of the principles of ethnographic fieldwork is the observation that too much 'qualitative' research has become dependent on one data-type. This argument has been rehearsed in more detail elsewhere (e.g. Atkinson 2005) and I do not recapitulate it here in full detail. But a general overview of the current state of the art suggests strongly that too many studies are based on single-method designs, and on single forms of data. Too many studies, for instance, are based solely on interviews with key informants, or with groups of them. Equally, we find too great reliance on recorded talk. Visual materials may, likewise, be granted a prominent or privileged place in the repertoire of research methods. The collection and analysis of material culture or its representations is also a prominent approach.

Now each of these data-collection strategies is valuable. To varying extents, they form the major contents of the remaining chapters of this book. But they do not make ethnographic sense in mutual isolation. It is of the very essence of ethnographic fieldwork that we need to be faithful – as far as possible – to the complexity of everyday life. There is a recurrent danger of reducing the social world to a single dimension by the use of single modes of data collection. In recent years it has become fashionable to reiterate the merits of 'multi-method' research designs. In many contexts, this seems to amount to advocacy for quantitative and qualitative research methods in combination. There is, perhaps, nothing intrinsically wrong with that, although in practice the results often seem jejune, especially when it comes to the 'qualitative' aspects of the research. And there is clearly no merit in treating the qualitative data as an adjunct to quantitative studies, with a vague appeal to rich data or the use of qualitative information merely to illustrate and flesh out the bare bones of quantitative findings. Equally, there is little merit in using qualitative case studies merely to establish hypotheses that can then be studied through quantitative research (such as sample surveys).

Ethnographic research is always potentially multi-method. In fact one can argue that the most significant exemplars of multi-method research are always to be found in ethnographic field research, and owe little or nothing to the sterile contestation between 'qualitative' and 'quantitative' research strategies. But the crucial difference here falls between multiple methods and multiple modes. Here I want to reiterate the main theme of this book in order to make this specific point. The social world is enacted and represented through multiple forms and multiple cultural codes. Social organisation is realised in complex ways that depend on multiple forms, conventions and principles. Social and cultural orderliness is made with symbolic means, with material artefacts, with linguistic repertoires, through spatial and temporal frames of reference. The proper conduct of ethnographic work, therefore, needs to do justice to those modalities of social and cultural organisation.

Ethnography depends on participation

I am convinced that some form of participant observation, as it is conventionally known, remains central to the ethnographic enterprise. Without that degree of engagement, ethnography remains all but impossible, and any kinds of social research that do not incorporate that core of fieldwork are not worthy of the name of ethnography, and – more importantly – can rarely if ever do justice to complexity. Clearly, there are many connotations to the notion of participant observation. It is at the heart of fieldwork, however, and subtle differences in interpretation or execution of participant observation are trivial compared with the massive commonalities, and its huge significance for the practical conduct of research. There have been various attempts to define different varieties of participant observation, or to distinguish different degrees of participation (from complete participant to complete observer). These distinctions are virtually useless for practical purposes: in the course of practical fieldwork, the modes and intensity of participation are contingent and protean. Degrees of intimacy with or proximity to one's hosts are equally variable.

Participation in this context clearly means more than just physically 'being there'. The underlying rationale of field research can be understood in terms of the homology between the everyday social actor and the ethnographer. Fieldwork is possible because social actors can 'take the role of the other'. That is, it is a human capacity to be able to perceive the world not only from one's singular perspective, but also – however imperfectly – from the perspective of others. This basic tenet of interactionist sociology, deriving from Mead and Cooley, is also another expression of the reflexive principle that underpins our understanding of the overall ethnographic enterprise (Hammersley and Atkinson 2007). It does not mean, of course, that we are capable of some mysterious act of mind-reading, or that we can perfectly intuit others' motives, emotions and understandings. Indeed, we should not be trying to do so.

What it *does* mean is that we can enter into a world of others. We can engage with them in their everyday lives. We can interact with them. As the sociological phenomenologist Alfred Schütz would put it, we can 'grow old together' (Schütz 1967). We can, in other words, occupy a shared social world. We can engage in mutual attention. Participation in that sense, therefore, is a fundamental human capacity. It is through such participation, in the most general sense, that we, as ordinary men and women, can ever learn anything. We become enculturated – whether it be in our own culture or a strange one – through participation in a social world. In other contexts, we are used to the recognition that socialisation takes place by participation in a *community of practice*. Well, ethnography is entirely based on that self-same principle. To that extent, fine distinctions between observer-as-participant and participant-as-observer (and so on) vanish into insignificance. Furthermore, we need to recognise that the element of participation is far more than simply being present, in order to do other things (such as the conduct of interviews). Participation with our research hosts implies a personal and even existential commitment on the ethnographer's part. To participate in a form of life, in a community of practice, within an agency or organisation, a work-setting or a sub-cultural group is to do far more than merely collect and record data. We engage with the rhythms of everyday life, with its material circumstances, its spatial and scenic arrangements, its interactional ceremonials. Such participation is not merely personal or experiential: it is an analytic resource in understanding and documenting everyday life in its local forms.

Ethnography depends on observation

If participation is fundamental, so too is the element of observation. This is too often interpreted literally, as if observation meant merely watching, or concentrating on the purely visual aspects of everyday life. The latter is patently absurd. Participant observation is certainly not just about looking at purely observable phenomena. It means being attentive to the multiplicity of actions – spoken and unspoken – and of social actors, material culture, spatial and temporal arrangements that together constitute the field. Observation clearly implies visual acuity, but equally clearly it goes beyond just seeing. It encompasses listening, and it also implies a full awareness of the many sensory channels through which one might grasp social settings. So it means hearing, and listening to, not just talk but *soundscapes*. It means a sensitivity to physical environment and material things. It means a sense of taste and smell: the full range of senses is implied. They are not necessarily drawn on in equal measure in all fieldwork projects. But the general point is: the ethnographer's participant observation is, in principle, faithful to the inherent and ordered complexity of the social world.

Note here that I want to insist yet again on the potential for *order* in these sensory domains. Participant observation is certainly not about gaining a series of impressions about a given social situation. One does not advocate a complex sense of participation and observation merely in the interests of a vaguely rich sense of a social setting, or of a group of actors. Our task as ethnographers is not to be the equivalent of a diarist or newspaper columnist, providing personal reflections on equally personal experiences. Ours is an *analytic* attention. Sensory exploration of the social world is a way of making systematic sense of it. We do not need to be 'positivists' (of whatever stripe) to recognise the degree of pattern in the social world. Social life includes routines, conventions, and codes that furnish *forms of action* that simultaneously enable and constrain social activity. Event-types (encounters in medical clinics, classrooms, legal proceedings, political disputes and so on) are robust in their form, in any given society, and often display shared properties across cultural boundaries. We do not have to claim that they are all the same in order to recognise the predictability and stability of social cultural forms. Social encounters are highly structured, whether through the interaction rituals that Erving Goffman (1967) so elegantly described, or the sequential patterning of spoken activity, as documented by Harvey Sacks (Sacks 1992). Social institutions and organisations are highly predictable, through the ceremonial cycle of meetings, the documentary practices of recording organisational facts, or the temporal cycle of hiring, firing and socialisation. While we always seek to capture and convey what is particular, specific and local, our primary purpose is to seek out those regularities that make social life relatively orderly, predictable and, indeed, observable in the first place.

Ethnography uses multiple technologies

It follows from what I have just suggested that the conduct of ethnography draws on multiple modes of recording and representation. It is easy to think in terms of text, and ethnography is undoubtedly a predominantly textual mode of inquiry. The 'traditional' ethnographic strategy has been based on the transformation of participant observation and interaction in the field into the textual form of fieldnotes (Emerson et al. 1995, 2001). From this point of view, there is always a process of translation – from our observations (in the broadest sense) to a written narrative, summaries, commentary. Fieldnotes can never be a perfectly transparent reconstruction of all that happened in the field on any given occasion. Such a perfectly faithful transcription would be impossible in practice. It would also be well-nigh useless by way of data, as it would provide little opportunity for the ethnographer to be adequately selective, guided by her or his developing analytic perspectives. So fieldnotes are not data in the sense of being independent of the very considerable interpretative and translational work that goes into their construction. They *are* in themselves preliminary reconstructions of the social world, that feed into further translations and reconstructions, not least in the ultimate composition of an ethnographic monograph or journal article. Criticisms of fieldnotes as inadequate records of the details of encounters can therefore be wide of the mark. They are intermediate texts, not imperfect forms of transcript. Our engagement with fieldnotes is always an act of retrieval and reconstruction, of memory as well as reading (Taussig 2012).

This compositional work is by no means the only technology of ethnography. Indeed, as we have argued at considerable length elsewhere, contemporary ethnography is and should be multi-modal in its deployment of technologies of representation (Dicks et al. 2005). Contemporary digital technologies provide unparalleled opportunities for many aspects of ethnography. They also feed into the possibilities of representation that complement and transcend the purely textual devices that have predominated in the past. We are now able to use small, highly portable devices to record still and moving pictures of remarkably high quality, and equally remarkably moderate cost, considering the functions they can provide. Video-recordings of close-to-broadcast quality can be obtained from simple recorders, while more highly specified camcorders are readily available. Digital cameras that yield publishable images – not least on the internet – are entirely commonplace. Mobile phone technology can yield data that can equal or surpass previous technologies. Visual data can be transferred to computer files and internet sites with great ease. Gadgets have now become so compact as to be wearable. Many of our research hosts and informants inhabit multi-media worlds, producing and consuming text and audio-visual materials through social media. It is up to us as researchers to do as much.

In the same way, sound recording of high quality can now be made digitally. Technologies have changed rapidly, of course. The mini-disk recorder proved a remarkably useful way of recording interviews and other sound materials with very small and unobtrusive devices that were in many ways a marked improvement over cassette recorders (such as the still-lamented Sony Professional Walkman). Digital voice recorders can now record and store long stretches of talk and other sound, without separate storage media, and can be downloaded into sound files for reproduction, transcription, or analysis without transcription into hard-copy text. The soundscapes of everyday life are within easy reach (Makagon and Neumann 2009). Given these opportunities it is now conceivable to develop one's fieldwork in digital terms. A full array of data types can be garnered through these devices, which are themselves highly usable. (The contrast with previous generations, when film-based cinematography and photography were necessary, is striking.) We can now assemble a multi-modal ethnographic assemblage within an integrated environment. In combination with data-management software and various forms of editing and presentation, we can now create ethnographies that can reflect just some of the complexity inherent in the social world (Dicks et al. 2005).

These technologies of representation do not substitute for the kinds of ethnographic imagination and analytic sensitivity that all fieldworkers have had to cultivate. We cannot re-define fieldwork as simply an exercise in digital recording, generating data that are then treated only in traditional ways. While technologically based innovation is by no means obligatory, we are clearly in a position to create genuinely novel, exploratory ways of reconstructing social worlds though digital means, and of representing them in ways that include digital forms. Equally, multiple channels of recording and data collection do not absolve us from the intellectual tasks of analysis and conceptual development: it is not enough merely to reproduce fragments of raw materials in whatever form they arise.

Ethnography requires multiple skills

It is clear that in the ideal world, ethnographic fieldwork depends on a variety of skills that mirror the various forms of everyday life. The conduct of ethnography is not a non-method. It is not an amateurish pursuit. The forms of everyday life call for disciplined inquiry, and that calls in turn for a variety of research skills. Unfortunately much of the training available, even at advanced graduate level, does relatively little to prepare field researchers in the range of research and analytic skills that they might need. It is, perhaps, not necessary for us all to become equally adept at everything, but a degree of advanced competence in a range of research approaches is useful. To take one example to begin with – the various forms of linguistic performance need some degree of specialist attention if the field researcher is to get the most out of those data. In the first place, language has its own organisation. Discursive structures and devices, rhetorical forms and interactional exchanges all have intrinsic forms of organisation – whether they be narrative structures or sequential order. If we are to make adequate sense of spoken activities, and we are to take advantage of digital recording opportunities, then we have to have an adequate grasp of the elementary analytic issues. We may or may not wish to commit ourselves to specialising in, say, 'narrative analysis', but we clearly need to cultivate a disciplined understanding of what narratives amount to. Equally, we may not have to devote ourselves on a full-time basis to discourse-analytic or conversation-analytic techniques in order to appreciate how spoken action is structured, and how it is used by social actors to achieve orderly social conduct.

Equally, we ought to develop some degree of competence in the analysis of material culture. Whether we are working directly with objects, places, or surfaces, or collecting representations of them (such as photographs), we need to develop some specialised competence in doing such analytic work. Clearly we need to be able to go beyond uninformed impressions. We need to cultivate the skills to describe and analyse the semiotics of cultural forms, an informed understanding of materials and their affordances. We shall need to have the skills not merely to collect records of material goods and physical artefacts, but also of the disciplinary knowledge of material culture in order to do justice to those materials. The same can be said of visual culture. Fieldworkers clearly need to be adept not only in the collection of visual records (such as photographs), but also need to cultivate an analytic machinery for describing visual codes, and translating images into anthropological or sociological analyses.

These are generic skills that fieldworkers clearly ought to cultivate. To them we need to add the disciplined and systematic study of spaces and places, the appropriate use of software to integrate spatial with other forms of analysis. The contemporary fieldworker probably needs to gain a working knowledge of several relevant software packages in order to develop adequate competence in editing and authoring multi-modal ethnographic representations. Now recommending these, and other, competences may, in their totality, be amount to a counsel of perfection. It is difficult to imagine too many younger researchers being able to develop all such skills to the highest possible degree. But in their absence, ethnographic research is going to remain underdeveloped, and will display an amateurish approach to everything. We certainly cannot afford to have social scientists less well equipped to study aspects of the social world than many of the people around us. There is certainly no excuse for failing to comprehend the inherent organisation of social forms solely because one has not mastered the technical resources adequately to analyse them. In the absence of technical, analytic skills and resources ethnographers risk reproducing the kind of impressionistic reportage that any person could generate on the basis of casual participation.

Ethnography is theoretical

If ethnographic research demands multiple skills, it also depends on a variety of theoretical, or conceptual, repertoires. There is a sustaining myth that ethnographic research is so purely exploratory that one does not enter the field with any prior concepts or hypotheses. It is perfectly true that one rarely has a particular 'hypothesis' to test through fieldwork. It is also the case that ethnographic fieldwork is more suited to the generation of ideas than the testing of hypotheses. Ethnography is rarely addressed to the sort of explanation that lends itself to hypothesis-testing – and very rarely depends on the sort of causal explanation that hypothesis-testing might call for. On the other hand, it is not the case that ethnographers typically embark on their field research without ideas. Equally, it is not the case that the conduct of ethnography is in any sense anti-theoretical. While ethnography is not tied to any single theoretical perspective in the social sciences, and there is no one-to-one correspondence between ethnographic methods and any given theoretical tradition, there are family resemblances between sets of ideas and ethnographic perspectives. If ethnography is not a paradigm or quasi-paradigm in its own right, it is a constituent element in a variety of theoretical packages.

I have already outlined a number of key commitments that underpin the ethnographic tradition(s). Here I want to put them further into context. It is my general contention that the contemporary ethnographer needs a working knowledge of a variety of analytic traditions. These are outlined below in no particular order of priority. In my opinion none should be pursued as a devotee or with all the purblind passion of a convert. Any and all should be drawn on for the right sorts of ideas to make sense of a social setting and social action. I do not want to suggest that these all constitute 'theories'. Some reflect distinctive theoretical perspectives, others less so. They are, however, repositories of ideas about the social world. Each has a characteristic research literature associated with it, as well as key concepts. Each therefore deserves serious attention. In combination they furnish repertoires of fruitful and productive ideas.

Symbolic interactionism

Interactionist sociology has a long association with ethnographic research, although the two are by no means identical (Atkinson and Housley 2003; Rock 1979). There is, in fact, a historical link between the ethnography of urban and organisational worlds and a set of ideas that derive from Chicago School sociology. The second Chicago School, led by Everett Hughes and his circle, is a particularly fruitful heritage of inspirations and ideas (Fine 1995). This broad interactionist strand pervades contemporary sociological work, even when not attributed directly to interactionism itself. Key ideas include a strong sense of the fluid, negotiated nature of social order. They also include an equally processual view of social identities. Indeed, there is a strong sense in which – from this perspective – social selves and social order are just two aspects of the same general social process (Atkinson and Housley 2003).

Dramaturgy

Interactionist ideas are closely related to dramaturgical ones. The key figure, Erving Goffman, is often treated as a generic interactionist, although his intellectual inspirations were somewhat different. The dramaturgical perspective adds to the interactionist interest in selves and situations, Goffman's analysis of the interaction order, and the everyday ceremonials of interpersonal conduct. The dramaturgical metaphor adds a specific stress on the performative nature of everyday life. Thought of from this perspective, social life is analysed in terms of its formal similarity to a theatrical performance. It also stresses the strategic nature of social interaction, thought of in terms of the manipulation of appearances and the control of information.

Social phenomenology

Phenomenological ideas are translated into social research primarily through the constructivist perspective popularised by Berger and Luckman (1967), in terms of the *social construction of reality*. The work of Alfred Schütz was mainly instrumental in marrying phenomenological ideas with the broadly interpretivist tradition of German sociology, derived from Max Weber. He introduced the significance of common sense and the creation of the 'life-world' of ordinary, everyday activity. Recipe knowledge is the basis for ordinary, habituated thought and action. In the 'natural attitude', everyday social actors engage in thinking-as-usual. They use a variety of methods of practical reasoning in order to make everyday life possible. Phenomenology also contributes to studies of embodied knowledge and practice. In the past a rather small number of exponents have advocated an *existential* approach to sociology, which has many affinities.

Ethnomethodology

Ethnomethodology's inspirations include phenomenological sociology, but also a number of classic sociological traditions, including the Durkheimian legacy. It is concerned with the fundamental and recurrent problem of how social order is possible. It shares with the phenomenological movement a concern with social actors' *methods* of sense-making, the *practicalities* of rule-use and the creation of organisational *routines*. Ethnomethodologically informed ethnography examines how local knowledge is created and used. It provides an especially useful repertoire of ideas for the analysis of work and organisations, social problems and institutional realities. The posthumously published lectures of Harvey Sacks provide ethnographers with a rich resource of insights into the imaginative analysis of mundane details, and how they can exemplify generic issues of social theory.

Ethnoscience

Etymologically related to ethnomethodology, ethnoscience is a field of specialisation concerned with indigenous systems of classification and knowledge-in-use. Its origin lies in cultural anthropology, and it has a strongly cognitive and semantic flavour. Specific interests in anthropology include ethnobotany, ethnoastronomy and ethnomedicine. It is not absolutely necessary to adopt the original approach of cognitive anthropology to recognise the potential significance of acquiring a comprehensive view of local, indigenous systems of knowledge. Of course, viewed from the appropriate perspective, *all* systems of knowledge are 'ethno' systems, including Western or cosmopolitan systems – so the sociology or anthropology of science is, strictly speaking, a study of ethnoscience (however widespread and potent a system it may be). While a generic ethnographic approach is not likely to depend on a restricted, semantic view of culture, and is more likely to stress knowledge-in-action, any fieldwork that takes account of local knowledge-systems (and what does not?) ought to be informed by at least an acquaintance with ethnoscience and cognitive anthropology and sociology more generally. There are close affinities with structuralism.

Structuralist anthropology

The heyday of high structuralism is over. Few anthropologists today would aim to emulate the work of a Claude Lévi-Strauss in analysing symbolic or textual materials (e.g. Lévi-Strauss 1963; Leach 1970). On the other hand, the broad tradition of Durkheim and Mauss has fed into a more pervasive structuralist sensibility. The sociological work of Pierre Bourdieu on cultural systems of taste and discrimination – notwithstanding his own accounts of it – owes a great deal to a distinctively French structuralist sensibility (e.g. Bourdieu 1986). Mary Douglas's work on purity, pollution and danger had a structuralist origin and has inspired a good deal of subsequent work that in effect gives a particular impetus to Durkheimian notions of the sacred and the profane (Douglas 1966). While structuralism *per se* may not be fashionable in contemporary anthropology or sociology, it retains the capacity to remind us of something fundamental: that cultural systems have their own internal logic, are organised as systems, are indeed structured. In other words, we do not need to subscribe to a grand narrative of universal structures to understand the formal properties of semiotic systems and cultural conventions. Whether they be narrative structures or systems of visual representation (such as colour-codes), cultural domains have their distinctive structuring principles. We do not need to be so wedded to the uncertainties of poststructuralism or postmodernism as to overlook such properties.

Interpretative anthropology

Strictly speaking there is no specific theoretical perspective of interpretative anthropology, but the ethnographer needs to be aware of a range of ideas that relate to anthropology (especially cultural anthropology) and are inspired by writers like Clifford Geertz (1973). This perspective treats the culture in question as if it were, broadly and metaphorically speaking, a set of texts to be inspected and interpreted for their primary cultural configurations, and in terms of the dominant cultural themes that they display. Geertz's own interpretative approach to Balinese culture or to the theatrical court culture are among key examples, as is Michael Herzfeld's work on the cultural idioms of masculinity (Herzfeld 1985), or the appropriation of the archaeological past on Crete (Herzfeld 1982).

Discourse and conversation analysis

This is not strictly a theoretical school – but the close analysis of spoken action is a vital resource for any ethnographer. As with other perspectives mentioned in this section, it is not always necessary to embrace all of the technical apparatus of these analyses in order to develop careful and methodical analyses of spoken activity and the relevant processes of the interaction order (Potter 1996; Potter and Wetherell 1987). While discursive analysis relates more directly to a social psychology of emotions, motives and the like, conversation analysis is more directly concerned with the achievement of orderly conduct through the sequential ordering of turns at talk, or turns at talk and unspoken activities. In both cases, however (and their differences can be exaggerated), analysis is directed to the intrinsic ordering of language in use. This is definitely not a matter of simply collecting spoken data and inspecting it in a common-sense way for what the actors 'really mean', or using language materials as transparent avenues to speakers' intentions and psychological states. Too much 'qualitative research' takes that latter (impoverished) form.

Narrative analysis

Again, not strictly a theoretical perspective, but a body of work that, like studies of discourse, acknowledges the ordering of spoken materials. Narrative analysis implies a systematic analysis of stories, accounts, memories and the like. It recognises that there are *forms* to narrative structure. Moreover, it therefore identifies the shared formats and genres of personal narratives. Even the most 'personal' narrative of experience and personal identity is, therefore, couched in culturally shared terms. Narrative analysis is, therefore, a particular example of the more general analytic issue: of recognising that cultural phenomena have their own forms of organisation, their own inherent logic. Narratives encapsulate the intersection of the personal and the cultural, the spontaneous and the conventional. Narratives frequently conform to elementary forms (cf. Labov 2013). The work of authors such as Labov (2013), Riessman (1993, 2002) and Cortazzi (1993) provides fundamental analytic tools.

The analysis of material culture

Cultural studies hardly constitute a 'theoretical' paradigm in their own right, nor does the more particular analysis of material culture. But in recent decades, material culture has become a particular focus of analytic interest. It pays attention to the role of goods and artefacts. These are not merely passive carriers of social relations (as in the gift or other ceremonial exchanges) but also have their own cultural significance, their own intrinsic systems of organisation, and occupy a distinctively material order. The detailed analysis of material artefacts is a counterbalance to accounts of social life that seem to take place in a material vacuum – peopled by disembodied and untrammelled individuals, who do not manipulate or make anything in the course of their work, who do not inhabit material environments and whose world has no substance.

Now I am not suggesting that this is a comprehensive listing. Equally, it is hard to suggest that each and every ethnographer ought to be thoroughly fluent in each and every one of these bodies of work (and of course there are others that could be added to this list). These packages of ideas and analytic strategies do not constitute mutually exclusive 'paradigms'. It is certainly not a matter of choosing between one and another. But any decent ethnographer ought to have a working knowledge of the core ideas and analytic procedures that derive from them. In many cases, it is clear that disciplinary and local boundaries impose unhelpful limits on scholars. Social and cultural anthropologists, for instance, routinely pay absolutely no attention to the work of sociologists or language analysts. (On the rare occasions that they do so, they re-brand them as anthropologists – as in the case of Pierre Bourdieu.) While sociologists are less restricted in their view, they also pay insufficient attention to anthropological research. Scholars who think of themselves as symbolic interactionists can be unduly blinkered, paying insufficient attention to other disciplinary traditions. And so on. While it may well be impossible for a social scientist to be equally *au fait* with all the possible analytic and disciplinary traditions, there is absolutely no justification for narrow-mindedness and ignorance.

Contrary to some accounts of the field, there is no sense in which we ought to be treating all of these perspectives as mutually exclusive. Some commentators try to derive complex typologies of traditions, 'paradigms' and the like. These are almost always unhelpful. I have only presented the listing above in order to advocate an eclectic appreciation of what they have to offer the ethnographer. I do not subscribe to the view that these are approaches to be chosen and adhered to as acts of faith. While there are, admittedly, some important differences between disciplines and theoretical perspectives, these are not such as to preclude a fruitful reading of them and a productive use of relevant ideas.

As a matter of fact, some disciplinary boundaries are not merely arbitrary, but positively unhelpful in making sense of the social world. In particular, the divide between anthropology and sociology is a silly one. While they may have had very different historical roots, anthropology and sociology have converged upon similar themes and issues increasingly. Ethnographic research methods have been pursued in both disciplinary traditions. Anthropology's stock-in-trade was always fieldwork with 'exotic' peoples and face-to-face communities. Sociology always included fieldwork with urban groups and sub-cultures, in work-settings and complex organisations, among professionals and their clients – indeed in most of the social settings of a complex society. The two were pursued in oddly separate ways. Anthropologists indeed have been especially reluctant to recognise the ethnographic tradition in sociology. In the course of a research conversation with a British anthropologist (in the context of a project on doctoral students and their supervisors), I was informed that ethnographic fieldwork was the unique preserve of anthropologists, while we sociologists – myself included of course – rely exclusively on surveys. This is not an isolated event. One finds again and again that anthropologists claim ethnographic fieldwork for themselves. If they acknowledge that other folk use it too, then they always add the rider that anthropologists do it in an ineffably different manner. (You might have thought that anthropologists above all others would be sensitive to such boundary-work.)

In the ideal world, social scientists who are interested in the (broadly speaking) interpretative approach to social life, and who adopt (equally broadly) qualitative fieldwork methods, would recognise common cause. They would not draw their disciplinary skirts about them and shrink from association with others. Sociologists of an interactionist or discursive bent would find themselves closely aligned with cultural analysts on the one hand and social anthropologists on the other. We would recognise that such sociologists frankly have little in common with political arithmetic and applied economics, or with political science (to which many sociologists aspire), and owe little or no allegiance to the second-rate philosophy that often passes for sociological 'theory'. They would all distance themselves from the sort of semi-scholarship devoted to expounding the ideas of dead Parisian *savants*, while celebrating the virtues of empirical social research. Sadly, it does not happen.

These various perspectives variously imply not merely different analytic strategies, but also call for different, complementary, techniques and modes of data collection. The conduct of fieldwork depends, therefore, on the simultaneous deployment of distinctive kinds of imagination and attention, on the one hand, and technologies of recoding, on the other. Fieldwork is not, or should not be, technologically driven in a technologically determinist sense. But there is no doubt that data collection rests on a variety of techniques. The traditional and still conventional approach to ethnographic fieldwork is the construction of fieldnotes. Fieldnotes are almost always the bedrock of ethnographic participant observation, irrespective of what further techniques and technologies might be employed. Fieldnotes have a very particular and distinctive character. They are not like other 'data', in that they are created by the ethnographer, translating what she or he has seen, heard and done into a textual form. They are rarely written *in situ* in their entirety. Even if one can write extensively 'in the field', because it is that kind of an organisational or professional setting, further note-making is almost always required. Fieldnotes are always selective. It is clearly impossible to make notes on everything that happens, and everything that is observable (as opposed to what is actually observed). On the other hand, the participant observer who is adequately observant, can create a degree of coherence by crafting fieldnotes that escape other forms of direct recording. In other words, there is a process of transformation that lies at the heart of fieldnote-making. Such notes are not raw data, and should never be thought of in such terms. While the fieldworker/author should try to retain as much detail as possible and create concrete notes of events, speech and material circumstances, the creation of fieldnotes is in itself an act of reconstruction. Fieldnotes are themselves textual forms, they are composed, and they should therefore be thought of as an especially artful aspect of a complex process whereby social scenes and social worlds are reconstructed. In other words, the creation of fieldnotes is to be seen as a work of textual reconstruction. It is the sort of work that many observers and participants do – travel writers for instance. It is none the worse for that. But it needs to be recognised for what it is. It is one of the stages in the longer, greater work of reconstruction, through the creation of extended texts such as the ethnographic monograph. To that extent, therefore, the fieldnote is different from other technologies and forms of recording – although as we shall see, these two involve a degree of reconstruction and textual convention too.

But as we have already seen, in order to do justice to the complexity of everyday life, and to social scenes, we need multiple technologies. We need to be able to record the visual order, the linguistic and interactional order, the narrative order and the material order. Fieldnotes can account for many of these phenomena in general terms, but they cannot do so in a way that permits enough retrieval of form and detail to sustain detailed analysis. Luckily we can avail ourselves of unobtrusive technologies that support such data collection. As I have suggested already, contemporary (and rapidly changing) digital technologies permit recordings that can be stored, shared, manipulated and displayed in a completely digital environment. They can be shared via the internet. They can be integrated in bespoke data-analysis software. Moreover, they also permit data-collection methods that are not totally dependent on the ethnographer alone. The contemporary investigator has an extraordinary array of easy methods available through which she or he can generate permanent recordings of events, actions, accounts and encounters. This does not mean, however, that these can all be used as data without further intervention. Spoken and visual materials need, in most cases, to be transcribed. The transformation of recorded digital information into usable text is not a simple procedure. In a way that is analogous to the production of fieldnotes, transcription requires a degree of intervention on the part of the author/analyst. Transcription conventions are just that – conventional. The transcription of recorded speech is now well codified, and conventions are widely acknowledged. The delicate transcription of naturally occurring interaction requires detailed, technically specified transcriptions. But that does not in any sense detract from the fact that transcription is itself conventional. The act of transcription is not innocent. There are many decisions (of orthography and punctuation among them) that impinge directly not only on the intelligibility of speech, but also on the identities of the speakers themselves. Likewise, visual data cannot be treated merely as surrogate recordings of observations. The use of visual materials requires several things: selection of excerpts and examples, editing, style of printing (for still photography), the relationship between text and image. Indeed, film, video, still photography and more – all these need some degree of transformation and selection before they can be used productively for ethnographic purposes. The transcription of visual materials – such as mapping movement – is far from straightforward. Equally, however, it is clear that the conduct of contemporary ethnography can – even if it is not obligatory – be developed into a technologically complex array of recording and analytic issues. Recording technologies do not substitute for the elementary disciplines of participant observation, though they can be vital and even necessary adjuncts to the ethnographic gaze. Observation is extended through a variety of devices, resulting in a complex array of data types, that in turn imply a complexity of analytic perspectives and strategies.

Increasing methodological awareness on the part of sociologists and others (even anthropologists to some extent) has led to increasing specialisation. So, for instance, we have a specialism of visual ethnography, or of narrative analysis. Equally, various opportunities of data collection, as well as more general developments in sociology and cultural geography, have led to an emphasis on mobile methods. The development of discourse analysis and conversation analysis is well known, and has also led to a highly specialised domain of research. There is clearly nothing intrinsically wrong in the development of specialised knowledge and expertise. The opportunities afforded by recording devices are not to be ignored: they should be exploited to the full. But in doing so we must avoid the danger of *technological reductionism*. By that I mean that there is a temptation to celebrate one variety of data collection, and hence one modality of data, so that the social world becomes reduced to a single dimension. Visual data and their analysis are undeniably important, and they call for a degree of expertise. But they do not exhaust the many forms of order and significance within a given cultural gestalt. It is wrong to treat spoken language as if it were the be-all and end-all of social life. Narratives are undoubtedly significant ways of ordering memory, expressing emotions and organising experience. But we have absolutely no warrant for treating narratives as special kinds of cultural phenomena that can, as it were, stand for the entire range of social actions and cultural forms.

Does this mean that we turn our back on, say, narrative analysis? Do we pay no attention to visual aspects of everyday life? Of course not. But we need to be clear about their potential significance. Narrative analysis is important if and only if narratives are a significant feature of the social world we are studying. If it is (and it is hard to think of social worlds where narrativity is not an issue) then of course we have to study those narratives properly. We do not celebrate them, in other words, but we treat them as kinds of social acts like any other. Moreover, we do not devote ourselves to narrative because that is our specialism and we are determined to stick to it. It is not a matter of a researcher's personal identity to devote herself or himself to one data-type, which becomes a Procrustean bed to which all aspects of the social are made to conform. Moreover, a proper analysis of 'narrative' is going to take us beyond those narratives themselves. Narratives do not exist in a social vacuum. We shall take account of the fact that narratives are enacted forms, with audiences as well as tellers. We shall have a properly ethnographic interest in their circulation. We shall examine how narratives of various sorts are embedded in a given culture – occupational, organisational or local. We shall inspect them for their cultural functions – as moral tales, confessions, testimonials and so on.

Now these preliminary remarks may seem self-evident. In many ways they are. But there are many versions of 'qualitative' research that seem to overlook the obvious. In too many of those versions, indeed, researchers depend quite disproportionately on interviews of various sorts. In essence, this reliance on the interview is the very antithesis of the ethnographic imagination. Reliance on interviews alone, however conversational or unstructured they may be, denies any chance of real attention to social action and social organisation. Again, this is not an argument in favour of mute, passive observation. It is not an argument against conversing with one's research hosts. It is not even an injunction against interviewing. It is a rejection of interviewing as the main means of data collection. As we shall see, the problems of data derived from interviews are compounded when they are not subjected to any systematic, detailed analysis, but are reproduced uncritically as unvarnished representations of personal experience (as if the latter were the main topic of social science research). It remains the case, however, that whatever data may be gathered, and by whatever means, our ethnographic purpose is to develop systematic understandings – densely inhabited with ideas, and empirically detailed – about the social settings and worlds under consideration. This is a thoroughly comparative and cumulative enterprise.

4
Analytic Perspectives

Ethnographic analysis has been led up some blind alleys in recent years. In particular, a recurrent emphasis in some quarters on so-called *grounded theory* has proved limiting. This is not an especially popular view, I realise, and it is not easy to sustain. As I shall suggest, in its simplest essence, the development of grounded theory is just a way of expressing what everybody does – or ought to do – anyway. At one level, grounded theory is the sociological equivalent of speaking prose. Recently, grounded theory has been complemented, or possibly countered, by appeals to *the extended case method*. Some authors have suggested, indeed, that these are the only analytic strategies available in sociology or anthropology. I shall discuss this assertion later. It is clearly absurd, except insofar as they are the two sides of the same, rather commonplace, coin.

Why start this chapter with a perspective I really want to depart from? Because its influence is so pervasive in sociology and other fields, such as nursing and education (though anthropologists seem to have got by quite nicely while ignoring it completely). There is a clear danger that textbook versions of grounded theory, in concert with some other taken-for-granted approaches (such as the over-reliance on interviews), has – in some quarters at least – deflected attention away from the fundamental goals of ethnographic work. The basic idea of grounded theory is, of course, simple and straightforward. It is derived more or less directly from an American pragmatist philosophy of science and of inquiry more generally. It values the active exploration of a field of research, and it values equally the generation of original ideas about that field. Equally, it encourages the development of general ideas that go beyond the particular research field in question. It is comparative, and it encourages the cumulative developments of ideas.

It can be approached from a very elementary question: Where do research ideas come from? We can call that the development of theory, but since so many people find 'theory' unhelpful – with connotations of 'grand theory' that is entirely divorced from real-world phenomena and associated with dead European thinkers – I prefer to think in terms of *ideas*. They seem more user-friendly. So at its simplest, grounded theory describes some of the heuristic methods that researchers (of any sort) use to engage with some empirical domain, and attempt to make some general sense of it. In formulating the basic notion, Glaser and Strauss (1967) were reacting against abstracted theory that related purely to other theory and had no direct engagement with any empirical research. The social sciences have indeed been bedevilled by grandiose theories, often directed at a macro-level 'social system' perspective, that do nothing to drive and inform real-world research. So grounded theory turns away from such abstraction. It suggests that there is far more to empirical research, moreover, than 'testing' pre-existing theories and hypotheses derived from them. The latter – a strictly deductive approach to the logic of inquiry – has a certain philosophical appeal, perhaps, but it has virtually nothing to say to the practising researcher. In essence, for example, a purely deductive approach tells us nothing about what is a plausible or fruitful line of inquiry to pursue. It has very little to say in guiding us in the concrete exploration of a social world. A purely theory-driven research agenda thus has little or no room for practical experience. Yet the researcher necessarily relies on some form of experience – a generalised experience with the academic discipline in question, and a more specific experience based on her or his general comprehension of the research topic. We do not pull theories and hypotheses out of thin air. We derive them from a variety of sources: our own prior exposure to phenomena, the work of others (published or otherwise) and our first engagements with our research field. Equally, there is no useful place for a completely sterile empiricism that simply gathers facts divorced from any kind of developing social theory. Grounded theory was never intended to justify inductive research. That is, it is definitely not a recipe for aimless accumulations of facts and observations, coupled with a hope that ideas will somehow 'emerge' from them (like eggs hatching out).

So far so good. To that extent, the original conception of grounded theory is unexceptional. In point of fact, it describes what any sensible researcher would do, and Glaser and Strauss transformed good practice into a normative framework. In keeping with their pragmatist inspiration, they stressed a cyclical relationship between ideas and data, in a way that introduced a sensible role for experience and craft knowledge in the logic of scientific discovery. The logic – as has been noted repeatedly – is essentially *abductive*. That is, on the basis of observation (in the most general sense), one draws out *possible* analytic ideas that speculatively answer the question: What might this be a case of? One considers what general pattern or configuration might give rise to the observed phenomena. That tentative identification then provides what Herbert Blumer (1954) called a 'sensitising concept' that can inform further data collection. Hence sensitising concepts are used in dialogue with data, in order to generate further elaborations of the guiding ideas, refinements or modifications to them. This mode of reasoning is so central and so pervasive to the tradition that I call it *ethnographic abduction*, recognising that there are multiple levels of social institutions and processes that call for such inference.

The 'method' is always comparative, in the broadest sense. One does not spend one's time examining only the same research setting, or devoting oneself solely to one's own data-set. After all, if one is asking oneself 'what might this be a case of?', then the analytic gaze is already a comparative one. One is – if only implicitly – drawing contrasts and comparisons with other research settings. This does not always mean, of course, that we have to conduct first-hand fieldwork in all the possible sites of relevance. It does mean working with ideas drawn, in principle, from a very wide variety of different types of social setting. The method is also comparative in the sense that one is always comparing across cases within one's own data – doing so in order to refine and modify developing ideas.

Again, this is fine. It seems to describe the sort of heuristic reasoning that most competent researchers would pursue, irrespective of the research topic, the field of specialisation and the kinds of data being collected. In the original formulations by Glaser and Strauss themselves, there is no inherent link between 'grounded theory' on the one hand, and 'qualitative' research on the other. It is a general description of the practicalities of research practice. But something seems to have happened to the general ideas in the decades since Glaser and Strauss first promoted grounded theory as a characterisation of research. In the intervening years, grounded theory has had an odd fate. It has become codified into some highly prescriptive, formulaic approaches. It has also been transformed into a distinctive kind of theory in its own right. Neither is helpful, and both can be antithetical to the ethnographic imagination.

Glaser and Strauss themselves turned out to embody a tension, one that has become increasingly apparent through their own work and the work of others. Glaser published several interventions that railed against the version of grounded theory being proposed by Strauss himself, with collaborators (Glaser 1978, 1992). There is no need to recapitulate that history in detail here, but its general direction is germane. In essence, Glaser argued (and I agree with him) that textbook versions of grounded theory, especially that by Strauss and Corbin (Strauss and Corbin 1998), translated a sensitising, heuristic approach to exploratory research into a codified protocol. In part, of course, that process would reflect a very general process that is visible in virtually any textbook. It is the process classically defined by Ludwick Fleck, in his pioneering study of scientific knowledge (Fleck 1979 [1937]). It is a trajectory of simplification, whereby knowledge is progressively transformed from innovative scientific discovery into textbook knowledge. There are, of course, levels of even greater simplification beyond Fleck's: there is the sort of taken-for-granted knowledge that is not really based even on textbooks, but based on second-hand acquaintance with simplified versions. The latter are often vulgarised and distorted versions, that can in turn be re-cycled into published literature. The consequences include misleading and unhelpful injunctions and prohibitions. As a consequence, 'grounded theory' has become fetishised, translated into a unique approach to social research in its own right (see e.g. Morse et al. 2009).

The problems have become compounded. First, naïve versions of grounded theory seem to imply that one enters the field with no prior ideas. Indeed, this fallacy is not confined to proponents of grounded theory *per se*. It is often attributed to ethnography, and to 'qualitative research' more widely. This is especially wide of the mark. There has never been a plausible suggestion that ethnographic research should be thought of as a purely inductive undertaking. Entering the field with an empty mind is guaranteed to result in empty notebooks. There is a world of difference between an *open* mind and an empty one. The productive researcher is by no means devoid of ideas, during fieldwork or before it. Ideas may be emergent from the interaction between theories and data, but that does not occur in an intellectual vacuum. One does not have to enter the field with tightly defined hypotheses in order to have sensitising ideas about it. Quite apart from anything else, nobody should be undertaking fieldwork without an adequate grounding in a relevant social science discipline. I have already sketched some of the general bodies of knowledge that inform the overall ethnographic enterprise. We embark on the fieldwork with a number of general intellectual commitments. We conduct our fieldwork in the light of those general ideas, and we interpret our field in accordance with those orientations – constructivist, interactionist and so on. In that sense, therefore, fieldwork is always and irreducibly saturated with ideas. There is nothing atheoretical about the fieldwork, and 'analysis' is pervasive, starting before and lasting during the fieldwork, as well as being undertaken subsequently. There is nothing more dispiriting than the assumption that grounded theory encourages the mindless collection of data, followed by an inspection of those data, on a purely inductive basis, in the search for emergent ideas.

Secondly, and more forgivably in the circumstances, is the belief that analysis consists of coding the data. This is undoubtedly a direct reflection of grounded theory texts, where there has long been an emphasis on coding. Indeed, Strauss himself promoted a somewhat complicated scheme of different kinds of coding. Now coding can have a number of connotations, irrespective of any given author's intentions. As I have remarked before, it too readily conveys an analytic culture of 'fragmentation'. The technology of coding all too easily leads the researcher towards a jejune form of thematic analysis, whereby a number of categories are identified, and instances gathered up to exemplify those categories. Analysis is thus interpreted as the identification and illustration of a number of themes.

Now this is a process relevant to ethnographic research, of course. At the very simplest, all data, whatever their type or form, need some degree of ordering, and *indexing* data is always useful. Indeed, before the development of bespoke computer software, or even the generic functions of personal computers, ethnographers did indeed index their notebooks and transcripts. The basic technology of index cards was sufficient to keep track of information garnered over a period of time. But nobody thought that such an activity constituted even an approximation of analysis. Analysis is certainly not to be confused with procedural tasks of coding qualitative data. Strauss and his collaborators did help to create that perception, as various types of coding are among the abiding preoccupations of Strauss and his co-authors, and some of his followers. Indeed, it is easy to get the impression that the core idea of grounded theory, coupled with an inductive logic, is the repeated and complex coding of data.

This preoccupation with coding has been compounded by the widespread use of computer software packages for the 'analysis' of qualitative data. Now, as I shall acknowledge later in this discussion, one cannot hold the contemporary software responsible for limited and unimaginative uses of it. And I do not hold it entirely so. But the development of CAQDAS indisputably enshrined a 'coding' technology. When the first software was developed, such as The Ethnograph or Kwalitan, there was a quite explicit intention to build a code-and-retrieve strategy. Kwalitan was quite deliberately created to mimic the principles of grounded theory, and it was that aspect of grounded theory that was most prominently inscribed in the software and its functions. Indeed, the early textbook versions of CAQDAS, such as Tesch's, were overtly organised in terms of code-and-retrieve (Tesch 1990). That is, coding was characterised primarily in terms of attaching identifying labels to segments or instances of textual data, so that they could be searched for and found, and then collected together under thematic headings. There was a clear strategy implied here. Data were to be *de-contextualised* out of their original location, and *re-contextualised* into a new environment of categories, in which examples of 'the same' code are collected together. Of course, nobody ever suggested that this was the end of analysis, which manifestly could never mean just sorting and collating data extracts, but as a major analytic step in the overall process, it clearly sets the ethnographer on a particular pathway.

Since those early days, software has developed into a much more complex array of possibilities, and I shall return to that theme later. But, *pace* the denials of Fielding and others, I remain convinced that there was a particular congruence between the codification of 'grounded theory' and the promotion of analytic software. As I have acknowledged (e.g. Weaver and Atkinson 1994), there are many other things that one can do with the software – and indeed there are even more interesting things that were not part of the origins of CAQDAS. But the combination of 'coding' and 'computing' has not been an especially beneficial one (Coffey et al. 1996). Part of the problem lies not so much with the software itself, nor indeed with the general strategy of coding on its own. It derives in part because too many studies – and indeed too many manuals of advice concerning 'qualitative' research – depend on rather simple notions of data, and consequently yield equally simple versions of analysis. As I have suggested already (e.g. Atkinson 2005), far too much reliance is placed on one-dimensional data, often derived from interviews, which results in equally one-dimensional kinds of analysis. As a result, what we get is the *thematic* treatment of respondents' accounts, all too often treated as proxy information about reported events, experiences or feelings. Now interviews and conversations are by no means irrelevant to ethnographic fieldwork. I shall discuss them in more detail later in this book. But clearly a series of interviews with separate informants does not constitute an ethnographic study of their everyday social worlds. It can tell us little about social action within a given setting. It can tell us nothing about how people actually engage with one another. It tells us little or nothing about the achievement of social order within a given setting. Moreover, dealing in interviews primarily, or as the sole source of data, too often glosses over the nature of the interview itself. The interview is itself a social encounter. Interview-derived narratives and accounts are performances in their own right. They are, or contain embedded within them, speech events. They contain stories that reflect common genres. They construct biographies and identities. They deserve attention from *those* analytic perspectives. They do not deserve merely to be chopped up and coded thematically without proper regard for their forms and functions *as* narratives and accounts.

To return to the central argument, then, I am recommending an ethnographic analytic perspective that tries to do justice to the complexity of data that, in turn, do justice to the complexity of everyday life *in situ*. This is not in itself an argument against 'grounded theory', but it is an argument against vulgar versions of it and the effect they have had on research in practice. In particular, as I have argued, too much of what passes for analysis is unhelpfully flat, reducing the complexity of everyday life to a set of themes that remain otherwise under-developed. Moreover, an implicit emphasis on inductive logic, rather than the abductive logic in the original pragmatist tradition, can easily have a deadening effect on the conceptual complexity of the analysis. An adequate and sensitive understanding of a given cultural system or social setting may emerge from the ethnographer's thorough knowledge of it, but it will not emerge from peering at 'the data'. So we really must free notions of analysis from a close dependency on 'data'. This in fact reflects an implied congruence between ethnographic and other forms of social inquiry. It can convey a spurious sense of rigour, by creating a system of data-management, even of data-mining, analogous to that carried out with large quantitative data-sets. This is a misguided approach. I am not accusing everyone who appeals to 'grounded theory' of sharing these weaknesses, but I am suggesting that *in use*, the danger is there, and it does owe a great deal to subsequent versions of grounded theory. It would be safer to drop the term, and it would certainly be safer to avoid treating grounded theory as something special, as a kind of theory in its own right, and as something to be followed slavishly. We could therefore do very well with far fewer secondary sources about it, and more thought as to how good ethnographic work might get done.

The same might be said of notions of *theory-building*. This again is a formulation that has gained particular currency in recent years, and is also built into the logic and the rhetoric of computer-aided data analysis. The imagery of 'building' theory always seems odd. Ideas are rarely built. As I have argued, a purely inductive approach to analysis just does not wash, and has never been a part of the ethnographic tradition. While it is an exaggeration to imply that all notions of theory-building are indebted to an impoverished view of ethnography, *in practice* there is too simplistic a view, and it is one that draws on the sort of code-and-theme 'analysis' I have just referred to. When embedded in the logic of CAQDAS, theory-building frequently relies on a notion of linkage between themes – and hence on linkages between codes. Now the creation of complex relationships between ideas is always useful, indeed imperative, and there are many ways of representing that process. But, just like the fallacy of 'emerging' ideas springing from data, the idea of building theory by successive acts of linking codes and themes, is profoundly limited. Both seem to imply that the processes of analysis and theorising are performed on an otherwise inert data-set, after it has been collected. It pays insufficient attention to the pervasive nature of speculation and theorising that is embedded in the ethnographic enterprise at every moment, and it too readily implies a quite inappropriate periodisation of fieldwork, whereby data collection precedes analysis.

Now, there are certainly many heuristic devices that can be used to promote the development of ideas. The use of 'theory-building' functions in software is one way (so long as one is not seduced into thinking one is actually building anything), so too is the creation of 'mind-maps' and other visual devices. These are perfectly useful as heuristic methods. They can certainly prompt one to think creatively. But they do not embody the creative process themselves. This is partly because the end-point of analysis is *not* a knitting-together of coded themes. There is no single form of analysis, of course, but all valuable analytic forms transcend mechanistic, code-based strategies.

Why have these precepts and principles come to occupy a dominant and potentially unhelpful place in the methodological literature? The answer is not far to seek. Methodology has become a major industry in recent decades. The numbers of students following methods training – particularly at the postgraduate level – has grown exponentially in all countries where the social sciences flourish. So too have journals that publish the work, summer schools and short courses. These have all been underpinned by a publishing industry that has thrived on the back of methods textbooks and the like. This is a movement that feeds off itself. Textbooks and handbooks on research methods proliferate. Oral traditions of apprenticeship are translated into explicit advice and methodologically rule-governed behaviour. Where once the proof of the quality of research lay in its outcomes (a doctoral thesis or monograph), now it resides in the processes that went into it. We care more about people's adherence to proper codes of behaviour – ethical and procedural – than we do about the quality of their imagination and scholarship. (That is perhaps a bit of an exaggeration, but only a bit.) Consequently, every aspect of the research process can become codified and enshrined in textbooks or journal papers at every level of specificity, at every level of readership (from beginning students to expert practitioners). There is nothing more susceptible to codification than a system of data analysis. This is especially so, given that so many students find that analysis is at best mystifying, and at worst terrifying. So it is better to have some practical activity to get on with, like coding, and procedures, like theory-building, to embody the work of analysis. They act like a comfort-blanket.

To that extent, grounded theory is unremarkable. If it does provide ways of going on for a large number of people, then it is difficult to argue against it. But it is equally hard to see that following the sort of recipes outlined by Corbin and Strauss, or Charmaz (e.g. 2006) are actually conducive to the very best kind of sociological or anthropological imagination. This does not, of course, mean that it is impossible to think about analysis. Or that it is impossible to give some sort of constructive advice. It does, however, mean that the most important issues concern the sort of 'big picture' ideas that ought to suffuse and inform the analysis, rather than the essentially clerical work of managing data.

I am down-playing the management of data here partly to reinforce the notion that ethnography inevitably and desirably gives a very particular, and distinctive, understanding of a social world, and it is not one that is strictly confined to written or otherwise recorded data. Transcripts and notes, photographs and videos are important – do not misunderstand me. But they do not and cannot capture the entire range of knowledge and understanding that the ethnographer acquires and then brings to bear. There is, moreover, a recurrent need to return, if not to 'grand theory', then at least to theories of a generality beyond merely ideas of 'the middle range', useful though they are. We need constantly to push our ideas as far as they will go in any direction – from the finest grain of everyday life and culture to the local manifestations of global phenomena. Neither of these is guaranteed by moving fragments of data from one field to another, nor indeed by attaching labels (codes) to those fragments, however interesting those labels might be.

The so-called *extended case method* explicitly seeks to locate the ethnographically local within a broader – even global – analytic framework. The phenomena of classic anthropology, for instance, would thus be located within an understanding of colonial or postcolonial dynamics. Local manifestations of social and cultural systems would be interpreted in the light of global economic and political phenomena. The local is therefore always redefined as a moment in a wider social or cultural process. The origins of the extended case method lie with the Manchester School of anthropology, and with a characteristic preoccupation with conflict, notably in ethnographies of African society. Methodologically speaking, its proponents reacted against a purely structural-functional form of anthropology, which assumed a stable social system and culture, such that any specific events (cases) are regarded as exemplars of that culture. Analysis thus resides in the retrieval of 'the culture' through the accumulation of episodes and events. The Manchester model, by contrast, emphasised a much more dynamic social and cultural process. Cases and events are thus analysed in terms of their reflection of conflicts and strategic interests. (In fact, this view of the social process is close to that articulated by the Chicago interactionists, who partly inspired the grounded theory approach.)

In recent years, the work of Burawoy and his colleagues has provided the most sustained attempt to develop ethnographic work through the extended case. It has, of course, great appeal. Burawoy (1998) has suggested that the extended case method be adopted in order to enable ethnographic sociology to move from the 'micro' to the 'macro', which he expresses in terms of being able to 'extract the general from the unique'. In turn, in Burawoy's hands, this means an engagement of the ethnographically local with broader societal, even global, forces, and with economic, political and other systems. Sociologists in particular have often felt uncomfortable in dealing with the fine grain of the particular. They frequently want to extend their explanatory scheme to incorporate the grand themes of sociological theory – social structures and processes of transformation that can be identified at or beyond the level of the nation-state. Anything that remains at the level of 'middle-range' theory seems inadequate and immature. The solution is, therefore, an appealing one. The value of ethnographic work is, of course, to free the analysis from a totalising application of ideas like 'globalisation', that are always in danger of explaining everything and nothing. (The same is true of ideas such as 'postmodernism', having a protean character, capable of application to virtually every cultural form and ultimately often divorced from any empirical, concrete application.) Insofar as the ethnographically local does not merely illustrate the taken-for-granted categories of terms like globalisation, then we remain on ethnographically firmer ground. There remains, however, the danger that the complexities of ethnographic representation are sacrificed in the interests of analytic inclusiveness. In reality, extended cases are a bit like grounded theory – the sort of sensible thing that practical researchers do as and when they are able to and when their study permits. But when elevated to an orthodoxy or a strict methodological regime, then it outgrows its usefulness and becomes a straitjacket. Burawoy's own formulation is misleading. He equates the ethnographic exploration of the generic and the local with a sociological rhetoric of macro- and micro-levels of analysis. In this formulation, moreover, the implication is that the ethnography should always be linked directly to existing theory. It is clear that this is intended, in the work of Burawoy and his colleagues (e.g. Burawoy 1991), to furnish the wherewithal for a critical sociology.

In recent commentary, grounded theory and the extended case method have been proposed as the only games in town, the only two available models, competing for allegiance and legitimacy (Tavory and Timmermans 2009). This is unhelpful. In the first place, the distinction is over-drawn. It is all too easy to infer that grounded theory is inductively generated and always local in nature, while the extended case is always theoretically driven. In practice, real ethnographies are derived from *local* circumstances and *generic* ideas. Both 'methods' (and of course they are not methods or procedures at all) actually depend on very similar intellectual and imaginative processes. I repeat myself here. Both approaches to the relationship between ethnography and theory depend on answers to the research question: What is this a case of? Now what might be a 'case' does not receive a single answer. It is not the case that the whole ethnography or the research setting should be categorised in terms of just one 'case'. There will be multiple answers, many possible patterns that can be invoked or constructed to make sense of observed events.

Indeed, the whole thrust of this book is to remind us of how potentially complex a social setting may be, and hence of the role of complexity in ethnographic inquiry. In consequence, there may be many ways of asking 'what's going on here?' and of answering such a question. For instance, observed phenomena might be held to be cases or classes of a form of social *process*. They might equally be thought to be enactments of a kind of *strategy*. They might at the same time be couched in *ceremonial forms* and distinctive *speech acts*. And so on. So we are not searching for a reductionist answer to our analytic question. There are not simply multiple social or cultural forms in play, but our analyses can clearly operate at multiple levels of generality. The distinction between the local and the generic is, of course, not an absolute one. It is a heuristic distinction that establishes a dimension of reflection, not an absolute difference. So the analytic process can be taken in several different directions, with different levels or layers of generality, and with multiple forms of social action or cultural forms.

In that sense, therefore, the distinction between grounded theory and extended cases is an unhelpful one. In many ways they are both retrospective accounts that justify normal intellectual processes and elevate them to a prescriptive orthodoxy. Each formulation stresses just one version of the essential tension between generality and specificity, and the creative moments that are derived from the repeated juxtaposition of ideas and data. The iterative process that is an ethnographic project is constantly and necessarily suspended between the two extremes. In reality, therefore, the two approaches converge. As we have seen, the pragmatist tradition that inspired the Chicago School and grounded theory always demands that the fieldworker should ask herself 'What might this be a case of?' Moreover, the view of social and cultural reality is always processual. No version of grounded theory would be adequate were it predicated on a static view of social structure, or a cultural system of fixed categories. The emphasis of extended case analysis on social process, negotiation, dispute and so on in no way separates it out from interactionist sociology. It is noticeable that Burawoy makes an unsustainable equation. He creates an equivalence between 'micro' or 'local' on the one hand, and 'macro' and 'generic' on the other. Now, as I have stressed already, the principles of grounded theory always imply a dialogue between the local and the generic, the context-specific and the context-free levels of conceptualisation and abstraction. The principle of constant comparison is predicated precisely on the necessity to transcend the purely local, and to seek a dialogue of ideas between the local and the generic. Indeed, there is nothing in grounded theory *per se* to deny the possibility of relating local processes to wider processes, or to insist on a restricted sociological perspective. Admittedly, in practice, there are perhaps too many ethnographies that do not venture sufficiently far into the realm of ideas. But any implication that ethnographers who do not explicitly endorse the 'extended case' method are therefore unable to engage with generic sociological or anthropological theory is patently nonsense. On the other hand, the extended case method is also a statement of the obvious, in that it enjoins the ethnographer to treat local circumstances in terms of a wider significance. So much would seem uncontroversial, to say the least.

The honest answer to these and similar strategies – such as the closely related procedure of *analytic induction* – is to say that ethnographic analysis is never achieved or exhausted by the application of a rule-bound set of procedures. Rather, it resides in our capacity to generate reconstructions of social processes and social actors, in such a way as to remain faithful to the complexities of the particular setting, while drawing out the generic links and comparisons. Ethnography works towards broader conceptions of social processes, social forms, processes of identity production, sources and types of knowledge and so on. In so doing, ethnographic accounts inescapably engage with the broadest possible intellectual frames. But we must equally be resistant to any suggestion that ethnographers are beholden to 'grand' theorists, such that they have to mould their ideas to suit the often un-grounded accounts of late modernity, globalisation.

So, what kinds of ideas, or sets of ideas, are we aiming for? They certainly correspond to well-established types of social science theory. They are not different in kind from the sorts of ideas that might inhabit any discipline, or indeed be derived from any methodological tradition. So far I have suggested, in a rather jaundiced way, that grounded theory and extended case methods are equally unhelpful. Both formulations suggest a rather narrow interpretation of the interpretative act. We are in danger of losing sight of the role of imagination in the ethnographic enterprise. In contrast, we need collectively to encourage the sort of extrapolation and speculation that a thoroughly abductive logic implies. We need to use our imagination, drawing on the imagination of others, and using a genuinely comparative style that ranges widely across disciplinary and substantive fields. There needs, as we have seen already, to be a cyclical dialogue between data and ideas. Indeed, we probably need to go further, and stop going on about 'data' altogether. It is too redolent of an inert mass of information, akin to the sort of materials to be found in archives and large surveys. Rather than just focusing on data, then, we need to think about our detailed knowledge of the local, of the field. And our analysis therefore resides in the skill with which we interrogate simultaneously the local and the generic. This is not the analysis of obsessive peering at data, or constructing multiple linkages and annotations. It is not derived from repeated memo-writing, nor yet from the multiplex codings beloved of grounded theory devotees. Equally, it is not a whimsical or mysterious process of intuition.

I have elsewhere referred to my own version of what might constitute 'thick description', which is yet another version of ethnographic analysis – or at least an ideal of ethnography. Rather than recapitulating Clifford Geertz's anthropological formulation of the idea (Geertz 1973), I want to counsel against yet another vulgar version of analytic perspective, and then to suggest how it relates to the ideas proposed in this book. The vulgar version of thick description implies a rather trivial notion of detail. In this version, the idea of thick description implies an ideal that is no more ambitious than to provide a richly detailed account of a given setting. Now it would be hard to quarrel with that aspiration (vague though it can often seem), but it is by no means adequate. From my perspective, the notion of 'thickness' implies a commitment to the exploration of the multiple forms through which social life is enacted – material, visual, spoken, embodied and so on. It also implies a *systemic* view of culture and social action. By that I mean an analysis that pays regard to the relations between the different modes of organisation, or the organising principles that are in play at any given time. The semiotic codes of cultural significance need to be anchored in the social relations between individuals and groups, the institutional arrangements through which collective action is accomplished, and so on. The interaction order may be a level of analysis that is relatively autonomous in terms of its organising principles, but that does not mean that it can be treated in complete isolation. Selves and biographies may have their intrinsic principles of temporal and narrative ordering, but they do not play themselves out in a social vacuum. And so on.

Reductionism of various kinds is a recurrent danger in conceptualising analytic strategies. I have already dealt with this, in discussing the necessity for multiple modes of data collection, and hence of understanding the dimensionality of everyday life. Let me therefore repeat the message in this context. We do a disservice to ethnography – and indeed to social science in general – if we transform the glorious variety of social forms to a single mode of understanding. Far too much contemporary work, for instance, apparently seeks to boil it all down to personal experience, and to represent the end of ethnographic analysis as merely biographical. It is, of course, important that lives should be documented. It is vital that our ethnographies are peopled by social actors who have biographical trajectories, and whose lives are shaped by personal and institutional frameworks. What is *not* desirable is the equation of social life in general with 'lives'. Equally, it is important to document how social actors construct their own and others' 'experiences'. But the ethnography of everyday life is far more than the documentation of people's reported experience – and much more than the autobiographical experiences of fieldworkers themselves.

Many of the 'theories' and 'models' that are derived from ethnographic research take the form of ideal-types. There is, of course, a voluminous literature on the history of this sort of theorising, and I do not intend to enter into a detailed discussion of that sort here. But it is necessary to point out that very many of the most powerful ideas in the social sciences are *de facto* ideal-types. For instance, Goffman's famous formulation of the *total institution* is a classic case in point (Goffman 1961). It reflects the way in which a constant comparative method is used to illuminate a given setting. It shows the productive use of generic ideas in illuminating the specifics of a given research site. It also shows how ideas always transcend the detailed particularities of an ethnographic 'field'. The substantive, local detail on which Goffman's analysis was based was a single mental hospital. But the ideas go well beyond that particular setting, and they go beyond other kinds of mental (or other) hospitals. Goffman develops the idea by making explicit comparisons with other types of institution – military installations, religious orders, prisons and the like. He derives a model that is delineated by a small number of dimensions: a common timetable, a common round of rules and regulations, a small staff managing a large number of inmates, physical and symbolic boundaries between the institution and the outside world. In a way that is perfectly characteristic of ideal-typical analyses, this model is not based on a piecemeal comparison of specific sites and situations, but is itself an abstraction that is derived (abducted) from a rich variety of sources. It is not a theory that is 'built' from instances, cases or themes. Furthermore, it embeds other ideal-typical models. For instance,

Goffman develops the idea of mortification of the self – a process of role-stripping and identity-transformation: again, this is something that may happen to institutional inmates, and takes common forms, such as head-shaving, removal of everyday clothing and so on. Ideal-types may well enclose other ideal-types.

Goffman's analysis was not derived in a cultural vacuum. At almost precisely the same time as he was developing the argument of *Asylums*, Julius Roth, a sociologist trained in a very similar tradition, was undertaking ethnographic research on tuberculosis hospitals (Roth 1963). His ideal-typical analysis also drew on comparisons with other institutions, focusing primarily on their temporal order. Hence *Timetables* (the title of the monograph) captures the significance of time, the control of time and the experience of time in a variety of institutional settings, not just TB sanitaria. Of course if we were repeating the analysis today, we would have the advantage of reading Foucault's invocation of the *panopticon*, not merely as a model for the rational prison, but – by extension – as a model or metaphor for modern institutions more generally, and by further extension as a microcosm for modernity itself (Foucault 1970).

Let us consider a more recent example, from anthropology. Appadurai's idea of *tournaments of value* is an ideal-typical concept that he derives from a variety of well-known examples (Appadurai 1986). Indeed, this is not derived from his own ethnographic case study, but is in the tradition of comparative ethnology. He suggests that one can think of ceremonial or ritualised occasions, with a competitive element, in which symbolic goods are exchanged. He refers to classic anthropological cases such as the *kula* or *potlatch*, while suggesting that occasions such as fine-art auctions may display similar characteristics. The idea is taken up by Moeran in a discussion of book fairs (Moeran 2011). Moeran suggests, *inter alia*, that events like book fairs can be thought of as crucial nodes within the *value chain*. Here we can see how one comparative concept can generate others, and how productive cross-site comparisons can be developed. Taking a cue from Appadurai, therefore, one might think of all sorts of performative events where cultural values are displayed and that have an agonistic aspect. Music and singing competitions would be a classic case in point, while public masterclasses have some features in common with overtly competitive events. Book prizes and art competitions have similar forms and functions. I would try to develop this comparative perspective, therefore, by thinking about *pageants of performance*, to capture some of the ceremonial as well as competitive elements of such occasions of cultural enactment.

Note here how close is the relationship between the local-specific research setting, and the comparative-generic frame of reference. It is not the case that one builds up from case to case (as if it were a larger-scale version of inductive theory-building). The ideal-typical concepts and models feed directly into the analysis of the local case, while the particularities of the local setting(s) contribute to an elaboration of the general model. This is entirely in keeping with the general pragmatist legacy that inspired interactionist sociology and that informed Glaser and Strauss. It is equally congruent with the logic of anthropology as an essentially comparative discipline. A general ethnology has always been founded on the development of generic analytic concepts that transcend the particularities of particular cultural systems. There can be few, if any, productive accounts of a single case that do not – however implicitly – draw on generic ideas of social process, social order and cultural significance. Equally, there are few ideas of any generality that have force and impact in the absence of concrete detail and specificity of application. The generic and the local depend intimately and inextricably on each other if they are to work analytically.

By no means coincidentally, to return to the total institution, the cases of Goffman, Roth, Foucault and others influenced by them, illustrate the multiple modalities of the ethnography. We cannot capture the complexity of the total institution without a clear and systematic understanding of its temporal and spatial orders, its material as well as its symbolic boundaries, or its visual codes of dress and décor. The sensory order and the soundscapes of the total institution help constitute its distinctive local culture. The institution is a repository of stories: inmates' stories of hard luck and victimhood, staff members' atrocity stories, complaints, accusations and similar forms of accounts. Reputations – inmates' and staff-members' – circulate and are part of the linguistic and performative repertoire of the setting. These multiple codes of order in turn call for systematic, sustained ethnographic analysis. This in turn calls for multiple technologies of recording and reconstruction.

Ideal-types imply typologies as well. We are not engaged in generating only overall characterisation of institutions or organisations. Analysis also implies a systematic understanding of types and sub-types, and of the systemic relations between them. But this is not – or should not be – a static exercise in mapping cultural categories. This is not equivalent to a semantic anthropology of fixed categories. We need a clear sense of varieties of social action precisely so that we can demonstrate how they constitute a repertoire of acts, recipes for practical action, resources of cultural knowledge and the like. They need, in other words, to be grounded in a thorough sense of *action*, that recognises simultaneously that actions are constructed out of shared cultural resources. For instance, if we are in a position to gather and analyse narratives of personal experience, then we need to be able to identify their distinctive genres and formats. In other words, even the most deeply felt and personal narrative is shaped in accordance with cultural types and precedents. Stories have shape, and those shapes (and their functions) reflect genres of story-telling. Again, we are dealing with repertoires that social actors can draw on in constructing their biographical work. Likewise, we may identify a repertoire of techniques that actors may employ in order to perform some significant form of work or action. These in turn may be linked to local inventories of tools and other material resources with which practical actions can be accomplished. I do not want to recapitulate all of the comments made about these and similar things in previous chapters. But I do want to remind us that these kinds of analytic issues can be, and should be, in our minds throughout the fieldwork, and not just during the 'analysis', treated as a separate phase.

Analysis in these cases therefore does not mean an obsessive sorting and inspection of 'the data'. It depends on the ability to rise well above the minutiae of fieldnotes and interview transcripts. Indeed, it sometimes means setting those aside. In fact, setting the data aside can be a very valuable discipline. It forces us to *think* rather than drowning under a surfeit of information. I would, therefore, advocate a periodic removal from the field, and from whatever data have been collected. Then we have to ask ourselves: What is really going on here? What are the big picture issues? What are the leading motifs here? What are the recurrent images that capture and encapsulate central cultural themes? Of course, some of these issues *can* be derived from coding and similar procedures. But they are better thought about by taking a bird's-eye view, rather than a worm's-eye view of things. We need to cultivate moving between the detail of specific events, situations and actors, as recorded in our data-sets, and the broad, generic analytic issues that will guide our most productive analysis, and will probably drive our monographs or papers.

Often, these dominant ideas will be metaphors and images. They cannot be 'built' as theories, from bits and pieces of information. They have to be 'found' through the imaginative work of abduction, whereby general categories are drawn out from the particularities of local situations and settings, events and activities. Oscar Lewis, after all, did not 'build' his theoretical construct of 'the culture of poverty', and derive its ideal-typical features, by an obsessive inspection of the details of ethnographic fieldwork on Mexico City and elsewhere (e.g. Lewis 1959, 1968, 1972). The notion comes from that ethnography, but it is not simply inductively derived, and its characteristic features are themselves abducted from the empirical details. Again, therefore, we need to recognise that a guiding metaphor or model (they come to much the same thing) are bird's-eye and not worm's-eye kinds of perspective.

Scepticism about procedural approaches to ethnographic analysis clearly does not imply a lack of rigour or a lack of ideas. On the contrary, in the absence of comforting textbook prescriptions we have to work extremely hard in creating adequately thick, complex characterisations of social worlds. That work calls for well-developed analytic frameworks, through which we pay serious attention to principles of organisation and forms of social action. For that reason, the following chapters outline just some of the ordering principles of everyday life through which ethnographic fieldwork can be conducted, and ethnographic analysis organised.

Some of the observations in this chapter may seem grudging, even grumpy. My remarks are not based on a resentment of popular ideas about analysis. The ideas that I have referred to and criticised in this chapter are clearly very useful, *provided they are regarded as heuristic and not prescriptive*. My overall intention is positive, and not based simply on negative critique. I want to free students and researchers from undue reliance on other people's procedures and formulae. We need to ensure that research in general and analysis in particular are not hobbled by slavish adherence to such prescriptions. I want to encourage us all to use our social science imagination to work with ideas, recognising that ethnographic fieldwork is not an end in itself, but is completed by the quality and fecundity of the ideas that are derived, and indeed that are brought to bear. There is no need to feel overwhelmed and intimidated by the demands of theory (too often brandished as a sign of potency) if one can feel empowered by the need to work with ideas. Ethnography is, if it is anything, a process of exploration, discovery and creativity.

5

Interaction and the Ceremonial Order

If ethnographers are to take seriously the intrinsic, indigenous modes of social organisation, then they need to pay particular and distinctive attention to the patterning of interaction in social settings. This seems entirely obvious, of course, but in recent years the undue emphasis on individuals' experience and the collection of interview data in pursuit of those experiences has meant a correspondingly reduced emphasis on social encounters and the processes of interaction between their members. Perhaps this also accounts for what seems a creeping neglect of many of the key themes of interactionist sociology (broadly defined), including the distinctive contributions of Erving Goffman. In this chapter I want to remind us of one of Goffman's most important observations. That is, that there is an *interaction order* that exists relatively independently of other social orders: the political order, the economic order and so on. Patterns of social interaction obey their own logic, based on socially shared conventions and understandings. These occasions are not confined to spoken interaction, such as dialogues or meetings. I shall also commend serious attention to performances and similar kinds of social activities or events.

We do not need to focus exclusively on spoken activities, although the use of language is self-evidently significant: we need to pay serious attention to the forms of speech. But we do not have to focus obsessively on conversation-analysis or discourse-analysis, except insofar as their general principles can be used to develop and inform our ethnographic analytic strategies. The close analysis of encounters and performances is, however, one field of analysis where the use of permanent recordings is – where possible – especially valuable. As digital recording devices become ever more cheaply available, and taken-for-granted features of everyday life, so we can use them to help us develop systematic analyses of the many modes of social organisation.

So a properly complex ethnography needs to address the interactions that occur within any given social world: encounters, meetings, confrontations, consultations, ceremonials and the like all imply forms of interaction that are constitutive of the cultural and social order. The ethnography therefore needs to pay serious attention to these interactional features. Self-evidently, there are many ways in which the interaction order also implies the orderliness of spoken interaction, and clearly spoken action is a key feature of the interaction order. But in this chapter I want to remind us that the ethnography of any given setting must take systematic account of processes of interaction. While spoken discourse is a fundamental part of that interaction order, an ethnographic understanding of interaction can be broader than the analyses furnished by conversation analysis or discourse analysis alone.

A fundamental understanding of the grammar of social interaction furnishes much of the conceptual apparatus of interactionist sociology, and goes back at least to the formal sociological analyses of Georg Simmel – a key influence on the early interactionists, and a clear precursor of Goffman's intellectual style. Both Simmel and Goffman point the way towards an analysis of the forms and styles of interaction, whether they be face-to-face or (as they increasingly are in contemporary society) mediated. Here is clearly not the place to review all of this tradition. Rather, I want to highlight some of its distinctive features that seem especially pertinent to the conduct and analysis of ethnography. In two of his key papers, Goffman outlined a programme of systematic attention to what he referred to as *the interaction order* (Goffman 1983), and before that as *the neglected situation* (Goffman 1964). Let us consider the second of those first, and ask ourselves whether 'the situation' might still be neglected, even by ethnographers. It reflects a more general orientation that runs through Goffman's work, and it is one that is widely misunderstood. It is far too easy to assume that Goffman's extraordinary attention to micro-level phenomena means that his is a humanistic or individualistic kind of undertaking: that it is about social actors thought of as social atoms that come together and interact. But that is a poor understanding of his work. For the unit of analysis is not really the social actor, but the situation, the encounter, the event. In other words, 'the situation' here is a social phenomenon that is *not* reduced to its participant actors. The situation has, of course, occupied a potentially central place in sociological analysis since Thomas's famous dictum concerning its reality: 'situations are real insofar as they are defined as real and are real in their consequences'. To that extent, therefore, situations, events and encounters have a social reality that is relatively independent of the individual participants. However, some constructivist approaches to sociological analysis have led to an undue emphasis on the 'definition' aspect of Thomas's dictum, as if situations could be endlessly defined and redefined indefinitely, with no regard to their conventional forms or actual participants. We need, perhaps, to remind ourselves of the social reality of the situation itself, which displays cultural regularities and social practices. After all, Goffman proposed an interaction order that is a relatively autonomous order of organisation (analogous, for instance, to the economic order). It has its intrinsic organisational and formal properties, its ceremonial forms and ritual observances. The unit of analysis is thus the encounter and not the individual participant. Encounters and social interaction are, therefore, fundamental to a properly sociological or anthropological understanding of social conduct and social ordering. The analysis concerns itself with the properties of the interaction order itself, relatively independently of the idiosyncratic characteristics of the individual participants.

Faced with the sheer variety and complexity of encounters and situations, would-be ethnographers too often shy away from their analysis, falling back on extracts from interviews in which informants give accounts about encounters, and their retrospective understandings of situations. One example that could stand for many is the study by Ruchti (2012) of 'intimacy' and its management by nurses. Obviously nurses are required to work in close proximity to their patients, to work on their body, to which they have privileged access by virtue of their occupational duties. Such intimacy can call for careful management, especially in the context of a female nurse and a male patient. The author of the study tells us that she spent some 800 hours observing nurse–patient encounters in hospital settings. And yet the monograph has virtually no analysis of such observed interactions. What we are treated to is extracts from interviews with the nurses. Now such accounts may be revealing in their own right, and they may help to illuminate aspects of the observed activities. But the absence of truly observational analysis means that most of the opportunities are missed, and we are left wondering just *how* nurses manage themselves and their patients in order to achieve certain kinds of work while avoiding other kinds of intimacy. Equally, of course, we are robbed of any understanding of *how* patients themselves initiate or otherwise engage in 'intimacy'. We also learn next to nothing about patients' perspectives on intimacy with nurses. The issue is that intimacy, or something like it, is a property of the encounter, not something that is confined to the reported experiences of individual actors.

Now it might be thought that this is self-evidently the stuff of ethnographic analysis. The micro-level of social interaction is surely the field where the ethnographer typically observes and participates. Moreover, in the many intervening years since its publication, the increased popularity of ethnographic and other kinds of qualitative research might lead one to expect a great deal of emphasis on interaction and encounters. In part, that is true, of course. And Goffman himself is a taken-for-granted point of reference for many such studies. On the other hand, far too much qualitative research seems preoccupied with the individual actor (often in the guise of an interview informant). As a consequence, the interaction order itself can be overlooked in the conduct of general ethnographic analysis. Experience shows indeed that it is much, much easier to write up interview data in which informants talk *about* events, rather than reporting them on the basis of direct observation. Extracts from interviews can be pasted into the text with relative ease, and so used as illustrative examples and vignettes. On the other hand, transforming observations (which include photographs and recordings) into textual representations (such as detailed descriptions of events and/or transcripts of recordings) and *analysing* what is going on, in terms of formal properties, takes rather more effort. It can also call for more technical competence than many researchers seem willing to acquire. It is incumbent on practitioners and teachers of ethnographic fieldwork to ensure that these more demanding aspects of field research are properly engaged in.

This stricture does not apply equally to all varieties of sociological work. Studies of interactional work have become the stock-in-trade of research in the tradition of ethnomethodology. Indeed, one can argue that the ethnomethodologists and conversation analysts are the true heirs of Goffman. On the other hand, many ethnomethodologists explicitly reject general ethnography, and seek to maintain something of a niche for their own emphasis on the local production of social order. My contention here is that ethnographers do need to pay serious attention to the forms of interaction, of social encounters and of social events. But these analyses do not need to be confined purely to conversation analysis, and – more significantly, perhaps – they ought to be embedded in more general ethnographic accounts of social worlds. In other words, we ought to respect Goffman's suggestion that there is an interaction order, and that an adequately thick description of everyday life must incorporate a sustained analysis of the conduct of social events and situations (Goffman 1983). These should also include proper attention to the enactment of performative encounters within the fabric of mundane social activity, as well as more overtly ceremonial events. We need to examine how social actors perform themselves, and how they collaborate in sustaining those enactments. It is, I suggest, not enough merely to invoke some sort of dramaturgical metaphor, to assert that performativity is of fundamental importance: we have to *analyse* how performances are put together. We also need to examine properly how embodied competences are deployed in such performances. The physical work of self-presentation requires proper attention to the body and its use. Situations and encounters are physically embodied and material; they are not just disembodied speech.

Social encounters have their own forms, even though they are improvised in real time by their participants. There are shared assumptions, for instance, concerning the definition of the situation. To take one key dimension: encounters and situations differ according to the degree of *formality* that is enacted. Formalised institutional settings are recognisable and are constituted by conventions of comportment, as well as by local rules of language-use. The achievement of formality in courtroom settings is a case in point (Atkinson and Drew 1979). Formality is conventionally expected, and participants orient their activities to such conventions. These are performed through conventions of speech and silence. They are also managed through the scenic arrangements of courtrooms. The *mise-en-scène* and the distributed rights and expectations of speech are constitutive of legal proceedings, and are features that participants draw on in constructing such occasions.

The scenic arrangements and discursive conventions of the courtroom are just one very obvious example of the cultural resources that are used to create a given type of encounter. Formal encounters are useful analytically because they help us to identify some elementary forms of such situations, and therefore to raise ethnographically relevant questions. Organisational and professional encounters demonstrably have distinctive forms of interaction. They have been widely documented in detail. Pedagogic encounters have characteristic structures of spoken interaction. These typically include cycles of elicitations by teachers, responses by students and teachers' evaluations of the students' responses. These triadic structures can be, and are, used by the participants to generate long sequences of classroom talk that sustain extended periods of classroom or seminar talk. Such encounters are, however, not just about sequences of talk. The classroom encounter enforces sustained and close interactions between teachers and students, in which displays of authority and of character are performed. Teachers, for instance, often work at constructing a distinctive classroom identity, a persona that is crafted for pedagogical purposes – perhaps with a degree of eccentricity – that constructs a protective personal front. Classroom encounters can be dangerous places: teachers and their students are exposed to mutual gaze and stringent evaluations. They can create self-presentations that provide protective camouflage. In just the same way, encounters between professionals and clients display characteristic forms and structures of interaction. Studies of clinical encounters now constitute a genre of publication analogous to the studies of classroom interaction. The structure and implications of these and similar encounters I shall outline below.

Encounters and their management involve issues of politeness. In point of fact, interactants do not have to be egregiously deferential for politeness or mutual attentiveness to characterise the encounter, and for a degree of tact to permeate it. This underpins what Goffman (and then others) referred to as 'face-work'. That is, a degree of interactional attentiveness to the presence and actions of one's fellow participant(s). Social actors are capable of taking the role of the other. Indeed, this has been a tenet of interactionist sociology or social psychology since its origins. Consequently, social actors are constantly monitoring their own performances and those of others. The social encounter is not just a behavioural enactment. It has profound implications for the *moral order*: that is, the maintenance of or challenges to identity and personal worth. Consequently, ethnographers need to pay close attention to these features of social encounters. They are at the heart of everyday life. They display formal features, and they are the interactional engines that drive concerted social activity.

Exchange has been at the heart of ethnography since the classic anthropological studies of the gift and the social relationships that gift-exchange creates and sustains. Speech-exchange is one of the primordial forms of interaction, and speech-exchange systems have now been widely documented. They are especially important in their own right, and also insofar as they demonstrate the orderliness of social encounters. While social situations, including face-to-face interactions, are normally improvised, that does not mean that they are without structure. Indeed, the example of speech-exchange should guide us towards the investigation of formal regularities, conventions and structures throughout everyday life. Studies of the interaction order, including the mechanisms of spoken interaction, are, therefore, at the heart of the ethnographic enterprise. Oddly, these analytic issues are too often treated as the esoteric preserve of conversation- or discourse-analysts. Clearly, this is unduly restrictive, and can rob more general ethnographies of one of their most significant modes of analysis. Yet the current opportunities afforded by digital recording mean that we can – subject to the usual caveats of research ethics and participants' consent – gather and analyse materials relating to a wide range of encounters and interactions. The ethnographic imagination also brings to such analysis an acute awareness of the subtle intersections of talk, action and talk-in-action (cf. Martens 2012).

Technologies now mean that the ethnographer can certainly complement general participant observation with participant recordings of encounters. We can be faithful to Goffman's recommendations regarding the *situation* and the *encounter*. That is, we can examine the means and methods employed by parties to the encounter to display mutual attention. The intersubjectivity of the encounter is not, therefore, merely a vague (if productive) idea, but subject to empirical investigation and analysis. Enactments of mutual attentiveness, for example, can be explored, identifying mutual gaze, attentiveness, body posture and proxemics (cf. Kendon 1990). Likewise, the relationship between speech and gesture is available for close analysis. While spoken action may well be regarded as the principal means of social interaction, it is always enacted in an embodied fashion. My own analysis of master-classes for young opera singers illustrates the point (Atkinson 2013b). Such classes have a very distinctive form of pedagogy. Typically, the young singer (student) performs a chosen aria without interruption from the teacher or mentor who is conducting the masterclass. Then the young performer is invited to repeat the piece, but this time the teacher interrupts the performance to make detailed suggestions. These are typically technical, relating to voice production and pronunciation, musical, relating to phrasing and shaping the vocal line, and expressive, concerned with the musical and vocal display of character, emotion and dramatic intention. Teachers characteristically attempt to convey their pedagogic intentions through a multi-modal enactment of spoken and physical action. Teachers display their close attention to the student's performance through gaze and their physical, bodily orientation. They employ a repertoire of gestures in order to convey matters of vocal production, such as miming a more 'open' sound. They use gestures of the hand and the arm to mime the shaping of a vocal line. There is a dialogue of mutual attention between the singer and the teacher. The singer is frequently stopped in her or his aria, so that the teacher can provide spoken and gestural commentary on some aspect of the piece and its performance. This is an intensely focused encounter. It is based on complex exchanges between the student and the teacher. The fact that such classes are often conducted before an audience (other singers and/or members of the public) means that the sense of performance is heightened.

Informal encounters and more focused encounters provide especially significant exemplars of fine-grained analysis of speech-exchange. The inspection of such interactional materials has developed as a distinctive, even esoteric, specialty, devoted to *conversation analysis*. Now it is my contention that ethnographers should pay far more attention to the kinds of formal properties uncovered by conversation analysis, build them into more general ethnographic studies, and so pay far more sustained attention to the nature of social encounters. Equally, speech-exchanges do not exhaust the nature of social encounters, and therefore a broad perspective on their character is needed.

Clinical encounters between medical practitioners and their patients or clients provide obvious and classic examples of focused encounters that have been thoroughly documented. The speech-exchange system of the medical consultation has its own distinctive (but by no means unique) characteristics. The characteristic structure through which the practitioner elicits the medical history creates a distinctive form of encounter, through which the patient's personal feelings and symptoms are formulated and re-formulated in terms of standardised biomedical categories. It is permeated therefore by what Mishler (1984) called 'the voice of medicine'. In eliciting clinically relevant information, the clinician leads and dominates the form of the interaction, and the content of the consultation. The patient's everyday experience and knowledge tend to get side-lined in the process.

Focused encounters like these alert us to a wide range of phenomena. We find that they are occasions for the display of authority and expert knowledge. What we might call the pedagogic format and the professional format are interactional devices that facilitate particular types of work: interactional work, professional work and face work. These are all particular instances of generic forms of interaction. So here I want to commend serious attention to the systematic study of spoken activity. As I have indicated, such analytic issues have too often been treated as specialist interests, confined to conversation analysis. At the same time, conversation analysts have sometimes been unwarrantably reluctant to engage with broader ethnographic forms of inquiry. This is to the detriment of both, and does not serve the yet wider interests of sociological or anthropological analysis.

Issues of speech-exchange can display interactional issues of considerable import, going well beyond purely 'technical' issues. For instance, the analytic topic of *repair* can seem at first blush to be an esoteric issue. Here repair refers to occasions where a speaker corrects or reformulates an utterance. Clearly, such repair-work can be undertaken by the speaker herself or himself (self-initiated repair) or by an interlocutor (other-initiated repair). Now clearly, there are profound moral consequences attached to such work. In most everyday speech contexts, there is a preference for self-correction. This is a demonstrable, distributive and formal feature of everyday conversation. It is also one of the many ways in which a speaker displays her or his competence and agency. Self-correction performs actors' capacity to monitor their own speech, and to evaluate its referential value, or its potential significance for their hearers. It displays a degree of self-management; it is an element in persons' self-presentation. By contrast, the initiation of repair by another can potentially threaten such agency, calling into question the other's competence. In other words, apparently very fine-grained matters of spoken interaction can be examined for evidence of what might otherwise be glossed as face-work and issues of moral worth. Equally, there are occasions that are distinctly marked by other-initiated repair. I have already referred to pedagogic encounters, where teachers normally repair their students' utterances (and where students rarely repair their teachers'). The organisation of correction thus enacts the asymmetry of such encounters, as it does in socio-legal and medical settings. It is not sociological nor anthropological news to note that law courts, clinics or seminars are interactionally asymmetrical. What we need to know is just *how* difference is performed. We need to understand how social positions are established, maintained, or threatened through speech-exchange. Likewise, we need to examine how repair-work is used interactionally to establish what is judged 'correct' in context. Moerman (1988) provides a classic example of this sort of analysis. He provides a commentary on extracts from a legal hearing in Thailand, in which he demonstrates precisely how a counsel's concentrated repair-work is oriented towards a desired formulation of the case in question. Skilful use of repair is deployed in order to shape the legal proceedings and the record of the case. The case proceeds through sequences of questions and answers, and repair is used to ensure that favourable versions of events are entered into the record. An equally classic example is provided by Goldman (1983), writing on disputes among the Huli of Papua New Guinea. Goldman displays the complex discursive practices that characterise such adversarial encounters. Moreover, he demonstrates the cultural homologies between talk about pigs, decoration and discourse ('pigs, paint and parlance'). Adversarial discourse is predicated on the management of a speech-exchange system, coupled with specific culturally derived contents.

Very similar issues can be identified in the fine-grained analysis of *interruption*. While the exchange of speech displays a high level of orderliness, that does not mean that at the very finest of levels it proceeds without overlaps, hesitations or interruptions. Such perturbations – fleeting and barely noticed though they may be – can be highly implicative interactionally. Let us take medical encounters once more. Mishler writes about the 'voice of medicine' interrupting the 'voice of the lifeworld', and although his observations are grounded in transcribed medical encounters, his use of 'interruption' is as much metaphorical as literal.

On the other hand, West (1984) has a precise, conversation-analytic account of interruptions in the course of medical encounters. Amongst her other findings is the demonstration that (American) medical practitioners interrupt their patients much more frequently than patients interrupt physicians, *unless the physician is a woman,* in which case male patients reverse the emphasis and interrupt the physician. Self-evidently, this can tell us a great deal about the intersection of professional status and gender in such encounters. Again, we see how formal aspects of spoken interaction can tell us important things about significant social categories and their encounters.

These few examples illustrate the degree to which ethnographers, interested in social encounters and situations, can benefit directly from a close acquaintance with conversation analysis – or, more generally, the detailed analysis of spoken activity. Although many conversation analysts themselves have declared a radical difference between ethnography and their own intellectual enterprise, this seems to me to be unnecessary. As I have indicated, analytic interests converge on the analysis of action and the nature of encounters. Some analysts have acknowledged the possibility of such symbiosis. Moerman (1988) is quite explicit. He commends embedding conversation analysis within a broader ethnographic analysis of culture, suggesting that: 'Ethnographers comment on, translate, and embellish the native world. The transcripts will anchor us in that world. Rather than pretending to read a culturally standardised finished text over the shoulder of an imagined native, we will be living in the line-by-line production of actual native talk' (p. 5). In other words, close attention to actual spoken activity allows ethnographers to escape any tacit assumption that culture and social order are finished products, as it were. Rather it forces us to undertake detailed observational analyses of the means whereby the phenomena are brought into being.

The dramaturgical metaphor, developed so successfully by Goffman, has become something of a commonplace in the interactionist tradition. In recent years, perhaps, the rhetoric of 'performativity' has become more fashionable. There is a danger, however, that such ideas become either so taken-for-granted, or so pervasive, that they lose a good deal of their analytic edge. So here I want to concentrate on encounters that are emphatically performative, and to remind us of their analytic significance. If Goffmanesque dramaturgy is the obvious point of reference for sociologists, anthropologists may find a different point of departure. But both disciplines converge on a current interest in *performance*.

I start with a social world that is, perhaps, not the obvious starting-point for performance-studies – science. Ethnographic work on the natural and biomedical sciences in fact reminds us of how thoroughly performative is the social world of scientists. All those in the academic world know that they are regularly called on to 'present' their work. Conferences and seminars, for instance, consist of encounters between scientists and their audiences. Considering how routine these occasions are, we have remarkably few published accounts about these performative aspects of science. The scientific conference is, for example, an occasion for scientists to 'show off': they present their latest findings and lay claim to originality; they showcase and acknowledge the work of their colleagues; they show due respect to others in the field; they distance themselves from competitors; they pay their dues to their funders. Audiences are by no means passive recipients of these presentations. They display interest, or the lack of it, through unspoken activities: sleep (actual or feigned) can be a devastatingly silent criticism. Members of the audience can also display affiliation or antagonism through questioning strategies. They can counter the presenter through their choice and style of question. In other words, these are supremely performative encounters. Scientists are impresarios for their own and others' work. They use visual materials as well as the spoken word to provide plausible accounts of their own work. The conference 'presentation' is also a case of *self-presentation* in which the moral worth of the individual scientist is promoted, endorsed or challenged. These are ceremonial occasions in which the participants are often engaged in ritualised exchanges of value.

Intriguingly – perhaps unsurprisingly – there is a considerable similarity in these approaches to scientific and political discourse and that adopted by Pinch and Clark (1986) in their analysis of market-traders' patter. They studied the kinds of traders that drum up custom for the sale of household goods (bedding, pots and pans, china – that sort of thing). Successful traders are rhetorically skilful, building up and drawing an audience of passers-by. They often use accomplices who may start the bidding for items, and who provide the initial growth-points for the small crowds on whom the traders rely. Formally, as well as commercially, these performances have much in common with those of confidence-tricksters and card-sharps, as described by Erving Goffman. Again, their enactment depends on the participation of 'audience' members. These and similar kinds of encounter have features in common. They depend on a degree of rhetorical skill on the part of the main protagonists, designed to display the performative skill of the performers/celebrants. Nowadays one can witness similar kinds of selling performance on auction TV channels. The jewellery channels are especially rewarding from this point of view. The presenters repeatedly enact breathless delight and enthusiasm, coupled with incredulity at how low the prices have dropped for (what is always) such a stunning piece of jewellery. But the presentations are always more subtle than just shows of excitement. They position the unseen television viewer and potential buyer as a knowledgeable 'collector', and presenters invite viewers and bidders to think of themselves as cognoscenti, able simultaneously to appreciate gemstones and their settings aesthetically and in terms of their market value. (The fact that most items are apparently more or less given away at prices far below their true worth gives the more detached observer an immediate sense of these performances' dramaturgical qualities, as well some clue as to the gemstones' true worth.)

In other contexts, performances display what might be thought of as more conventional performative skills. Dramatic and musical performances provide cases in point: musical concerts or competitions; concerts, performance art. They celebrate a specific genre of cultural performance. They are often celebrations of a particular style or tradition (national, artistic, local, historical). Participation in them calls for 'stylish' performance. Participants are often expected to perform in a perceptibly felicitous way – displaying more than mere technical competence, but also expressive capacities. In some cases, such as instrumental or singing competitions, auditions, or first nights, style may be adjudicated and/or commented on by senior exponents – such as competition judges and casting directors – or by critics. Some of these are formalised and ritualised into what I call *pageants of performance*: that is, formal occasions where individuals or groups engage in self-presentations of technique, interpretive skill and expressive mastery. They can bestow honour and prestige on their participants. They are productive of that prestige, and in turn are warranted by the prestige that they bestow. They can have multiple functions. They can be rites of passage for participants, who can 'win their spurs' through skilful performances. In martial arts events (like the *capoeira batizado* or 'baptism' event) they are accompanied by formal status passages (moving up from one belt to the next); in art-music competitions, they can 'launch a career' by transforming the inexperienced performer into an internationally recognised one, and in doing so they can endow the successful performer with a distinctive persona. They are often what Appadurai calls *tournaments of value*, in which the symbolic value of performative excellence accrues honour, as well as possible material rewards (Appadurai 1986).

Performances and equivalent forms of focused encounters characterise many professional settings in contemporary society. The worlds of bureaucracy and management are suffused with such events. Indeed, the very notion of 'the presentation' (nowadays accompanied by visual or audio-visual scenic arrangements) has clear connotations of dramatic performance. So too does the academic conference, where 'presentations' are also ubiquitous. Knoblauch (2013) provides an especially pertinent account of PowerPoint culture and its representational conventions. In such settings the dramaturgical quality of the speaker's enactment is striking. Saunders (2008) gives us a vivid sense of such encounters in a medical setting. Hospitals and medical schools have dense schedules of conferences, reviews and rounds at which cases are 'presented' and in the course of which professional colleagues are quizzed and grilled by their peers and their superiors. Saunders conducted an ethnography of radiology, based on the 'CT suite', where trainee specialists learn how to 'see' and to 'read' images generated by computerised tomography. As Saunders describes it, regular conferences can take the form of an *inquisition*, where the senior (attending) physician cross-questions a more junior practitioner.

These overtly performative events serve to remind us that in everyday life, there are equally performative encounters. We might therefore want to take an extended dramaturgical metaphor and ask ourselves of any such encounters, formal or otherwise, the following sorts of questions:

- What forms of rhetoric do actors use to engage, persuade, impress or otherwise influence their 'audience' (which might be an audience of one)?
- How do actors use embodied skills and techniques to accomplish this?
- How do audiences collaborate in endorsing or appreciating others' performances? What criteria of evaluation do they apply? How are their judgements made visible (if at all)?
- Are there local judgements of skill and felicity on the part of performers and others?

Of course, not all types of interaction need to be viewed as 'performances', but they do provide a familiar and productive entrée to the general approach to the interaction order. We can ask ourselves perfectly similar kinds of questions about the dramaturgy of everyday life. This is an area in which it is easy to be imprecise. Together, the notions of self-presentation, or Bourdieu's concept of *habitus*, can be remarkably vague. The latter in particular seems to mean virtually everything and anything wanted by any given author. It can certainly encompass the physical embodiment of a culturally specific array of dispositions and activities. We can therefore make these broad generic categories yield more concrete and local observations. In other words, the ethnographer who is committed to detailed, concrete observation ought to be able to go well beyond such catch-all notions as 'habitus'. To say that an actor behaves in a certain way because he or she has internalised an appropriate habitus is often to say nothing or to offer a circular kind of description. To say that an orchestral conductor acts in a certain way because he has imbued the habitus of the dominant male maestro (say) is merely to restate the topic, not to analyse it by examining closely the how and the when of such activity or the processes of acquisition. As ethnographers, therefore, we need to examine the performative competences – successes and failures – of embodied identities, or the management of appearances, of dramatic enactments.

In summary form, we can focus our observations on topics like these:

- How do actors use their physical appearance and their body to create distinctive performances of personal identity?

- How do they arrange their surroundings to create a distinctive *mise-en-scène*?

- How do they use their body – expressively and instrumentally – to create a characteristic appearance?

- How do social actors create appearances of adequate self-control and competence?

These general questions call for close observation and concrete detail. They are among the many reasons why a complex multi-modal ethnography is especially important. We need participant observation if we are to develop a strong, practical sense of encounters and performances. We need visual data in order to capture matters of posture and embodiment. Likewise we need to be able to record matters of appearance – clothing, hair, body-modifications. We need, of course, permanent recordings of spoken activity too. Everyday performances are quintessentially complex and multi-modal enactments. In principle, therefore, they need to be matched by ethnographies of equal complexity. It may not be practical, in practice, to gather permanent recordings that cover all the possible modalities of activity. A minimum requirement is close *in situ* observation and careful recording in the form of detailed fieldnotes, perhaps accompanied by sketches of embodied activities.

As Goffman pointed out, the social self is a *ritually delicate* one. In other words, we do not need to confine our sensibilities concerning 'rituals' to the overt, sometimes exotic, forms that have permeated classic anthropological texts. The latter do, however, have their methodological value as well as their intrinsic significance. The classic ceremonies and rituals that ethnographers have studied display a degree of orderliness and structure that we do well to reflect on. For instance, we know that *rites de passage*, or status-passages, have an intrinsic structure. This was, after all, the great contribution of van Gennep's original ethnological analysis. The rituals that demarcate the transition from one social position to another, whether they be collectively or individually undergone, have common properties. There is a recurrent, underlying grammar to them. They recurrently – and unsurprisingly – enact ceremonial observances of separation and segregation that are mirrored by ceremonial observances of inclusion and integration. These observances provide a form of performative punctuation in the passage of mundane time and the life-course of the initiates. They are often marked by symbolic forms of reversal: special clothing that demarcates the sacred time of the ritual from the profane time that precedes and succeeds it, special foods that do likewise, music and noise that mark off special periods of time. There are ceremonials of cleansing and emptying – whether they be based on washing or on vomiting. Anthropologists and sociologists are familiar with the notion that time and celebrants are suspended in *liminal* states, often in highly sacred and/or dangerous circumstances, between the 'before' and the 'after' of the transitions. Now the point here is that rites of passage and similar occasions are structured. They have formal properties. Their celebrants perform within the constraints of ritualised frames.

We can identify similarly patterned activities in less exotic settings. Goffman's classic accounts of role-stripping and mortification of mental-hospital patients (Goffman 1961) is another case in point, as is Garfinkel's analysis of degradation ceremonies (Garfinkel 1956). While these may not have quite the formalised ceremonials of religious observances or rites of passage, they clearly have their own recurrent patterns. They too involve processes of removal: former identities are removed or redefined, and new attributes are assigned. Characters are rewritten, and new identities are promoted. This applies to destructive processes, such as those just mentioned, or to more positive promotions.

In other words, the ritual and ceremonial order is one of patterned, structured activity. It is not just a matter of improvised action that is created *de novo*. And it is certainly not a matter of formless personal experience. It is grounded in socially shared conventions that shape and frame action, that give form to collective identity-work. They are *situations* in every sense.

Our ethnographic emphasis on real-time observation and recording should not blind us to the broader cultural, social and historical contexts in which ceremonial and discursive orders are created and sustained. Horodowich (2008) explores the management and control of speech in the Renaissance Venetian Republic, demonstrating how propriety in matters of speech was implicated in social control and state formation – among courtiers, between the sexes and between different social estates. Her discussion extends the historical sociology of Elias (1978) on management of bodies and politeness in the European 'civilising process'. One of the classic Italian sources – Castiglione's advice to the courtier (*Il libro del cortegiano*) – is itself a Goffmanesque commentary on the interaction and ceremonial orders. Indeed, Goffman's accounts of everyday ceremonials and the interaction order in contemporary or recent urban society is a manifestation of a long-standing preoccupation with personal comportment and social position. Of course, the courtly self-management of the Renaissance has, in Goffman, become an issue for the common man and woman. But there are enduring preoccupations: the control of the body and its margins, the tactful management of personal space, the proprieties of spoken interaction.

The same sort of Goffmanesque tradition gives us insight into a constellation of features that deserve attention. That is, the distribution of knowledge and awareness among and between networks of social actors. Goffman referred to *strategic interaction*. Again, Simmel's sociological imagination also provides a valuable set of parallels. The general set of issues concern the distribution of knowledge. Simmel's classic work in this area concerns the nature of the secret, and the opportunities given by dyadic and triadic relations. Gross (2012) provides a useful summary of Simmel, who outlined not merely a model of interpersonal relations, but also an analysis of the distribution of knowing and not-knowing. Human competence includes the ability to dissemble. Secrets and evasions are remarkably pervasive. Indeed, some degree of evasiveness seems to be a necessity in everyday life (although degrees of directness do seem to be culturally specific, as national differences in the exercise of politeness and indirect formulations can cause acute discomfort and embarrassment). Harvey Sacks once famously suggested that 'everyone has to lie', and all that we know of face-to-face encounters suggests that 'tact' calls for a degree of dissembling. We do not in everyday life say all that we might, and we do not give overt expression to all that we think or feel. The maintenance of others' sense of worth is partly dependent on mutual tact. We all have to be inattentive to the imperfections (physical and moral) of others. Otherwise normal social interaction is virtually impossible.

The general perspective was given a very pointed significance in the famous studies of death and dying in American hospitals by Glaser and Strauss (1965). Amongst other things, they developed the idea of 'awareness contexts', to express the distribution of awareness or expectation of impending death. The parties that constitute the context include the patient, family members, nurses and medical staff. While the analysis does not in fact explore every possible variation, key configurations include: 'closed awareness' (when impending death is kept secret), and 'suspicion awareness' (the meaning of which is pretty obvious), and a context of mutual pretence (where all the parties know, but keep up the appearance of a more optimistic state of affairs). The point here is that these are formal definitions, and reflect the *distribution* of knowledge within a given nexus of social relations.

Our own studies of families with inherited, genetic medical problems and risks suggested very strongly that 'communication' between family members is rarely, if ever, a matter of 'open' talk (Featherstone et al. 2005). If you or I have a known genetic condition, or are known to be a carrier for a defective gene, or have inherited a risk that can be estimated by the medical profession, then that knowledge can have profound implications for our immediate kin, not least our children – born and unborn. Yet 'telling' other people is just not simple or straightforward. Our families seemed to be characterised by 'secrets and lies' rather than a complete sharing of the possible information and its implications. What was left unspoken was just as important as what was said. Moreover, family members engaged in what we called a *moral calculus* to try to estimate who in the family could best cope with the information, and – in the case of offspring – when best to broach the topic with them. The control of knowledge, information or awareness among members of a group or network is intimately bound up with issues of trust, as well as a shared sense of intimacy and mutual obligation. Studies of phenomena such as 'coming out' by gay individuals also display such patterning of differentiated awareness among social networks. Not everyone is equally involved or made aware at the same time. Close friends may be disclosed to differently from close family members; work colleagues may be treated differentially again.

In other words, fields of social relationships have contours. Things like information, awareness and trust are patterned. They are differentially distributed. The interaction order must be thought about and investigated in terms of such patterning. So in any given social milieu, we need to ask ourselves the following kinds of questions:

- Who knows what about her or his fellow participants?
- How is knowledge shared and withheld?
- What lines of secrecy and discretion can be identified?

Of course, strategic interaction is a normal feature of everyday life. The conduct of ordinary interaction is profoundly dependent on 'tact', which often includes some degree of reticence or even deception. As Harvey Sacks memorably suggested, 'everyone has to lie', to the extent that the unfettered expression of opinions and personal judgements can be deeply disruptive, while suitably tactful interaction normally requires, if not an outright lie, then less than the whole truth.

Attention to strategic interaction does not mean that we are trying to set ourselves up as omniscient observers of a social scene, so that we are trying to adjudicate on the truth or falsehood of people's claims and stories. Rather, we are concerned with what is observable in how people manage disclosure, how they justify non-disclosure, or how they manage their social networks in order to control information about themselves and others. Unpublished research with army veterans by Barrie Meek provides an especially telling example. Infantrymen on active service can experience many occasions of danger: they may receive injuries, their comrades may be injured or even killed. They do not want their mother, wife or girlfriend to know all the distressing details. Consequently, they construct stories to account for what they have been doing, or how injuries have been received. Moreover, these stories have to be agreed and rehearsed among platoon members, lest there be discrepancies if others meet one's mother or partner. This exemplifies just one aspect of strategic interaction: the occasional need actually to rehearse a cover story. The careful management of information among a network of friends and family members is, of course, captured vividly in processes of 'coming out' as gay (or the management of equivalent self-disclosure). Who one comes out to, at what time and in what sequence is often a matter of some significance; how one comes out, and what accounts of oneself are rehearsed, is also significant; so too are the narratives that one develops concerning the coming-out process itself (cf. Plummer 1995). For gay men and for military personnel, dramaturgical failure or under-rehearsed performance by collaborators can prove disastrous. Such performances also reflect the extent to which *accounts* are of fundamental importance to the conduct of everyday life.

Hence, Goffman's ideas concerning strategic interaction and Glaser and Strauss's formulation of awareness contexts can be productively deployed to analyse the information states between social actors, and hence the networks or encounters that they are party to. We are interested in what is told explicitly, and what is withheld, what is regarded as 'tellable' and what is treated as ineffable. Such distinctions can be of extreme significance in particular social milieux. For instance, we have evidence of processes of occupational socialisation in which the 'master' craftsman does not impart instruction to apprentices at all possible levels of expertise. The fundamental 'mystery' of the craft is retained by the master, while apprentices may have to resort to 'stealing' the knowledge of the master (cf. Herzfeld 2004; Jordan and Weston 2003). In summary, therefore, ethnographers may often need to pay attention to what is sayable as well as what is said, to what is unsaid or unsayable. Glaser and Strauss (1965) provided an exemplary analysis of the awareness states surrounding their dying patients, that included *mutual pretence* and *suspicion*. We can, without necessarily doing the detailed fieldwork, imagine the dynamics of intimate relationships, such as kinship networks, that are permeated by all sorts of states – of deceits, half-truths, speculations, or suspicions, as well as desires, hopes and expectations. These are not just about 'information' and its exchange, of course, and they have great emotional significance. Their dynamics also have major analytic consequences. Not just for families, but for complex organisations, workplaces, total institutions – indeed the entire gamut of social arrangements. Moreover, these arrangements are not just formal distributions of knowledge or awareness. They have profound moral implications: Who can be trusted with secrets? When is a young person old enough to be entrusted? What are the consequences of inadvertent disclosure?

Here, then, the ethnographer enters into the distribution of knowledge and awareness within a given social group or network. Such issues give a different twist to the methodological chestnut: How can you tell if your informant is telling the truth? We as researchers should be just as interested in asking ourselves: Who is our informant lying to? (Or, at least, is being economical with the truth.) If 'lying' is too harsh a term here, then we certainly need to ask ourselves what kinds of discretion and tact are being used, what management of disclosure or self-disclosure is being practised. The social management of informational and moral states is of far greater interest, ethnographically speaking, then a naïve reliance on simple notions of truth-telling. Strategic information-management is fundamental to the interaction order and to the moral economy that it sustains. By moral economy I mean the distribution and circulation of social actors' perceived worth, credibility and reputation; like other economies, it is sustained through circuits of exchange and accumulation.

6

Accounts and Narratives

A great deal of qualitative research is, of necessity, based on the collection and interpretation of language materials. That is because despite the apparent emphasis on participant observation, even research that calls itself ethnographic depends rather little on either participation or observation. Instead, what is attended to is conversational material collected in the field. Even more strikingly, qualitative research in general is widely equated with the collection and analysis of interview data. The fact that encounters are sometimes given the title of 'the ethnographic interview' (e.g. Spradley 1979) does not in itself make them any more authentically ethnographic than any other kinds of interview.

In other words, a great deal of information that is gathered in the course of field research consists of talk. Now it will be clear throughout this book that I disapprove most strongly of a complete reliance on interviews and the kinds of data that they yield. They provide little or no opportunity to investigate the multiple forms of social organisation and action that are the stuff of everyday life. They yield information (of sorts) in a vacuum, bereft of the sensory and material means of mundane reality. They furnish no opportunity to study the techniques and skills that social actors deploy in the course of their daily lives, or in accomplishing specialised tasks. Equally, however, I do not subscribe to the view that such spoken materials are entirely inappropriate forms of data. But they do not substitute for other sources of ethnographic analysis.

The crucial issue is the *analytic* use that is made of such spoken materials, and that in turn is predicated on what ethnographic attitude one adopts towards them. In part, the themes of this chapter re-visit the hoary sociological question concerning the appropriate relationship between participant observation and interviewing. As I shall go on to suggest, however, the real analytic issues go far beyond the treatment of interviews and conversations. It also involves the proper analysis of spoken actions *in situ*. Ethnographers really do need to pay sustained and systematic attention to the use that is made of language in naturally occurring settings. This latter topic is not simply or primarily a matter of spoken interaction in the form of face-to-face speech – in the form of conversation – but of the use of a wide variety of speech acts and performances. These include accounts, myths, narratives, religious pronouncements, political speeches, lectures, scientific demonstrations. The list is indeed virtually endless – and therein lies the ethnographic richness. Some of the examples will be collected via interviews, others will be collected through participant observation and participant recording. It matters less how the data are derived; it matters a great deal how they are addressed and analysed.

It is the recurrent theme of this book that the methods of social life need to be analysed in terms of their intrinsic properties and organisation. We also need not shy away from the fact that social actions also have functions. In other words, and echoing classic formulations of philosophical speech-act theory, we *do* things with language, and with other means of representation. So when we think about language-use in everyday life, we need to think in terms of both the *forms and functions* of that language. Language-in-use is never a neutral medium of representation. Moreover, language-use always does far more than merely describing or reporting actions, events or feelings. We must always, therefore, have a due regard for the fact that language accomplishes social actions and realities, and that it has its own organising principles. Language-use is always conventional, and those conventions are themselves socially shared phenomena. Unfortunately, whatever their overt assumptions about language in action, far too many qualitative researchers seem oddly insouciant about the properties of language itself. Far too often there is a complete disjuncture between researchers' stated theoretical or epistemological standpoints and their use of language in their social analyses. In practice, we too often find informants' accounts of events, or memories, or descriptions of social action, reproduced as if they were transparent representations.

Yet virtually every theoretical perspective on which qualitative research rests recognises a central and constitutive role for language, and would stress that language-use is one of the most pervasive means of accomplishing social action, self-presentation, consciousness and the like. Symbolic interactionism, phenomenology, ethnomethodology, varieties of constructivism – these all accord language a special (though not exclusive) place in making social persons and social activities. This is something of a paradox, and it is a frustrating feature of contemporary research. Far too much of the work that is described as 'qualitative' relies on extracts taken from spoken accounts – derived from interviews, as I have said – reported as if they were unproblematic and transparent. They are deployed to illustrate analyses of action, attitudes, values and so on. Little or no account is taken of their intrinsic rhetorical features. Of course, this is not a universal failing, but it is far too common. Ethnographers – alert to the properties of social conventions – should not have any excuse for treating language-use in such naïve ways. On the contrary, many of the best ethnographic opportunities are provided by a sustained, analytic attention to the forms and functions of practical language-use.

I continue with a brief recapitulation of the recurrent debates concerning interview data. In essence, this depends on the competing claims of interviews and direct observation as sources of information about a given social world or social phenomenon. Silverman and I (Atkinson and Silverman 1997) have lamented the almost ubiquitous reliance on interviews among the various communities of qualitative research. Indeed, we noted that in some quarters the very notion of qualitative research (not a term we endorsed there or since, except for purely pragmatic purposes) seems to be equated with various styles of 'open-ended', or 'in-depth' interviewing. Moreover, there is a tendency even to describe as ethnographic studies that are almost or completely dependent on interviewing. This latter usage seems – for the sorts of reasons I have given already in this book – to be entirely unjustified. We suggested that this undue reliance on interviews as modes of data collection reflected the pervasive cultural phenomenon we called 'the interview society'. We noted that contemporary society seems to place a particular cultural value on self-revelation, and the construction of accounts of personal feelings, experiences and preferences. We seem to be surrounded, in everyday life, through the mass media in particular, with broadcast and printed interviews through which private experience is translated into a public commodity. The interview-obsessed research community seem to be recapitulating those cultural patterns, often equating the ends of research with the investigation of social actors' personal, private lives. The interview seems to be a means of penetrating personal experience, giving access to the individual actor's 'point of view'.

Now I think that to be a sound argument: there is certainly an over-reliance on interview data, and there are certainly too many publications – methodological and substantive – reflecting an obsession with the contents of experience. But the interview society in its various manifestations should also remind us of a slightly different thing. The interview *is* a cultural phenomenon. It is accomplished through the use of various conventions of language and repertoires of speech act. There are culturally shared kinds of stories and rhetorics of emotion that are expected of certain kinds of interviews. (I shall expand on this point later in this chapter.) So we might need to think about things from a slightly different perspective. An ethnography of (say) sports performers, artistic performers, or celebrities ought to include an ethnography of the interview itself. It would be one of several, indeed many, kinds of performance and enactment that the relevant social actors would be party to. In its cultural embeddedness, the research interview is in itself an 'indigenous' method that is distinctive to contemporary Western culture. In other words, the interview is a distinctive kind of speech event. It calls on shared assumptions on the part of the interviewer and interviewee. In many contexts, there are preferred kinds of questions and preferred kinds of answers. They appeal to culturally shared frames of reference that hearers or readers will recognise. Interviewees can engage in various kinds of self-presentation and various kinds of rhetorical device in order to do so: they can elicit sympathy, seek self-justification, allocate responsibility and blame, and so on.

So, the interview in everyday life and the interview as part of the research process, are both particular kinds of spoken activity. They embody speech acts and performances. They reflect socially shared conventions of expression. They *construct* experiences, memories and the like. They contain accounts and narratives. They reflect conventional codes of comedy or tragedy. They elicit sympathy or repulsion. They draw on story-types: hard-luck stories, stories of success and failure, stories of troubles overcome, and so on. Now research interviews are deliberately designed occasions on which such performances are enacted, and to that extent there is no question: they do not constitute 'naturally occurring' sources of data. On the other hand, they provide occasions for the performance of events that rarely, if ever, occur under other (natural) circumstances. The life-history interview, for instance, rarely occurs in other social circumstances. Fragments of such biographical narration do occur of course: occupational interviews, medical histories and similar kinds of accounting can contain aspects of the life-history. But they are clearly nothing like the sort of extended encounter(s) through which hours and hours of talk are exchanged, and large tracts of a life are recounted.

So, if we cannot treat interview data as unproblematic forms of representation or reconstruction, then they become especially troublesome, especially if viewed as sources of information about informants' personal 'experience'. As Silverman (1993) points out, we cannot approach interview data simply from the point of view of 'truth' or 'distortion', and we cannot use such data with a view to remedying the incompleteness of observations. By the same token, we cannot rely on our observations in order to correct presumed inaccuracies in interview accounts. On the contrary, interviews generate data that have intrinsic properties of their own. In essence, we need to treat interviews as generating accounts and performances that have their own properties, and ought to be analysed in accordance with such characteristics. We need, therefore to appreciate that interviews are occasions in which are enacted particular kinds of narratives, and in which 'informants' construct themselves and others as particular kinds of moral agents. Examples here include the analyses of parents' accounts of life with handicapped children as analysed by Margaret Voysey Paun (2006) and of natural scientists' accounts of scientific discoveries by Nigel Gilbert and Michael Mulkay (1984).

When I was studying the Welsh National Opera company (Atkinson 2006) I did conduct interviews with a number of key informants, as well as a great many conversations that occurred in the course of fieldwork (between rehearsals, in WNO offices, at performances in the theatre), I also collected interviews from a number of individuals who were among the financial supporters of the opera company. I did not treat those interview materials as proxy sources of information about performances or rehearsals. I did, however, recognise that many people associated with the opera have stories and narratives to give, biographical work to undertake, and justifications to offer (for their aesthetic or other operatic commitments). Singers, for instance, draw on distinctive (but by no means unique) repertoires of narrative to account for their careers. Along with other performers, they do, for instance, have all sorts of stories about luck and success. Chance opportunities – lucky breaks – are presented as the origins of successful careers, for instance. These are among the well-rehearsed tropes of career-narratives. Similar accounts can be found in scientists' narratives concerning their scientific discoveries. In both contexts, these kinds of stories enshrine devices that allow the speaker to express her or his success, while allowing for a degree of personal modesty, rather than attributing success to brilliance. Culturally, such a degree of managed modesty is normally preferred; arrogance and self-praise are not. Obviously, this is not a question of accusing singers, scientists or anybody of misrepresentation. It most definitely *is* a matter of applying elementary analytic principles to such spoken materials. There is no merit in simply reporting what was said with no regard to how it was said, and what cultural conventions were deployed.

We should not, therefore, worry about whether 'the informant is telling the truth', if by that one understands the task of the analyst to distinguish factual accuracy from distortion, bias or deception. Similarly, ironic contrasts between what people do and what they say they do become less pressing. Rather, attention is paid to the coherence and plausibility of accounts, to their performative qualities, the repertoires of accounts and moral types that they contain and so on. It would be more fruitful, in a way, to ask 'How does the informant know s/he is telling the truth?' or indeed, 'How is truth enacted?' and 'How are plausible versions of persons and events conveyed?' Thought of in this way, interviews are approached as a form of social action. This approach to interviewing as action can be illustrated with reference to the topic of memory. One way of thinking about interviews and the data they yield is to think about informants producing descriptions of past events. In part, therefore, the interview is aimed at the elicitation of memories. Viewed from a naïve perspective, it also follows that one of the main problems of this kind of data collection concerns the accuracy or reliability of such recollections. Such a perspective certainly presents pressing problems if one is using the interview to gather information about past events. The same is true of the elicitation of experiences. It is possible to view the interview as a means for the retrieval of informants' personal experiences, if by that one means a biographically grounded and discursively constructed view of memories and past events. The analytic problems of memory and experience are equivalent from my point of view. It is possible to address memory and experience sociologically, and it is possible to address them through the interview (and through other documents of life). But it is appropriate to do so only if one accepts that memory and experience are social actions in themselves. They are both enacted. Seen from this perspective, memory is not (simply) a matter of individual psychology, and is certainly not only a function of internal mental states. Equally, it is not a private issue. (I am not denying the existence of psychological processes in general, nor the personal qualities and significance of our memories: mine is a methodological argument about the appropriate way of conducting and conceptualising social research.) Memory is a cultural phenomenon, and is to that extent a collective one. What is memorable is a function of the cultural categories that shape what is thinkable and what is not, what is counted as appropriate, what is valued, what is noteworthy and so on. Memory is far from uniquely (auto-) biographical. It can reside in material culture, for instance. The deliberate collection or hoarding of memorabilia and souvenirs – photographs, tourist artefacts, family treasures or other bric-a-brac – is one enactment of memory, for instance. Equally, memory is grounded in what is tellable. In many ways the past is a narrative enactment.

Memory and personal experience are narrated. Narrative is a collective, shared cultural resource. As authors such as Plummer (1995) have reminded us, even the most intimate and personal of experiences are constructed through shared narrative formats. The 'private' does not escape the 'public' categories of narrativity. Just as C. Wright Mills (1940) demonstrated that 'motive' should be seen as cultural and linguistic in character, and not a feature of internal mental states or predispositions, we must recognise that memories and experiences are constructed through the resources of narrative and discourse. A similar perspective has, much more recently, been articulated by Tilly, in suggesting that stories, big and small, can be understood in terms of the 'Why?' they implicitly address (Tilly 2006). Narratives and the resources of physical traces, places and things – these are the constituents of biography, memory and experience. When we conduct an interview, then, we are not simply collecting information about non-observable or unobserved actions, or past events, or private experiences. Interviews generate accounts and narratives that are forms of social action in their own right (Lyman and Scott 1968).

Gimlin (2012) provides an instance of how narratives can be treated in a sociological fashion. The substance of these narratives is women's accounts of cosmetic surgery. She identifies a number of narrative formats that are used to construct distinctive justifications and evaluations of cosmetic surgery. These are culturally shaped accounting mechanisms, not individual constructions alone. They include the trope identified in terms of 'surgical; otherness'. This form of contrastive rhetoric justifies the speaker's use of cosmetic surgery by juxtaposing it with extreme usages by others, such as women who are obsessive in their surgical transformations. Gimlin provides insufficient concrete data or detailed analysis to take this as far as she might, but it is a clear indication of how one might treat such accounts *as* accounts, and hence as cultural phenomena. In a similar vein, Taylor and Littleton (2012) treat interview data as accounts, focusing on the discursive resources through which their participants constructed autobiographical narratives. The materials are drawn from three complementary studies of creative workers at different stages in their career, from aspiring novices through to mature practitioners. They explore the discursive repertoires that are drawn on to construct career-narratives, including recurrent tropes that furnish biographical resources. Such career biographies include a repertoire of accounting devices that stress the early emergence of talent or a propensity towards creative interests. The biography is therefore, in part, constructed in terms of the revelation of creative talent – sometimes developed in the home, with supportive parents in childhood. This sense of continuity can be a significant aspect of identity-work, legitimating career-choice and aspirations. Accounts of biographical trajectories and career contingencies emphasise the actuality or possibility of good fortune and a 'big break', but also of the importance of continuing hard work. Participants also use a contrastive rhetoric that distinguishes their 'real' creative work from more mundane paid employment.

In these analyses of accounts, sociological and anthropological perspectives are informed by narrative analysis and discursive psychology. This is one among many cultural domains for which ethnographers need a sophisticated grasp of a range of analytic issues. At this point I return to the original formulation offered by Becker and Geer (1957). They refer to the study of 'events', arguing that observation provided access to events in a way that interviews cannot. In one sense, that is self-evidently true. We can observe, and we can make permanent recordings of events. On the other hand, we need to ask ourselves what constitutes an *event*. Clearly an event is not merely a string of unrelated moments of behaviour, nor is it devoid of significance. In order to be observable and reportable, events in themselves must have some degree of coherence and internal structure. An event in the social world is not something that happens: it is made to happen. It has a beginning, a middle and an end. It is differentiated from the surrounding stream of activity. Its structure and the observer's capacity to recognise it are essentially narrative in form. In that sense, therefore, a radical distinction between events that are observed and accounts that are narrated starts to become less stark, and the boundary maintenance more difficult to sustain.

Does this mean that we still acknowledge the primacy of particular kinds of social actions? Not necessarily. By acknowledging that accounts, recollections and experiences are enacted, we can start to avoid the strict dualism between 'what people do' and 'what people say'. This is a recurrent topic in the methodological discourse of social science. It rests on the commonplace observation that there may be differences or discrepancies between observed actions and accounts about action. They are different kinds of enactments, certainly, but I argue that the specific dualism that implicitly asserts an authenticity for what people (observably) do and the fallibility of accounts of action is both unhelpful and 'untrue'. By treating both the observed and the narrated as kinds of social action we move beyond such simple articulations, and instead reassert the methodological principle of symmetry. We should therefore bracket the assumption of authenticity, or the 'natural' character of 'naturally occurring' action, and the contrasts that are founded on that implicit dualism. If we recognise that memories, experiences, motives and so on are themselves forms of action, and equally recognise that they, like all mundane activities, are enacted, then we can indeed begin to deal with these issues in a symmetrical, but non-reductionist, way. In other words, it is not necessary to assert the primacy of one form of data over another, nor to assert the primacy of one form of action over another. Equally, a recognition of the performative action of interview talk removes the temptation to deal with such data as if they gave us access to personal or private 'experiences'. We need, therefore, to divorce the use of the interview from the myth of interiority – the essentially Romantic view of the social actor as a repository of inner feelings and intensely personal recollections. Rather, interviews become equally valid ways of capturing shared cultural understandings and enactments of the social world. Now, in a way, this discussion of a classic dilemma is a diversion, because it leads us to a much more general point. I have now suggested that there is not necessarily any radical difference between an interview account and any other naturally occurring speech event in the field. Consequently, this means that ethnographers really ought to be paying serious attention to precisely those stories, narratives, accounts and spoken performances of all sorts. Moreover, they need to be observed and recorded in order to capture and analyse their formal properties.

Let us continue by considering stories. The world is full of stories. They circulate endlessly, sometimes within small networks of friends and family, sometimes they travel over long distances and assume socially significant proportions. In recent years it has become commonplace to assert that the social world is quintessentially 'storied'. Narrative is held to be an especially significant way for actors to organise their lives, their experiences, their feelings and so on. So it is. That gives us every reason to study stories, narratives, accounts with every seriousness. Too often, however, narratives and other kinds of spoken performance are celebrated but not analysed. Narratives have form and they have functions. They circulate. They both reflect and shape social relations and social networks. They convey and embody personal reputations. They enshrine morals and other cultural values. They are the vehicles for socialisation, and rumours or gossip are means of social sanction. In other words, stories and similar kinds of spoken activity are far too important to be treated merely as the undifferentiated repositories of actors' personal experiences.

Most importantly, stories have structure. There is an inherent organisation to them, and through that organisation their social functions are accomplished. In other words, there are socially shared conventions that are used by social actors in order to accomplish a range of activities. Stories therefore create structures of plausibility, and they also enact persuasion, justification, legitimation and the like. Ethnographers, therefore, need to be especially alert to the stories that circulate within social worlds, and to analyse the kinds of work that they perform. The structural properties of personal narrative have been examined over a long period of time by William Labov, and his work is in many ways summarised in his monograph, based on stories of life-and-death experiences (Labov 2013). Linking his ideas explicitly to analyses of oral epic, Labov points out how thoroughly personal and emotional accounts display recurrent structural properties. Narratives are not streams of consciousness. They are organised in accordance with culturally shared conventions. Labov also discusses the profoundly significant theme of *credibility*, although his treatment of it is limited. As I have already acknowledged, social scientists have long grappled with the issue of whether informants' accounts can be treated as reliable. But the point here is that credibility is a property of narratives themselves. Consequently, the ethnographically productive question is 'How does the informant construct a plausible account?'

Analytically speaking, it is not necessary to believe an account in order to appreciate its formal properties of plausibility. I have had occasion recently to examine some published stories from victims of alien abduction. There are many individuals who recount the experience of being extracted in some way from their everyday life, a period of lost time during which alien beings sequester them, and physical evidence of aliens' inspection or invasion of their body. Alien abductions provide rather useful exemplars for analytic purposes. They are recounted by people who clearly feel the reported experiences deeply, and those experiences are extremely personal. But that does not mean that they do not display characteristic, conventional features. It would be wrong to suggest that these accounts are simply incredible because they confound our everyday understandings of what is possible. They provide an excellent example of the truth-telling issue. As I have already suggested, the old chestnut of 'How do you know if your informant is telling the truth?' can more fruitfully be replaced with 'How does your informant know s/he is telling the truth?', or even 'How does your informant tell plausible stories?'. The latter depends on no adjudication of truth by the researcher, but they do open up more productive avenues of inquiry. This is not to imply, incidentally, that lying or self-delusion or boasting do not take place. Of course they do, and there is an anthropological literature on lying and deceit (Barnes 1994). There are many cultural settings where lying, in one form or another, is highly valued in itself. Equally, therefore, we can make such deceptive acts into topics of inquiry in their own right (e.g. Morrow 2013), but that does not absolve us from approaching such materials from an analytic perspective.

Typically, the abduction stories implicitly address their own credibility in that they begin with a narrative that establishes the normality of events prior to the abduction itself. Tellers are engaged in unremarkable, ordinary activity. The story is also framed, however, in accordance with narrative conventions concerning the foreshadowing of strange events – lonely roads, bad weather, darkness, waking up in the middle of the night. These narrative forms represent what Labov would call the Orientation phases of the story: they establish the context as well as the dramatis personae, as well as the premonition that something newsworthy, remarkable is about to take place. The narrative thus posits a trajectory of normal time, which is then punctuated by a period of abnormal time. In narrative terms, therefore, the actual or presumed abduction stands in an equivalent position to religious conversions and similar extraordinary occurrences, in which the mundane is punctured by a sudden reversal and an inruption of the supernatural. The central action – what Labov would call the Complication – is framed as inexplicable, defying the normality that surrounds it. Complication is compounded with yet further complications, when the abductee seeks for evidence and confirmation – often found in physical marks on the body, or reconstructions of the interrupted journey, and checks on the lost time that elapsed. The extraordinary is thus bolstered with further demonstrations of normality and evidential accounting. By no means all abduction stories are the same, but they often display common structural properties and narrative themes. Such stories illustrate one of Labov's observations: that what is reportable as newsworthy contrasts with what is so ordinary as not to be worthy of narration. In abduction stories, the contrast between the mundane and the extraordinary is central to the accounting process. The stories are structured around a series of implied contrasts: ordinary *versus* extraordinary; darkness *versus* light; ordinary time *versus* lost time; mundane explanation *versus* the inexplicable.

It will be apparent that abduction stories are not unique in their components. In some ways they closely mirror that widespread genre of stories collectively referred to as *urban legends*. The latter differ in terms of their narrative framings, however. Abductions are narrated by people who experience them, while urban legends are recounted as second- or third-hand accounts (the events having happened to a friend-of-a-friend). As I have already hinted, they also have common properties with stories of religious conversion and miraculous intervention. All of these accounts *can* be deeply felt and regarded as entirely factual by their tellers. Equally, they can be recounted with a degree of caution or even scepticism. Their narrative structure does not depend on the degree of credence vested in them. Narratives are not the means for researchers to gain access to informants' personal experience. The task is rather to understand how experience is framed, constructed, shared and transmitted.

Mythic structures are pervasive in narratives and stories that reconstruct the past. While it is not in itself an example of ethnographic fieldwork, a recent monograph on the legends surrounding John

Coltrane's recording of 'A Love Supreme' provides an especially telling example. That recording is, in several senses, 'legendary' in jazz circles. And as Whyton (2013) demonstrates, those legends capture a series of oppositions in myth-making: the music was fully devised, the music was improvised; the recorded version was direct and spontaneous, there was over-dubbing of Coltrane's own voice; it was a unique performance, it was recorded in a different version again the following day. The contrasts that are embedded in the legends of the recorded music, Whyton argues, allow its hearers to frame an appreciation of the work and of jazz more generally through a mythic resolution of paradoxes and dualisms.

Equally, we can recognise that there are distinctive types or *genres* of narrative. Abductions and religious experiences can clearly be grouped in terms of revelation or conversion stories. In many settings we can identify a variety of stories about professional or personal reputations. For instance, in the course of my own ethnography with the Welsh National Opera Company I spent time with singers – guest artists and members of the company's chorus – before, during and after rehearsal periods. Inevitably, indeed in common with all such work settings, talk would include stories in the form of personal reminiscence or reported events concerning performers, directors, conductors and others in the opera world. These are often moral tales that are used to establish and to share the character of key individuals. For instance, such stories can construct individuals as 'difficult' or 'impossible' people (a category not at all rare in opera and other performing arts, but equally known in many other occupational settings). The story was told of a well-known American soprano who was known to be so 'difficult' that companies were unwilling to engage her. It told of the singer complaining that the limo sent to pick her up from her hotel and to take her to the theatre was late. She was sitting in the back of the car, and phoning her agent, ordering the latter to phone the limo company to instruct the driver to drive faster (rather than deigning to speak directly to the driver herself), only to be reminded that the only reason she was running late was because she had sent away the first limo that had arrived – on time – because it was too small, although she was travelling alone. This was just one anecdote told about the pathologically picky behaviour of this particular artist, told so as to construct her behaviour as manifestly unreasonable through implied contrasts with what was expectably normal behaviours. These kinds of stories have distinctive functions in the working context of the opera company: they portray the stereotypical *diva* as an alien and monstrous character, implicitly compared to ordinary, hard-working singers and musicians.

Some individuals can be assembled through series of anecdotes that mingle respect, admiration and a hint of terror. The late Sir Charles Mackerras was just such a character among members of the opera company. He was always regarded with great respect and even affection. In the course of my fieldwork I was struck on more than one occasion that when Sir Charles arrived in the rehearsal studio or in the orchestra pit in the theatre, in the course of rehearsals, he could – apparently by just his charismatic presence – inject a sense of urgency and a lifting of the performers' collective spirits. He also enjoyed a distinctive reputation as a conductor who mingled the authority of his musicological knowledge with an intensely practical approach to rehearsal and performance. He was also a demanding music director. Consequently there were repeated stories of Sir Charles's stern criticisms of singers. Characteristic comments were reported: 'Yes, this *could* be very good. It isn't any good at the moment. But it could be good.' One singer reported Sir Charles whispering detailed criticisms to singers even while they were hand-in-hand bowing and taking their curtain-calls in the theatre after a performance: 'Would you take a closer look at bar one hundred and thirty-two, please?'

Likewise, there were multiple stories about opera directors. I was told that one internationally famous director stormed out of rehearsals when he discovered that he could not have a performer throw himself off a high place on the set without a safety harness and health-and-safety approval. Or another director who discovered that a spiral staircase that had been specified in the design of the opera had been constructed spiralling in the wrong direction, and as a consequence he had locked himself in his hotel room, refusing for some time to come out. Yet another reportedly shouted at the leading lady 'Why don't you just go shopping, and get yourself a brain?' (These stories did not relate to any of the directors I actually observed.) These and similar stories were part of the collective folk-memory of the opera company. They were exemplars of a genre that is found in many organisational settings: they are the sort of *cautionary tale* that enshrines key values and breaches of occupational morality. They are akin to the occupational *atrocity stories* that Dingwall (1977) documented. They are also reputational stories, used to key newcomers (like myself) into a distinctive aspect of occupational culture, and to reinforce shared understandings of significant figures in the professional field. Stories like this circulate within occupational networks and organisations.

Here, of course, we have moved from narratives collected in the course of interviews to those collected as they arise more spontaneously in the course of ethnographic fieldwork. We need to note that this is one of the key modalities of everyday cultural performance, and these narratives are themselves a significant type of ethnographic data. Ethnographers therefore need to pay analytic attention to several things simultaneously. They need to be alert to the circulation of stories: who tells them to what audiences, their paths of transmission. They need to examine the social functions that stories are used to perform: enculturation, blame, sanction and so on. They also need to examine them for their formal properties: how they are constructed, how they represent events, how they construct actors and how they embody tellers' evaluations of the reported activity. These call for sustained analysis. It is, in other words, of little value merely to collect and to reproduce narratives, and to offer them as exemplars of 'experience'. We need, as researchers, to demonstrate *how* they are enacted, *how* they are shared, and *what* they accomplish in context. Moreover, experience is something that is itself constructed through acts of memory and telling. By recounting narratives of one's own past, or by passing on stories from elsewhere, the teller establishes her or his own stock of occupational and personal experiences.

Analytic attention therefore calls for an understanding of how narratives and accounts perform distinctive kinds of *speech acts*. We have already seen that such accounts – whether they are derived from interviews or from naturally occurring events in the field – accomplish things. If people 'do things with words', then they also 'do things with narratives'. People construct complaints, confessions, boasts – indeed the entire gamut of possible activities. These are all accomplishments, performed through the use of social and discursive conventions. Amongst other things, therefore, it is as important to know *how* an event is transformed into an experience, or *how* it is memorialised in personal narratives and biographical accounts, as it is to know *that* somebody reports an experience or a memory. Indeed, it is more important to do so: the conventions and techniques of everyday rhetoric are socially shared. They are the cultural resources that make possible a shared social world of motives, biographies and justifications that are the stuff of a *sociological* analysis. Equally, of course, forgetting or the suppression of memory can be an important function in the construction and circulation of stories (cf. Blenkinsop 2013).

From a complementary perspective we can see how biographies, lives or identities can be fashioned through narrative means, and through more specific speech acts. Life-history interviewing, and the collection of life-histories within a broader ethnographic context do not merely document a life that pre-exists independently of its telling. Recent intellectual interest in biography and autobiography has contributed to an undue emphasis on issues of personal experience, and of the individual social actors. What can get lost in such a perspective is the existence of narrative conventions through which the (auto)biography is assembled, narrrative coherence is accomplished, turning-points are portrayed and events are assembled. We need to analyse how narrators justify themselves and their actions, how they formulate their evaluations of others, and thus how lives are matters of celebration or regret, as tragedies or comedies of manners, as stories of victimhood or triumph.

In other words, the very notion of a life or a biography implies a narrative form. Lives, temporal markers of change and development, and the unfolding of narratives is, therefore, a fundamentally important set of ideas for the contemporary ethnographer. What it does *not* mean is that we should simply take such things as given, as unmediated phenomena. Too often, ethnographers and other qualitative researchers assume that they are dealing with social actors whose lives and identities are relatively stable. Now this is, of course, something of a paradox, since the underlying assumptions of interpretative or interactionist social research is that lives and identities are fluid and processual. Hence, if we take seriously that latter tenet, then we need to ask ourselves – ethnographically speaking – just *how* such fluid identities get accomplished. There is no single asnwer to that deceptively simple question. Clearly, they are emergent properties of interactions and chains of interactions. They are also accomplished through performances whereby they are collaboratively worked on by actors and their immediate collaborators. So, if we routinely collect and co-construct with our research participants documents of life then we certainly cannot think of those materials as speaking for themselves. Indeed, thinking that any data speak for themselves has several consequences. First, it means that we absolve ourselves of the need actually to do anything with those data, encouraging under-analysed studies. Secondly, it robs us of the intellectual work – the fun even – of finding challenging and innovative ways of undertaking a thorough analysis.

Here I have been alluding to the long-standing sociological interest in the nature of accounts and social actors' accounting methods. In itself, this is not especially startling. In essence, this standpoint implies that accounts are always constructed from a particular point of view. Moreover, they are always constructed from culturally available resources. Consequently, they are simultaneously social constructions in their own right and they are the means whereby social construction gets done. Accounts, therefore, do not merely report events. They shape them, they *make them into* events. They construct – for the teller and for the hearer (or reader) – what is tellable and what may be newsworthy. They provide evaluative and moral frames within which to place the account.

They position the teller of the account as a particular kind of person, and give them a standpoint or a distinctive perspective. Moreover, accounts are constructed in accordance with narrative conventions and from culturally shared resources.

Accounting in action can be witnessed vividly in the professional work of *making a case*. We know that it is the task of the ethnographer constantly to ask herself 'What is this a case of?'. This can equally be a practical matter for the social actors themselves. The construction of accounts and similar kinds of speech events is a professional matter, for instance, for social workers, the police, lawyers and medical practitioners. They all need to take whatever 'evidence' is to hand, and to transform it into the sort of account that constitutes a 'case'. Hence, professional workers are often engaged in what is essentially *narrative* work. A pertinent case is furnished by Gathings and Parrotta (2013), who document lawyers' constructions of courtroom narratives about their clients, in order to secure leniency in sentencing. These narratives are constructed in accordance with normal expectations concerning social worth, and consequently they reproduce normative assumptions concerning gendered social performance. So, it is argued, men are constructed as good workers and good providers, while women are narrated as good mothers and carers. Men are victims, women are dependent. Such professional narratives are part of the lawyers' stock-in-trade, and they help to create institutional realities of identity-work, labelling and sentencing in the criminal justice system.

I and others have frequently commented on such narrative case-construction on the part of medical practitioners. Hunter (1991) provides a valuable point of reference. She documents how profoundly medicine is predicated on narrative competence. Especially in settings such as major hospitals, there are multiple occasions on which medical practitioners and students are called upon to summarise and 'present' patients as cases. There are shared formats for such cases, and there are many occasions, of varying degrees of formality, at which they are presented to colleagues and superiors. Moreover, the construction and delivery of such a case calls for rhetorical skills, and individuals are evaluated on the basis of their performances and their narrative competence. These skills are acquired, and they are differentially distributed. Equally importantly, they are among the means whereby medical knowledge is constructed and shared (Atkinson 1995).

Consequently, we as ethnographers need to pay sustained, analytic attention to the nature of accounts and narratives, whether they derive from interviews or are recorded in more 'natural' circumstances. We need to address *inter alia*:

- How are accounts constructed: what are their formal properties?
- What accounting devices are deployed?
- What functions do they perform?
- How do they construct or portray their teller(s)?
- How are they constructed from cultural conventions?
- When and how are they recounted?
- How do they circulate?

If we take such issues seriously, then we do not need to base our ethnographic understanding on crude distinctions between speech and reported events. We can treat narratives and accounts as events, or as speech-acts, in their own right. This does mean that we should not merely reproduce extracts of speech as if they were straightforward representations devoid of social convention or function.

Forms of talk are, therefore, embedded in the social worlds in which we undertake our fieldwork. They are not sources of unmediated access to individual persons' interior lives and experiences. They are as much cultural artefacts as a pot or a carpet. We need to pay analytic attention to their construction, reception, and their circulation. They have form and function that are thoroughly dependent on shared cultural conventions. It may, perhaps, not be necessary for all would-be ethnographers to become fully expert in the analysis of documents of life and personal narratives. Equally, however, it is simply not good enough to treat such materials unproblematically. There is currently a vast amount of published research that is, by any criteria, scientifically unsound. By neglecting the internal organisation of spoken activities, and by taking the content of narratives or accounts at face value, researchers manifestly fail to commit themselves to an adequate level of analysis.

7
Aesthetics, Artefacts and Techniques

Sociologists and anthropologists have not always been sufficiently alert to the aesthetics of their research settings. In some ways this is understandable: aesthetics always imply value-judgements, and the principle of cultural relativism provides a strong injunction against such value-laden preoccupations. On the other hand, all social worlds imply aesthetic values. We are surrounded by artefacts, cultural activities, people, that we differentially value for their beauty, grace, taste, felicity and so on. We cannot be blind to the aesthetic dimension. Of course, viewed ethnographically, there is no real paradox in recognising the pervasive nature of aesthetic judgements and the avoidance of inappropriately judgemental attitudes of our own. What we, as anthropologists or sociologists, are interested in are what we might call the ethno-aesthetics of any given social setting.

Historically speaking, there have been a number of points of confluence between the ethnographic and the aesthetic. For instance, as Kelly (2007) describes, French avant-garde artists, including the surrealists, were directly influenced by the aesthetics of African artefacts that were assembled in the course of the French Dakar–Djibouti expedition, and their display at the Trocadéro museum, precursor of the Musée de l'Homme. Likewise, encounters with 'exotic' cultures, through anthropology and museum-culture, exerted a powerful influence on visual artists – painters and sculptors – elsewhere. The 'primitivism' of, say, Epstein in Britain clearly reflects a sensibility that was alert to exotic cultures. Much more recently we have seen new forms of congruence between art and ethnography, with a number of commentators examining the 'ethnographic' connotations of site-specific art works and installations. And yet it is fair to say that very many ethnographies of the last century paid relatively little attention to matters of aesthetics. Too often, we have found that aesthetics have been treated within highly specialised genres of research and writing: ethnomusicology and the sociology or anthropology of art are among the latter.

Yet there are of necessity many settings in which attention to aesthetics is of paramount significance, and I shall discuss some of the relevant issues below. There are, however, many aspects of aesthetics and aesthetic work – including notions of performance, felicity and technique – in a host of other settings as well. It is hard to think of many social worlds in which there is no room for aesthetics, at least in the sense that they have some culturally shared values concerning appearance, beauty, elegance. These do not have to be treated as separate matters ('art') although there are many contexts in which something approximating to art and craft – including music – is culturally recognised as a distinctive domain.

Let us begin with ethnographic settings in which aesthetics of performance and cultural production are central. I begin with a discussion of one of my own research sites, which I introduce by way of a critique of some recent work on the sociology of art. Largely influenced by the huge contribution made by Howard Becker, it has become conventional to discuss art (in the broadest sense) in terms of 'art worlds' (Becker 1982). From this perspective, the work of cultural production, such as that of the visual arts, is no different in principle from any other form of socially organised activity: this perspective derives from the sociology of work and professions characteristic of the Second Chicago School of sociology, associated with Everett Hughes and his circle. In and of itself, of course, this is an important perspective. It reminds us forcibly that, analytically speaking, we cannot and should not privilege 'art' works, on the assumption that they are intrinsically significant, or that they embody special values, cultural or aesthetic. It is important to recognise that art worlds and the works that they contain are created through socially organised activity. The artist is not to be seen in an unduly Romantic light, as a lone creator, whose efforts transcend social convention. Art worlds depend on often dense networks of collaboration – not just between artists, but also between them and dealers, galleries and curators, patrons and collectors, paid assistants and artisans. Sculptors, for instance, often depend on skilled assistants, specialist foundry-workers and the like to transform their models (maquettes) into full-sized sculptures. Likewise, artists' lithographs and screenprints are often created by skilled printers, and fine-art print studios constitute art worlds in their own right. Clearly, art worlds also imply markets, in which objects and commercial values circulate, and they are powerful aspects of art worlds.

This is, of course, a valuable antidote to any kind of analysis based on the assumption that art is dependent on the intrinsic and transcendental merits of the art work alone, or that it is the ineffable product of a solitary artist. On the other hand, there is a danger that the analysis becomes so thoroughly based on generic social processes that it could apply to virtually any and every form of cooperative work and collective social action. It was one of the insights that Everett Hughes promoted, and that has been taken up ever since, that the sociologist can find common properties between the physician and the plumber, the psychiatrist and the prostitute (Hughes 1971). In many ways that is true, but it can mask important differences as well. The production and circulation of an art work is thoroughly dependent on the circulation of aesthetic judgements about the art work, evaluations of the artistic worth and integrity of the artist, the validation of authenticity and so on. I take it that this is, in part at least, at the heart of the possible critique that is the rationale of the collection of papers edited by Becker, Faulkner and Kirshenblatt-Ginblett (2006), with a new emphasis on the 'work itself', even though – as Becker's own contribution to that collection of papers makes clear – the idea of a 'work itself' remains sociologically problematic at best. The work never stands independently of social networks, cultural contexts and shared (and contested) judgements. Never the less, if we reduce the content and organisation of the work or the production to a mere epiphenomenon, then we lose many of the features of the social action and organisation that frame the work, and the significance invested in the work – by producers, performers, critics, consumers, collectors and others – becomes just as mysteriously invisible as a Romantic appeal to intrinsic artistic worth.

Of course, we are not to be seduced into accepting every or any aesthetic judgement as if it accounted for the art work; nor should we impute some intangible quality to the art work (such as its *aura*). On the other hand, we need to make sense of what we might call the *ethno-aesthetics* of artistic and cultural productions. We need to recognise – and therefore to study systematically – the socially shared and collectively organised practices that underpin the aesthetic judgements that are invoked to endow performances and products with value. If we do not, then we have no way of making sense of the collective commitment to art and performance, of the socialisation of the artist, or of the circulation of value that attends the enactment of art works and art worlds. Let me try to illustrate what I mean with reference to some recent work we have been doing in Cardiff on masterclasses for young opera singers. Cardiff University's International Academy of Voice is the brainchild of the internationally famous tenor Dennis O'Neill. It was founded quite explicitly, by O'Neill, in order to foster a particular vocal style in younger singers. He is not alone in believing that too many younger singers are not benefiting from the sort of vocal technique that previous generations were taught, and that as a consequence, young voices are put at risk. In part, this commitment reflects the *bel canto* tradition – which is at once an aesthetic and a technical approach to singing and voice production.

If, therefore, one is to make any sense of the masterclass as a particular kind of event – simultaneously performative and pedagogic – one cannot overlook or wish away the aesthetic aspects of music and singing. Equally, one cannot ignore the extent to which aesthetic issues are simultaneously matters of technique. For opera singers, singing itself is an intensely practical, embodied matter. In other words, aesthetic and technical interests are mutually constituted through the local practices of singers and coaches. Masterclasses, including public masterclasses enacted before an audience, have some common features, even though the detailed content varies depending on the individual teacher. Typically, singers perform their chosen 'piece' in its entirety, and are praised for their performance. Then the performance is repeated, but the teacher stops the student at intervals, and makes suggestions or criticises the student's performance. This is often accomplished through a repertoire of physical gestures that constitute a register of didactic resources. Full explication of this needs more space than is available here. But in brief, there is a dialogue of music and singing, explicit advice – sometimes in the form of maxims – and physical gestures (see Atkinson 2013b; Atkinson et al. 2013).

Gestures are used by singing coaches and masterclass mentors to convey technical advice. For instance, there are characteristic hand gestures used to convey matters of voice production. For instance, in the *bel canto* tradition, singers are encouraged to visualise a continuous wheel of breath in front of them, on which they place the note. This can be represented not only in explicit verbal instruction, but also through a characteristic wheeling motion of the hands. Likewise, teachers make hand gestures – usually near their own face – to encourage the student-singer to sing on the note, rather than scooping at it from beneath. They use physical gestures – including physically touching the student – to encourage her or him to support the voice on a column of breath, from the diaphragm. These, and many other combinations of talk and gesture, are deployed in the interests of beautiful singing. Apparently small physical adjustments can result in audibly different voice production in the course of a single masterclass. The purely technical matters blend into matters of interpretation. For instance, singers are encouraged to *interpret* their music as well as being technically precise. Technique and interpretation are inseparable in practice, as the ability to shape a vocal line depends simultaneously on vocal technique and interpretative confidence.

Now these issues deserve much more detailed exploration than I can give them here. For the moment I want merely to use them to illustrate some more general points. First, it is clear to me that aesthetic issues are at the heart of our understanding of any such performative work, and of any encounter such as the masterclass. Secondly, the aesthetic and the technical or practical are mutually constitutive. Here, aesthetics does not inscribe an appeal to general canons of beauty. The styles of operatic singing in general, of the *bel canto* tradition in particular, are highly context-specific (and reflect highly evolved performance conventions). They are examples of ethno-aesthetic codes. Moreover, the work of singers and teachers in encounters like masterclasses highlight the importance of *felicity* in performance. Felicitous enactments are simultaneously technically accurate, interpretatively sensitive and produced with the appearance of effortlessness. The requirement for such felicity is not confined to the world of performative art. Indeed, composure and felicity are among the features of everyday action that are available to reflection and evaluation, by actors themselves or by others.

My point here is this. We cannot make sense of what our young opera singers are doing without some regard for the aesthetic evaluations and criteria that are being deployed by their teacher, and are recognised (even if not always perfectly reproduced) by the young singers themselves. Of course, we cannot simply read off those aesthetic values from our own appreciation (or dislike) of the performance, or of the cultural genre itself. In that regard, there are problems with some studies of cultural performance. For instance, Jones's study of torch-singers tells us a great deal about *her* passions and responses. We read a good deal of her (somewhat breathless) reactions to particular singers and their performances (Holman Jones 2007). But quite what actual qualities of enactment the singers themselves value, or what criteria might be invoked by audiences in general, or by critics, or booking agents, and indeed anybody, are noticeably absent. It is not our job to be amateur critics of music, visual art, dramatic performance and so on. It might, by contrast, be very much part of our job to *study* the work of critics, judges, casting agents, directors and the like. We certainly ought to be interested in the cultural values displayed by connoisseurs and enthusiasts. We really ought to be attentive to the aesthetic values of performers themselves.

There are, luckily, many ethnographies that we can look to for some degree of guidance and inspiration. A recent ethnography of opera fans gives us some insight into the obsessive preferences and commitments of the sort of enthusiasts who inhabit the standing-room spaces at the Colòn opera house in Buenos Aires (Benzecry 2011). They combine passionate value-judgements about opera in general, repertoire and performers, in a way that constitutes an identity based on an obsessive identification with the art-form and its local realisation. Such obsessive audience members embrace a form of everyday musicology and theatrical critique that far exceeds in its level of enthusiasm and vehement partisanship anything that a professional expert or critic could possibly muster. Some of these enthusiasts are referred to as 'addicts'. Benzecry's study parallels the earlier observations published by Vail (1999), who also studied opera fans. Vail's main research topic has been the culture of body-art (tattooing), and he makes a telling comparison between the two categories of enthusiasts. Like Benzecry's fans, Vail's opera enthusiasts and body-art aficionados share a rhetoric of commitment and personal identity. Their calculus of commitment includes a recounting of how they were inculcated, and by whom, how many operas they have attended or how many tattoos they have acquired, and – most importantly – what pain and personal cost they have suffered in pursuit of their passion. Both, of course, also invoke aesthetic evaluations of the music-theatre on the one hand, and of their own and others' body-art on the other. These are among the many social settings that one might seek to study, where aesthetic values and judgements are fundamental. There are, for instance, plenty of occupations and professions in which an aesthetic judgement is central. For instance, Cottrell's ethnography of professional musicians in London includes a commentary on their deployment of the notion of *musicality* in their evaluations of performers and performances (Cottrell 2004).

Aesthetic work itself is a key feature of many professional and organisational settings (Fine 1985). The fashion industry and its associated trades are fundamentally preoccupied with aesthetic values and judgements. Fashion worlds draw together aesthetic judgements and social networks, often in spatially close occupational and organisational networks (Villette and Hardill 2010). The point of these observations is to direct attention not merely to the facts of aesthetics in ethnography, but also to some of the ways in which they can be studied in a rigorous fashion. We can start to identify some of the pertinent questions that the ethnographer-in-the-field might address in order to make sense of some of the cultural conventions that underpin any such aesthetic issues. What criteria are mobilised? How are form and function related in the ethno-aesthetics of a given social world? How are these recognised in terms of schools, traditions, genres or styles? It is possible to develop such questions into the entire substance of ethnographic inquiry. For instance, a study of folk-pottery of Mexico documents a complex typology of vernacular designs. Relatively slight (to the outside observer) differences in shape or decoration relate to local distinctions and the work of individual artisans (Kempton 1981). Such aesthetic issues can be highly significant cultural phenomena in their own right. Consider, for instance, the creation and circulation of carpets in various societies. As Spooner

(1986) suggests, Western aesthetics of Oriental carpets inscribe a variety of judgements concerning authenticity and connoisseurship.

How does each maker or artist or performer develop and display what we might call their idiolect of style? There is no doubt that in many cultural contexts, the distinctive markers of individual performance and production are recognisable – at least to aficionados if not to every cultural member. So for a serious collector, the work of individual studio potters in post-war Britain, or the work of glass artists in the United States can be identified in terms of the individual artist (Bernard Leach, or Dale Chihuly) and also the period in their artistic career at which a piece was created. This is not because they are idiosyncratic or egregiously different from all other works. On the contrary, they clearly partake of traditions, and reflect well-established techniques in their making. But the relatively small differences that are identifiable between the works of different artists are the stuff of what Bourdieu (1986) identifies in terms of *distinction*. Experts, collectors and other members of artistic circles can establish their credentials and accumulate capital by using this knowledge. The ability to make fine discriminations is a marker of taste. The music fan or collector can relish fine discriminations between and within genres. The opera 'buff' can wax lyrical (as it were) about singers, performances, recordings, productions – terrible and good. The jazz aficionado can name the sidemen featured in studio recordings. The serious film enthusiast can identify actors, directors, cinematographers, cast members and so on. Moreover, he or she can discuss directorial styles, in terms of shots, framing, timing and the like. These fine distinctions – aesthetic through and through – are often lost on the audience-member who does not possess such cultural capital.

Again, my point here is not merely to point out that some people have specialised, esoteric knowledge, but rather to add that these forms of aesthetics and taste are based on culturally shared codes that are used to express and display those value-judgements. There are characteristic vocabularies of taste, codes of appreciation, and distinctive modes of attention. Lehrer's study of the language of wine appreciation provides a particularly telling account of how such a cultural system can operate (Lehrer 2009). These are not matters of individual, individualistic preference. They are framed by socially shared conventions – which are, as we have suggested, differentially distributed. One can – and should – therefore be attentive to these contours of cultural competence, and simultaneously to the codes that inform and sustain them. This is a far cry from imputing particular values to art works and performances. We do not have any need to try to read particular cultural values directly from the works themselves. We should not ourselves endorse the hierarchies of value that are enshrined in cultural codes. We clearly need to suspend any evaluations of our own, and treat the codes of cultural convention as topics of systematic investigation.

The cultural conventions of aesthetics are vividly illustrated in the 'historical ethnography' of traditional Japanese painting (Jordan and Weston 2003). This makes clear the rigid aesthetic and stylistic codes of Japanese art, and the strict canons of production and appreciation that prevailed. In consequence, the methods of apprenticeship in painters' studios were based on strict regimes of dutiful copying of exemplars and established forms. This was an aesthetic regime that valued existing aesthetic criteria, and did not encourage novelty or the development of highly personalised styles. Novelty is celebrated in the world of contemporary fashion, on the other hand. Aesthetic work is documented in detail in Entwistle's ethnography of fashion clothing and modelling (Entwistle 2009). She shows how very contextual are notions of 'beauty' in the context of modelling. Fashion models are selected on the basis of very different criteria of attractiveness from those applied to 'everyday' beauty, and are quite different from models selected for 'glamour' work. Moreover, aesthetic criteria differ geographically: the male models that are preferred in Los Angeles have a different 'look' from those employed in London. Different commercial brands can also be associated with distinctive looks. Likewise, her analysis of fashion-buying at a large retail store in London (Selfridges) explores the tacit knowledge and aesthetic expertise of the buyers. As Entwistle herself puts it, while her own experience was an undifferentiated array of sensory impressions when viewing clothes, the buyers' expertise allowed them to apply aesthetic classificatory systems in order to identify trends and thus to make informed commercial decisions. This is, as Entwistle emphasises, tacit knowledge: it is not formulaic. Nevertheless, it is a matter of acquired expert knowledge that both reflects and shapes what counts as marketable fashion. The aesthetics of the fashion world are, moreover, matters of economics. Designers, fashion houses, model agencies and retail buyers are all engaged in the maintenance of aesthetic markets. Aesthetic values and exchange values are closely intertwined. The same is true of art worlds. The aesthetic judgements of art-dealers, critics, collectors and artists themselves are crucial resources in the creation of markets and the circulation of artistic value. The tacit knowledge of styles, trends, movements and so on is a key aspect of the cultural capital deployed by aesthetic entrepreneurs and brokers, and is transformed into material capital through the operation of aesthetic markets.

There has long been a danger that ethnographers pay insufficient attention to the embodied presence and actions of everyday social actors. We need to avoid populating our ethnographies with disembodied actors, who merely have experiences, make decisions, or speak. We need to recognise that people are embodied presences for each other as well as for us as observers. The aesthetic aspects of self-presentation and mutual evaluation need to be assessed systematically. We need to remember the sting in the tail of Goffman's account of spoiled identities (Goffman 1963). He points out that there are few, if any, unblushing social actors, perfect in every respect. Appearance, as well as other components of identity and esteem, is always vulnerable. In an important sense, we are all always 'passing for normal'. It is not just the singer or musician who displays *sprezzatura* (the appearance of effortless competence).

What are the key methodological issues that confront the ethnographer, then? Alertness to the ethno-aesthetics of a given cultural world or domain implies the following:

- What canons of appearance, normality and beauty are shared, contested, endorsed, or challenged?
- What criteria are used to assess aesthetic values?
- Who exercises judgement and who enforces those judgements?
- What are the codes of aesthetic value that are in play? How are they expressed and used in context?

This is, of course, one of several ethnographic layers that is rendered possible by newer technologies, and that therefore lends itself to a multi-modal approach. Aesthetic criteria, as well as the processes that go into aesthetic work, are well captured by means of digital photography and video-recording. Multi-modal ethnography or micro-ethnography is well suited to the examination of aesthetic artefacts and values (Hurdley and Dicks 2011). The topics lend themselves to a detailed analysis of visual records, material goods, recorded sound – indeed the entire range of data-types and recording modalities. It seems odd that many ethnographers seem rather reluctant to deploy this remarkable array of possibilities, preferring instead to rely solely on the spoken word, collected through interviews or recordings of naturally occurring interaction.

When Marcel Mauss gave the lectures that became his own *Manual of Ethnography* (Mauss 2007) he had no hesitation in providing prospective anthropologists in the field with instructions as to the what and the how of ethnographic collecting. The aim was to furnish practical guidelines for the field anthropologist or the colonial administrator to compile an inventory of material culture. Nowadays, however, we are not likely to think of the ethnographer as a collector. The fieldworker working in his or her own culture is, perhaps, especially unlikely to see herself or himself as a collector or to think in terms of museum-like assemblages of artefacts. By contrast, the specialist study of material culture has become a field of expertise in its own right. Unfortunately, in too many cases, 'material culture' has become divorced from the many modalities of social life in which it is embedded in studies of material culture *per se*.

We need, as social scientists, to undertake ethnographic work that strikes the right analytic, methodological balance. We must avoid reconstructing social worlds that are devoid of materiality. At the same time, we do not want to create a special study of material goods that are devoid of a social world. As ethnographers, we need to approach material goods and culture from exactly the same perspective as any other form of social life.

- Things are social and cultural.
- They are made in accordance with socially organised practices.
- People do things with things, just as much as they do things with words.
- People endow things with special significance.
- Things are used to evoke memories, and to enshrine emotions.
- Things are used to accomplish work and mundane tasks.

So we need to pay adequate attention to tools and manufactured goods, to sacred objects, to personal adornments and ornaments, to art objects, to physical memorials, to displays, to industrial, corporate and state artefacts. But things do not speak for themselves, whether in material form or as visual representations (such as digital images). They need to be studied within the contexts of everyday life: of work, art, domesticity, public display, private experience (Hurdley 2013).

If things are used to do things, then they are certainly used to make other things. The study of material culture, therefore, is often embedded in studies of work. Tools are typical of the sort of analytic stance that I am advocating here. There is a smallish number of monographs in which we gain detailed acquaintance with a skilled craftsman or artist. A classic example, that deserves to be better known than it seems to be, is Harper's study of a rural workshop (Harper 1987). The ethnographer focuses on Willie and his workshop. He repairs agricultural machinery and pretty much anything else that needs fixing. Anthropologists and others are familiar with the term *bricolage*, used metaphorically by Lévi-Strauss to evoke cultural processes of signification. The term literally refers to the handy-man's capacity to adapt and improvise, using whatever materials are to hand, to create practical solutions to practical problems. It is the sort of tinkering work that keeps machinery, especially vehicles, going. It cannibalises parts from whatever can be salvaged. It improvises repairs and modifications, rather than bespoke spare parts. The ethnography is an exemplary study of working knowledge (the book's title), of which Harper says:

> The basis of Willie's working knowledge is his deep understanding of many materials. It is knowing how metal, wood, plastic, or even paper and cardboard respond to attempts to alter their shape, density, or pliability. The knowledge is so detailed it leads to engineering: forming materials into machines or correcting design problems in the process of repair. Fixing and making are often very close together on the continuum of Willie's working knowledge, both grounded in a basic knowledge of the materials. (p. 31)

This working knowledge is very different from the sort of knowledge that might be deployed in more formal engineering sites, or that would be taught in classes for automotive maintenance. The point for the ethnographer is that the knowledge is expressed in a highly practical manner, and on a case-by-case basis. Consequently, Harper's ethnography proceeds very much on a case-by-case basis as well. Harper documents a number of Willie's projects. Moreover, he does so through a photographic record as well as by means of the written word. Harper's book exemplifies the merits of a multi-modal approach. The concrete detail is fundamental to an understanding of Willie's improvisational skill. Admittedly, Harper's photographs are illustrative rather than sufficiently dense and analytic to fully merit being called a thoroughly multi-modal strategy. The monograph is, however, exemplary in its attention to the concrete, practical activity that Willie engages in. In a very different work setting, Hamilton (2013) describes the 'magic' of things in a rural veterinary practice.

The artisan and bricoleur have a practical understanding not only of their materials, but also of the tools that are used *on* those materials. The artisan's, craftsman's or artist's tools are, therefore, among the most significant kinds of things that we can study in many working and artistic settings. Many tools are impressive artefacts in their own right. They can be aesthetically pleasing, just as pleasing as the objects that they help create. There are, for instance, many craft materials that are associated with Japanese arts and crafts that are clearly akin to art works in their own right. They contribute to the aesthetic ambience of the craftworker's studio, as well as being strictly functional. (Form and function are usually closely aligned in the domain of tools, which are usually highly evolved in the interests of efficient working.) Tools and machines deserve their own attention in the right sorts of settings. They are productive, in that they make possible certain kinds of work – symbolic and economic – and they also limit productive activity, in that they constrain *what* can be achieved, and equally they shape *how* things can be enacted. In that sense, tools and machines can implicitly inscribe certain kinds of work, as well as implying distinctive social relations and divisions of labour. If the bricoleur or the craft-worker has an intensely personal relationship with tools and materials, the industrial worker may have an equally impersonal relationship with technology and tools. If we pay serious attention to the means of work, therefore, we can do justice to the kinds of skills and competences it takes to use them, the kinds of social relations that they sustain and the kinds of labour that they embody.

This is not, however, an argument in favour of ethnographic research that is primarily appreciative of material objects and their aesthetic or cultural values. And it is not an argument in favour of a study of material culture that is divorced from social relations, modes of social organisation, the social arrangements of work and other cultural codes of significance. In other words, we do not need studies of material goods that are essentially reductionist in that they examine only one of the many modalities of social organisation, and hence that rely on just one mode of ethnographic apperception. If we take seriously the need for an ethnographic analysis of things and their use, therefore, we ought to pay attention to the following sorts of research questions:

- How do material things reflect social relationships?
- How are materials and tools used to accomplish work?
- How is the body of the user related to the use of the tool?
- What are the temporal rhythms implied by using and making things?
- How does craft knowledge inform the use of tools and other things?
- How are material things arranged in space?
- What are the ecologies of places, spaces and things?

We know that social actors are highly knowledgeable and skilful. Simply by virtue of being socialised members of any given cultural group, we all possess and use rich repertoires of competence. Ethnographers need to pay systematic attention to the nature of such knowledge, and to its practical applications in collective action. We are interested in what knowledge is deployed, under what circumstances, and with what effects. We attend to the practical accomplishment of routine tasks and exceptional, expert activities. Practical knowledge-in-action relies on one of Marcel Mauss's major methodological themes: *technique*. The notion of technique links competence, skill, practical action and embodiment. The Maussian contribution became best known to a wider audience when anthropological and sociological interest in the body became fashionable. Mauss's essay on 'the techniques of the body' was identified as a classic, early contribution to the study of embodied action. Techniques, in the general sense, are often embodied competences, but their general analytic significance goes beyond studies of the body *per se*. Technique captures the intersection of the individual social actor with socially shared knowledge and skill, acquired through enculturation, applied locally and based on recipes of practical action. So issues of technique are fundamental to the ethnographic gaze. As we shall see, they encompass many different kinds of social setting, including those that deal primarily with esoteric knowledge (such as arts, crafts, sciences and professions), as well as more mundane settings of practical activity.

The practical use of technique and the accomplishment of competent social action require the truly ethnographic study of participant observation and participant recording. The possibilities of digital recording, especially still photography and video-recording, mean that it is now possible to document techniques in a way that is much easier than ever before, and it is also possible to integrate them into broader ethnographic analyses and representations. Such recordings also make tacit competence visible in ways that render them available for detailed analysis. We are thus able to take account of the entire range of 'methods' through which social actors accomplish their ordinary and their expert everyday accomplishments. As I shall go on to suggest, so-called *microethnography* gives us a way of conceptualising the analysis of technique. It also gives us a strategy of analysing some relationships between spoken action and practical actions.

All methods or techniques for everyday living and for specialised practice are folk methods, irrespective of whether they are found in 'other' cultures, or in Western societies, whether they be confined to small-scale and local cultures, or in cosmopolitan cultural systems. In that sense, therefore, *all* such techniques can be called ethnomethods, and to that extent, the inspiration of ethnomethodology could and should be pervasive. Likewise, *all* systems of science and medicine are ethnoscience and ethnomedicine. Analytically speaking, we make no radical distinctions between Western science and other knowledge-systems. Western biomedicine is just as much a culture-bound knowledge-system as any other. Consequently, we need to incorporate the analytic insights of ethnoscience into our ethnographic studies of knowledge and technique. This is not an advocacy for a full-blown ethnomethodological or ethnoscientific analysis as part of each and every ethnographic project. But it does mean that we need to pay serious attention to repertoires of knowledge and techniques. We also need to recognise that culturally shared resources have systematic properties. In other words, knowledge-systems have some degree of structure. There are patterns of knowledge. There are relatively stable recipes of action.

Such knowledge and practical skill are acquired through processes of enculturation and socialisation. Studies of occupational socialisation therefore need to include close attention to the methods whereby specialist knowledge and techniques are transmitted and acquired. This is not just a domain for specialised studies of education and socialisation alone. All knowledge is acquired – whether it be mundane skills and techniques such as driving a car, or more specialised knowledge such as becoming a master-butcher or baker. Ethnographies of everyday life can and should, therefore, pay attention to the modes of reproduction of technique and skill. We need to ask ourselves: How do social actors acquire such knowledge?

- How is it transmitted?
- How is it acquired?
- How is it evaluated?
- How is it socially distributed?

Consequently, ethnographies of cultural acquisition – socialisation or enculturation – can be of considerable significance.

Techniques typically involve the use of the body, language, tools and other artefacts. Studying technique therefore often calls for careful, detailed observation of detailed activities, often using recording devices to capture the intricacies of action. A recent example that captures some of these issues especially clearly is Heath's study of the work of fine-art auctioneers (Heath 2013). The auction is one of those occasions that Appadurai (1986) called 'tournaments of value'. This concept links auctions with a variety of disparate social settings in which monetary and/or symbolic value is established through public, performative events that include an element of competition: among classic anthropological descriptions, the *kula* ceremonial exchange of valued goods would be a prime example. Now, however insightful such a generic concept might be, it stops short of telling us *how* such value-relevant activities are actually accomplished, how the credibility of the vendor or exchange-partner is made visible to other parties. Heath, by contrast, develops a detailed account of just how the auctioneer and the bidders use clearly understood and visible mechanisms to sustain sequences of bids, to establish the visibility and transparency of the market process, and hence of the value of the objects that are bid for. Heath's detailed analysis of spoken and embodied activity, based on transcribed recordings, demonstrates precisely how such social and economic transactions are accomplished. Auctioneers display and use repertoires of activity that co-ordinate the activities of the auction room, generating smooth and rapid events.

Now Heath himself, working in the tradition of ethnomethodology, distances himself from ethnographic research, insisting that the latter does not typically include such attention to the local production of orderly activity. However, it is my contention here that these distinctions between ethnography and ethnomethodology are becoming harder to sustain. Researchers who think of themselves as ethnographers increasingly incorporate data derived from detailed recordings (audio and video) of interactions and encounters. Studies of technique can (and should) be embedded in broader ethnographic explorations of organisation and cultural knowledge. In the case of the fine-art auction, there are other contexts apart from the sale-room auction itself where value is established. They include valuations (for instance on valuation days, or valuations of estates), expert examination of art works and attributions of authorship, or evaluations of provenance. Moreover, there are contexts in which aesthetic judgements are applied and negotiated. In other words, art worlds and art markets are more diffuse than just the auction room. So a thoroughgoing ethnography of market-making in fine art and antiques might well encompass a variety of settings and encounters, within which might be embedded detailed, transcription-based examinations of techniques and cultural knowledge.

There are, of course, very many social worlds in which techniques are employed, especially the specialised techniques associated with a complex division of labour. It is part of the competence of the craft worker, the professional, the time-served master-worker and so on, that they use specific techniques. Moreover, they do so in effective and efficient ways, producing displays and enactments of smoothly competent activity. Consider, for instance, a market setting very different from the auction house. Lyon and Back (2012) provide a multi-sensory ethnographic study of fishmongers in a South London market. They draw on ethnographic observations, photography and video-recordings to document some of the skills and techniques deployed by two fishmongers on a local market – the one a market-stall trader and the other a shop-owner. What is striking is the description of the knowledge and craft skills of the market fishmonger. He has a thorough acquaintance with types of fish, their condition and the habitats they come from. Also, there are craft skills of gutting and filleting the fish. These tasks involve dexterity. They also depend on the use and care of specialist knives. Here knowledge and technique rest not only on dexterity and methods, but also on a working knowledge of materials (in this case, fish). From a very different cultural context, Nakamura (2007) details some of the techniques of Japanese calligraphy. She details the complex and delicate relations that the artist establishes with the brush, the paper, the ink and the ink-stone. These all require prolonged and intimate knowledge, so that the skilled practitioner can grasp the relations between them, the subtle differences that can be produced by variations in their use, as well as the embodied skill of making marks. Likewise, studies of Japanese potters (e.g. Moeran 1997) demonstrate the complex relationships between materials and techniques in the creation of material objects in accordance with well-established aesthetic conventions.

Multiple ethnographies provide us with exemplars of techniques and local knowledge. Foreman (2008) provides an illuminating account of the training of *geisha* (a category defined more by their musical competence than Western stereotypes suggest). The emphasis on technical mastery, dedication, personal investment and the devotion of time to musical training is striking. Japanese artistic and artisanal apprenticeships are, of course, proverbial for their rigour and duration. Haase (1998) furnishes an autobiographical account of being an apprentice potter in Japan (having previously trained as a studio potter in the United States). He provides an account that will be familiar to students of ceramics: he spent months repeating one basic, small shape of pot, repeatedly failing to satisfy the expectations of his *sensei* (teacher). The apprenticeship of the craft artist depends not on formal, explicit training, but on the observation of the master-craftsman and repeated attempts to emulate his (rarely her) exemplary pieces. Singleton (1998) summarises the 'folk model' of socialisation among folk potters: an early stage involves the repeated making of 10,000 copies of a single ceramic form, before moving on to another form. These apprentice pieces are not kept, and are not even glazed, being returned to the clay pit. Only after extended, repeated activities like this may the novice potter in any sense make his 'own' pieces. (Singleton points out that actual apprenticeships may not conform to this model in all respects.) Examples from Japan are readily to hand – presumably because the disciplinary regimes of that culture are so strikingly rigorous and demanding. To give further instances, the mastery of calligraphy (DeCoker 1998) or Noh-theatre performance (Rimer 1998) are equally based on protracted periods of demanding apprenticeship. The historical scholarship on apprentice Japanese painters (Jordan and Weston 2003) gives a very similar account of the process, in a tradition stretching over several centuries. What the Japanese models throw into relief is the extent to which successful enculturation depends upon protracted periods of repetition and personal commitment. The mastery and use of technique thus reflects what we might call cultural discipline, through which technique is honed and perfected.

These and many similar techniques are *embodied*, in that they are performed physically, their skills are bodily ones, and their competent use depends upon a well-drilled body, bodily discipline and routinised physical activities. The ethnographic attention to technique therefore necessarily incorporates detailed attention to such body-work. The skilled body is, therefore, an object of the ethnographic gaze, as well as being part of the ethnographer's reflexive self-consciousness. The embodied presence of the ethnographer in the field is as much an element in this conversation of physical co-presence with the research hosts as is the practised gaze or the inquiring conversation. This in turn reflects the fact that Mauss's treatment of 'technique' included, and indeed placed considerable emphasis on, the techniques of the body.

It is tempting for many observers to rely uncritically on Bourdieu's use of the term *habitus* to capture these aspects of technique (e.g. Bourdieu 1997). In many ways, of course, the term is appropriate, although it is worth noting in passing that the usage was not original to Bourdieu. Moreover, as I have suggested, Mauss's exploration of technique predates and anticipates some of the key aspects. I mention *habitus* here by way of a caveat. It is becoming too easy to invoke Bourdieu in such a way as to *avoid* giving proper analysis of technique and its physical realisation. It is all too easy simply to assert that a given competent or skilled activity reflects the *habitus* of a given social category – as if that constituted an adequate treatment of it. In such lazy usage (reflecting the currency of the idea) we find a reinvention of the over-socialised actor, who has internalised a set of predispositions and enacts them accordingly. Such a perspective accounts for everything and nothing. It is equivalent to saying that a substance makes us drowsy because of its soporific properties. The usage by-passes the need to examine technique in adequate detail, to examine its practical usage, the circumstances under which it is deployed and circumstances under which performance fails. It empties social action of its performative accomplishment, generating a kind of sociological or anthropological shorthand, akin to a functionalist catch-all mode of explanation.

Whatever theoretical perspective we endorse, however, it is clear that ethnographers ought to inhabit and document a social world of embodied, skilful technique. We can learn from studies that are explicitly concerned with embodied skill. The worlds of dance and sport furnish multiple examples of the body in motion, the trained and disciplined body, and indeed the wounded, injured body. These studies are not significant just because they are concerned with the body *per se*, but because they are thoroughly skill-full. Techniques imply embodied skills that are acquired through observation, mimicry and explicit instruction. I captured some of those processes in my own participant observation of glassblowing. As well as observing the work of makers in a glass studio, I also took a class in glassblowing techniques (see Atkinson 2013c; see also O'Connor 2005, 2006). Working with glass relies on techniques and technologies that have been in existence for centuries. Current practice derives from the glassmakers of Murano (Venice). One must learn how to gather glass from the furnace containing molten glass, how to work it – such as rolling it on the marble or metal bench (the marver), working it with hand tools, heating it in another furnace (the glory-hole) and blowing hollow vessels that can be shaped into a variety of objects. In manipulating the lump of glass on the end of my gathering iron or my blowing-pipe, I quickly learned that a crucial part of successful technique included *working the angles*. Various aspects to the process of making – gathering, controlling, rolling, getting the glass off the pipe, adding colour, blowing – are determined, or at least facilitated, by getting the angles right. To start at the beginning: if one takes the iron or the pipe from the glory-hole – where its tip has been heating – then there are ways of carrying it towards the furnace and the glass that are controlled and safe. One does not wave it around, or trail it. It is carried, sometimes like a pole-vaulter's pole, at a clear angle in front of the body and in front of the eyes. As one approaches the open door of the furnace, then the end is lifted (again, like planting a pole) the pipe is rested on the bottom shelf of the opening, and the tip of the pipe introduced into the molten glass. When the glass has been collected, then the pipe is removed, and turned, now kept on the level. When one takes the glass to the marver to roll it, then again the angle of attack is significant. To coat a lump of glass evenly all over, then it has to be rolled in the colour horizontally, but then to coat the far end, the proximal end of the pipe needs to be raised, so that the tip of the glass is rolling in the colour; then the pipe may need to be lowered, so that the end nearest the pipe is also coated.

We were instructed how to blow seated on the bench, leaning and blowing with the pipe resting on the right-hand arm of the work-bench. So the angle of the pipe is downwards. Throughout the process, therefore, the angle of the glass, the angle of the pipe, is crucial in controlling the glass itself, and in the process of shaping and colouring it. Using the wooden blocks was also dependent on getting various angles right – for instance, applying pressure with the block at a slight angle, so as to create a shoulder at the end of the pipe. A comparison with other sites of making and instruction (including dance classes) suggests that such postural issues can be crucial. In many contexts one has to learn to lean one's body *towards* the materials, or indeed to lean into one's dance partner. The novice tends to lean or to pull *away*. Getting the correct angles is also dependent on having a feel for the glass and for the tools. This is especially evident at the beginning of the day. Our first hands-on task was designed to introduce us to several elementary things. We collected a small amount of glass and then rolled it on the marver, producing a sausage-like shape or thickish rod. Taking it from the marver to the work-bench, via the glory-hole, we then used the piece to practise hands-on use of the jacks. The jacks are large divider-like objects, looking like over-sized tweezers. Our initial task was to use those to create two grooves in the rod, to create a series of rounded shapes. This is, therefore, an exercise in using the jacks. But, as a novice, one has no idea of how hard to press. Again, it is partly a matter of getting the angles right. The tool should be held firmly in the right hand, vertically. I learned, as quickly as I could, not to apply too much pressure. But equally, I discovered that if one does not have the jacks at the correct angle, or with the right pressure, then it can easily slip on the glass, especially as it cools and becomes less tractable. If it moves, then one can inadvertently create a corkscrew-like effect rather than a straight groove. Likewise, applying the various-sized wooden blocks requires a certain feel. As I have said already, the angle at which the block is held to the glass makes a difference. It is hard to judge what pressure to apply with the block – not least because the pressure is exerted from below. The same is true of using the tool to make flat sides and angles. It is hard to judge how much pressure to apply. The glass is resistant, and the right amount of pressure is not easy to estimate.

Likewise, when it comes to blowing a vessel: How much, how hard, or how long is one to blow? The effect of blowing is not instantaneous. How hard is it to get the air into the glass? Is it like starting to blow up a balloon, requiring a lot of puff to overcome initial resistance? Does it require a steady, extended breath, or a brief burst? The answer, I was instructed, is to breathe from the chest (just like singers, I thought at the time) and not to puff hard from the cheeks. I was also shown how to stop the mouthpiece with my thumb as the trapped air expands automatically when it reaches the hot glass, and it is easier to control the column of air. (Again, the use of a column of air is reminiscent of how young singers are encouraged to control their breathing.) There is, of course, a great deal more to glass-making than these small examples will suggest. But they start to capture some fundamental aspects of technique. Enculturation implies not merely learning the principles, but rests on the disciplines of the hand and the eye, of the body as well as sight. One learns how to *estimate* various things: the amount of glass to gather, the pressure to apply in shaping the glass, the angle at which to manage the iron, the amount of colour to apply, the volume of breath to impart.

These are not mysterious in themselves. But they call for detailed attention to how actions are performed. They also require analysis of just how they are transmitted. They do not necessarily depend on full participation. Close observation of everyday working and of the instruction of apprentices provides ethnographic opportunity to learn the practical routines and recipes of action that skilled and experienced technicians employ. These issues in turn lead us back to the issues of local aesthetics with which I began this chapter.

8
Structuring Forms

There is a recurrent irony that runs through much of ethnographic research. By definition, ethnography is based on the *local*, although I recognise that local relations may now be distributed and exist in virtual space (Boellstorff et al. 2012). While it is not necessarily confined just to one location, it is in most cases site-specific. On the other hand, too many ethnographic studies seem oddly lacking in a strong sense of place. Equally, there is, in too many cases, an absence of a full sense of space and of movement in space. Far too many classic and conventional ethnographies gave little sense of the specificity of place, and of the spaces (built and natural) within which social action takes place. One might think of many of the classic urban ethnographies of American and British city neighbourhoods that – paradoxically – have little or no real sense of the local circumstances. Equally, we often have little sense of the geographies of place and space – how people make us of places, how people navigate through those spaces, how changing and competing uses of place are accomplished. The counterpoint to space is time. The processes of everyday life are always temporal, and the intersections of time and space reflect motion – persons in motion and objects that circulate in time and space.

These are dimensions of structure that shape the organisation of everyday life *in situ*. It is a recurrent theme that runs throughout this book. Ethnographic fieldwork should be concerned with social organisation. Social life is not formless. It is about far more than 'talk' or 'experience'. It is about social action and cultural systems. These do not occur in a social vacuum. While we may freely accept that social actors *make* the social world around them, and that the objects of cultural knowledge are *socially constructed*, such creative work does not take place from scratch on every occasion. Nor does it happen in a social world that is lacking in order. There are clearly shared frameworks of time and space that simultaneously constrain and make possible orderly social conduct. While it is not the normal task of the ethnographer-analyst simply to record these temporal and spatial frameworks, we generate under-developed ethnographic analysis without due attention to these structuring and organising principles.

This is not a matter of background or context. Places and spaces are fully implicated in the organisation of everyday life and the enactment of everyday social action. Organisations and workplaces are physically embodied in their architecture, their internal divisions of space, their symbolic and physical boundaries. Public, ceremonial spaces – such as museums – shape trajectories of movement within them, and hence project temporal frameworks. Equally, of course, museums organise time through the display of artefacts, as well as shaping the time spent by visitors navigating their way through those exhibits. They create temporal frameworks of memorialisation and collective heritage too, of course. Places and spaces have their own intrinsic organisation. Organisational properties of space include the distribution of boundaries and the spaces that they define. These arrangements are in themselves ethnographically significant. Due attention needs to be paid to spatial arrangements. Temporal arrangements – such as timetables, calendars, routines, daily rounds – equally place boundaries around collective and individual social actions. They are among the significant mechanisms whereby actions are co-ordinated. Organisations, as social phenomena, may be defined largely through their temporal arrangements. Times and timescapes can be used by participants to define periods or activities as especially significant, marking them out from the normal temporal frames of mundane, quotidian social life.

Sociologists of organisations and work-spaces have long been informed by Goffman's fruitful distinction between 'frontstage' and 'backstage' regions. This is partly a metaphorical usage, of course – like so much of Goffman's work, it is suggestive and productive rather than precise in its delineation. But it is also a reference to physical spaces – reflecting the material and spatial realisation of a number of cultural categories and types. For instance, we are acquainted from many cultures with the clear differentiation between the 'home' and the 'street', with the further implication that the home is a site of trust and honour, the family and intimate relations. The street, on the other hand, is the site of strangers, of threat to family honour, of danger and so on. If the street is also masculine then the home is also the spatialised location of the feminine.

These kinds of examples are well known, but they are introduced here to make a specific point. That is, spaces have their own organisational logic and structure. They are, to be sure, thoroughly dependent on cultural conventions. They are, however, clearly structured, and in turn they actively help to shape the forms of social action and interaction. They are far from being a passive backdrop to everyday social life. They are themselves constitutive of it, insofar as everyday life is enacted in real spaces and places. There is, therefore, nothing optional about a close attention to the spatial arrangements of everyday life, or therefore about an ethnographic awareness of spaces and places. Moreover, as I have just suggested, these issues need to be approached in their own terms – with a recognition of the intrinsic and indigenous orderings of space itself.

Spaces can be analysed in terms of their cultural significance, and as metonyms for more general cultural phenomena. The hotel of European and American cities encapsulates a number of cultural themes and values. It was a space in which an urban middle class could partake of a semi-public form of luxury. It provided a space in which a form of conspicuous consumption could be pursued. The hotel was one of a type of urban architecture in which distinctive types of design and decoration defined a form of luxury. Department stores and restaurants similarly created highly designed and decorated spaces in which urban actors could engage in social, consumption activities in a new way. The department store not only helped to define the act of shopping, it also generated new opportunities for urban women to participate in public spaces. Shops, restaurants, hotels and similar institutions framed their clients' activities with versions of belle époque and art nouveau style – defining luxury and elegance in accordance with canons of fashionable consumption. Later in their historical development, more modern movements were enrolled, such as art deco, visible in such famous settings as the hotels of Miami, or London's Savoy. Likewise, commissions by leading architects and designers such as Frank Lloyd Wright brought contemporary style into semi-public settings. They were not simply passive sets for social actors, but helped to construct the *mise-en-scène* in which distinctive performances of urban modernity were sustained. In contrast to the private domain of the household, they created opportunities for a different form of respectable engagement in public spaces.

In ways that parallel shops and hotels, the modern art gallery was a similar example of a public space shaping cultural activities. The modern public gallery of the nineteenth and early twentieth century had a very distinctive style. In the classical style, it presented itself as a secular temple, furnished with an imposing stepped entry and portico with Corinthian columns. It invited a public attitude towards art works (or archaeological artefacts) that had previously been the preserve of private collectors, framing public reverence and rectitude. Architectural style invoked specific kinds of cultural framing. The interior decor (such as wall-coverings) evoked grand houses and stately homes, while the layout of interlocking rooms invited a sort of pedestrian grand tour through styles, periods and national schools of artistic tradition. The contemporary art gallery, on the other hand, evokes a very different kind of aesthetic. The 'white cube' frames a modernist aesthetic, and the minimalist interior style is in stark contrast to that of the nineteenth-century gallery. It also, however, creates the possibility of a space that serves its *own* aesthetic as much as – sometimes even more than – the art it contains. In recent years the art gallery itself has become the prime artefact, and a place of pilgrimage in its own right. The gallery at Bilbao, designed by the American architect Gehry, is a famous case in point. These spaces reflect changing aesthetics, of course, and they also help to shape their visitors' aesthetic responses to the experience of art. Indeed, they help to construct a distinctive type of 'experience', and a distinctive kind of reverence towards art works and their display.

A similar story can also be told about the opera house – a research setting closer to my own fieldwork experience. Famous older houses – such as La Scala (Milan) or La Fenice (Venice), or Vienna – can again frame the opera as a particular kind of social and aesthetic event. With plush and gilt interiors, and traditional, high horseshoe-shaped auditoriums they construct the audience in particular ways (vertically stratified) and invite particular perspectives on the operatic performance itself (including highly stratified lines of sight). Recent modernist opera houses can be equally famous as buildings in their own right (Sydney, Valencia), and can equally frame a different kind of aesthetic experience. Each opera house also defines (or at least helps to frame) the kind of experiences that opera-goers, tourists and others can expect and derive from visiting the opera house itself.

Ethnographic explorations of art worlds or of the opera as a field of cultural activity, then, need to pay due attention to the kinds of spatial arrangements within which cultural activities are conducted. These built environments do not, of course, exert an influence on users, visitors and workers through magical properties. Their symbolic significance and their practical arrangements are used and interpreted by those actors. They do so in accordance with socially shared symbolic codes that are interpreted and incorporated into broader frames of reference. Visitors may also be instructed to consume such spaces in particular ways: the opera house can become a tourist spectacle in its own right, independently of any actual operatic performance.

We know from cultural studies of phenomena like tourism that places and spaces are *marked* in various ways. The tourist experience is anchored to places of special significance that are in turn transformed into representations of themselves. Key places can 'stand for' places and destinations of special significance. They exist not only in themselves, but also as images and replicas, designed to furnish 'souvenirs' of holidays and travel. They include replicas of art works (small statues, cheap imitations of religious icons, museum replicas of archaeological objects), 'folk' objects (clothing in peasant style, brightly coloured ceramics). Places can, therefore, be endowed with special significance through a variety of cultural codes. Indeed, it is obviously the case that 'the same' place can be memorialised and marked in different ways by different people, simultaneously. Places may become special as places of cultural or religious pilgrimage, for instance, while retaining entirely secular attractions for others. To take just one possible example, Prague in recent years can be treated as a place of cultural heritage – with performances of Mozart's opera *Don Giovanni* at the Estates Theatre, where it received its premiere – while it is also a preferred destination for stag parties and similar trips for young people. Equally, it can be the site for artistic tourism – with travellers exploring the city's extensive legacy of art nouveau architecture and graphic art.

The point for the ethnographer is, of course, to pay close attention to the cultural codings and representations that are attached to places, and to the cultural practices that are used to accomplish those values and meanings. Equally, needless to say, the city is encoded – with greater significance – by its own inhabitants. The meanings of the *local* itself are of fundamental importance for the ethnographer. This latter has been a recurrent preoccupation for urban ethnographers. Classic studies of the neighbourhood, the slum or the ghetto have inevitably examined the notion of territory. They document the physical and symbolic markers of local territories, and the social organisation of local loyalties themselves. The great tradition of Chicago urban sociology was predicated not only on the sociological mapping of the city, and a strong sense of spatial distribution, but also of residents' own practical geographical sense of place. Intensely local understandings, entwined with ethnicity, class and occupation, were documented. In a similar way, the classic community studies that spanned anthropology and sociology, whether set in the rural periphery or in urban neighbourhoods, were firmly located in a firm sense of place. Indeed, the very essence of the 'community' so defined was its groundedness in a particular location. Now we do not recapitulate those classic interests, in order to observe that the sense of localism or boundedness of such 'communities' were not and are not 'given'. While some settlements may well be isolated physically and socially, the boundaries that define 'communities' are not.

To that extent, therefore, we might feel that any renewed emphasis on place might be redundant. Nevertheless, it is valuable to remind ourselves that, ethnographically speaking, place is not a 'given' or a mere background phenomenon. Recent developments and cases help us to establish some purchase on relevant issues. Stephens, Atkinson and Glasner (2008) use the notion of 'performative architecture' to capture some of the ways in which the organisation of space reflects and frames social action. The ethnography is of the United Kingdom Stem Cell Bank. This is an organisation established to receive cell lines from donating biomedical laboratories, and then supply cells to approved laboratories throughout the world. It is one of several such international depositories. The ethnography of the Stem Cell Bank emphasises the role of the Bank in guaranteeing the purity and provenance of the stem cell lines. Its physical, architectural design reflects and reinforces that function as guarantor of purity. Over and above the purely functional role of design, the Bank's internal structures provide a 'metaphorical vision of sterility' (p. 88). Stephens et al. refer to this as 'performative architecture'. They describe how, in the Bank:

> cells and persons describe circuits of separation and seclusion. These are pragmatic and functional, in that they separate cells and their custodians from contamination. They are also performative in that they provide *enactments of purity*. The physical and symbolic boundaries that surround the Bank and the observances that are attached to them construct a series of *rites de passage* that persons and cells go through. (p. 96, emphases in original)

These observations develop ideas from Nigel Thrift. Thrift's original ideas were also formulated in relation to some particular kinds of buildings designed to accommodate and celebrate bioscientific invention (Thrift 2006). He stressed the extent to which distinctive kinds of contemporary buildings, amongst other things, promote interdisciplinary working, promoting flows of persons and information, and the endorsement of sociability, through cafe-like environments. (Readers will recognise these as a distinctive type of modern building, often themselves regarded as 'iconic' and 'cutting-edge' that are distinctive of contemporary information-technology companies, academic 'resource centres' and the like.)

These buildings and others like them are, of course, deliberately designed to incorporate features of corporate and intellectual interests. Their effects are managed through various design features: the organisation of space, such as the creation of open public spaces like atriums, and the movement of people – workers and visitors – through spaces. Light is a key feature too. Glass is used extensively in order to create brightly lit spaces, contributing to the aesthetic as well as the functional features of the buildings themselves. These are among the cultural codings that are deployed in the creation of buildings. They help to shape their overall significance, as well as helping to prompt particular kinds of usage and mobility within them. They reflect (literally, sometimes) prevailing notions of taste, such as the use of materials (steel, glass, marble) and the arrangement of spaces (open-plan, flexible internal divisions). Colour is deployed in order to create contrasting internal divisions, to construct inviting spaces that evoke leisure uses in work settings. Public spaces (atrium, stairwell, escalator space) are often adorned with public art works that themselves evoke ideas of opulence and modernity. For the ethnographer, of course, none of this can be taken for granted, or simply read off from the designs themselves. In contemporary office settings, we know that workers can frequently subvert intentions by creating personal spaces and work-stations that contradict the open plan and the aesthetics of the original design.

Of course, no physical building can determine its usage or meaning, however carefully and self-consciously designed. Many spaces have multiple uses. Indeed, the multiple uses of space is one of the phenomena that ethnographers themselves need to pay close attention to. A setting like a shopping mall may have very different uses for different kinds of people. Shopping centres themselves are – like the spaces just referred to – designed as public spaces with connotations of consumption, in which particular kinds of sensory response (plenitude, opulence, openness) are evoked and invited. Shoppers and window-shoppers combine their experiences with eating and drinking in food-halls. Equally, and simultaneously, such spaces can be used by unemployed young people to 'hang out', being warm and dry urban spaces, with open access. In the same sort of way, outdoor urban spaces can be used simultaneously by a multitude of 'ordinary' people going about their ordinary activities, and by young people engaged in free-running, an outdoor urban pursuit in which participants use the urban landscape as a setting for expressive and athletic or acrobatic running. Urban ethnographies need to recognise that spaces and places have very different kinds of meaning and functions for different categories of social actor. The example of free-running is a useful one – as it shows us how spaces can be appropriated by particular groups for purposes they were never intended for: skateboarders in many cities are a parallel example.

As I have suggested throughout this discussion, we need to be attentive not just to general spatial properties of everyday life, but also to the intrinsic orderings that inhabit such places and spaces. The 'street' is itself more than a background feature of everyday urban life. Bittner's classic study of police work, for instance, gives us a powerful sense of how police officers scan and interpret urban landscapes (Bittner 1967).

In observing streets and similar urban settings, police officers cannot be attentive to each and every detail, and respond to every single stimulus. Rather, they have to use their occupational knowledge of urban scenes and the people in them in order to deploy a practical form of suspicion. This practical work reflects a sensitivity to people in places – including, of course, people 'out of place'.

Anthropological ethnographies are also replete with examples of analyses of places and spaces. One of the classic examples is the Trobriand village of Omarakana, first described by Malinowski, and then by Powell, and much more recently by Mosko (2013). The point of the successive versions of the village is not merely to chart the physical manifestations of social change (significant though they might be), it is also the derivation of underlying symbolic principles that structure the physical layout of the village. Mosko's analysis retrospectively answers Claude Lévi-Strauss's lament that Malinowski's original description of the village did not provide enough evidence to evaluate the Trobrianders' use of dual symbolic systems. Such underlying symbolic orders reflect the analyst's derivation of an ideal-typical spatial and semantic arrangement, suggesting underlying, generational *models* of spaces and meanings. A parallel ethnography, on the Panará people of Brazil, provides an equivalent account of the dual organisation of space and social categories (Ewart 2013).

Places and spaces have their own temporal order and their own cycles too. Bittner's practical police officers, for instance, will scan the street in different ways and will look for different kinds of events depending on the time of day, or time of night (Bittner 1967). Moreover, the time of night will make a huge difference to the very visibility of actors and actions. Here the repeated contrasts between light and dark can punctuate space, its use and its evaluations. The urban space after dark can be a very different environment, culturally and socially, from its daytime version. Lights and colours help to define the significance of locales – in terms of entertainment, shopping, or navigation. They obviously help to shape the meanings of space in terms of safety and danger. Light and dark, night and day help to define the timescapes of everyday life. As Melbin's classic study of night-time activity demonstrates, such temporal orders intersect with location to shape patterns of activity (Melbin 1987).

The underpinning ideas of ethnography are predicated on a strong sense of process, and of the fluidity of social action. And yet there is not always a strong sense of movement, through space and through time, or through social situations. Indeed, one can plausibly argue that too many classic ethnographies were unduly rooted in one place, and were unnecessarily static. Yet movement is a pervasive feature of social life, and so if ethnographic methods are to be faithful to the forms of everyday life, then adequate attention to mobility needs to be an aspect of the ethnographic enterprise.

Having drawn attention to the potential significance of places and spaces, I merely add the further, self-evident, observation that movement in and through such spaces is a significant aspect of the ethnographic enterprise. Additionally, therefore, attention needs to be paid to the possibilities of data collection and analytic procedures that do justice to mobility. In other words, we need to marry 'mobile methods' to the methodical analysis of mobility itself. The opportunities afforded by contemporary recording devices are themselves especially well suited to mobile methods, and this in turn reflects the fact that contemporary sociability is itself predicated on those self-same methods. In other words, contemporary mobility and the study of mobility stand in a reflexive relationship: they are homologous. In contemporary societies, mobile telephones, navigation systems, personal recording devices and the like all mean that mobility is not simply a matter of physical motion, but is an integral aspect of everyday life (Moles 2008).

This general observation stands in contrast to the implicit style of much ethnographic work, which seems to have a more-or-less sedentary approach inscribed within it. Yet much of social life is planetary, nomadic and fluid. I do not mean that ethnographers in the past have actually remained static. Indeed, it is clear that they have followed their informants in a variety of places and circumstances. Rather, I mean that movement has not been a visible part of the ethnographic enterprise itself. But just as places and spaces must now be accounted aspects of social organisation in their own right, so too must movement in, through and between places. This is, as I shall try to explain, not just a matter of movement, but also a question of *how* movement is managed, what its cultural significance is, and how it illuminates more general aspects of everyday life.

In recent years, 'mobile methods' have become more prominent. They are not endorsed here just because they are fashionable, however. Hall and Smith (2011) provide a clear case in point. Theirs is a field study of pedestrian practices in an urban environment (the city of Cardiff). The paper, intriguingly, partly recapitulates three walks through the city, In the course of these walks they sweep up in their ethnographic gaze encounters with welfare workers – people who keep the urban social fabric going – and their clients, such as the homeless. The paper is valuable for several reasons. Not least is the observation by Hall and Smith that grand themes, such as mobility and the good city, are susceptible to empirical research through ethnographic, street-level fieldwork. They draw, moreover, an explicit parallel between the footwork of ethnographic fieldwork and the everyday urban realities that such journeys encompass. In a quirky parallel, Gabrys (2012) develops the occasion of a moss-spotting nature-walk in London as the opportunity to reflect on urban settings in a way that escapes more conventional urban studies.

Such fieldwork also reminds us that the classics of urban sociology, such as those emanating from the city of Chicago, were grounded in a close acquaintance with the city itself, gained at first hand through a peripatetic engagement. Robert Park, a founder in so many ways, of urban ethnography, brought to bear his professional experience as a journalist who, by his own account, had tramped the streets in the search for stories. In the early years of the last century, after all, Chicago was traversed by a sociological gaze that encompassed the planetary motion of its teeming populace as well as its distinctive territories and neighbourhoods.

In recent years the long-standing interest in movement in spaces – especially but not exclusively in urban spaces – has been supplemented by the use of information technology. Qualitative GIS uses information technology to plot geographical position. GPS devices can therefore be used to plot spatial distributions and movements. Qualitative GIS is a relatively recent innovation, often used in 'multi-methods' combination with other strategies. In a similar vein, the analytic software Atlas/ti can integrate spatial data from Google Earth with other qualitative data, such as interview transcripts of visual materials. However, these forms of spatial representation do not answer many of the needs of ethnographic research. In essence, these types of research strategy contribute to *etic* categories: that is, they can tell us something of the observed patterns of movement and spatial distribution. But they tell us less about how social actors themselves organise space, or how they navigate between or through spaces. They can give us some clues – just as surveys can give us some potentially fruitful lines of inquiry – but they cannot answer the fundamental issues of social action, social organisation and cultural competence. Moreover, as Laurier (2010) and Smith (2010) have argued, we need to go on paying serious attention to what people actually *do* rather than linking spatial data to people's *accounts* of what they do.

In other words, we need ethnographically derived *emic* analyses of *how* social actors use space, navigate in socially and culturally organised ways, and how they use cultural knowledge to make such motion possible. This does not necessarily equate to the use of *mobile methods* themselves (although they may do so – see below). It does, however, mean that ethnographers need to be alert to two things simultaneously. First, the mobility of the social actors they observe and engage with. Secondly, they need to be equally sensitive to their *own* mobility in 'the field'. We are used to the idea that 'fieldwork' should not imply fixed, bounded fields that are pre-existent; we need to remind ourselves too that they are fluid. While ethnographic sites can be single locations, they are often multiple, or internally differentiated and bounded. They occupy spaces within which ethnographers themselves move, following the phenomena they document, accompanying the people they work with, and tracing the boundaries of physical or symbolic spaces.

The ethnographer who pays adequate attention to motion, therefore, needs to understand the navigational properties of everyday life. Navigation is based on specific knowledge and competence that allows the social actor to *make their way* across and between spaces. Local knowledge may permit actors to plot routes, to find locations, to avoid dangerous or troublesome places. Such navigational competence may, of course, be an occupational attribute. Demetry (2013) demonstrates the intersection of temporal and spatial orders in restaurant kitchens. She notes the extent to which time and space have been treated separately in many studies, and yet in concrete social settings, temporal and spatial frames simultaneously constrain and facilitate social action. They are constructed together, and they organise occupational action and talk (cf. Fine 1990). The kitchen is a place of choreography, in other words.

There are many urban occupations that depend upon a shrewd sense of place, and a well-developed navigational sense: the police, emergency service workers, cab drivers and many others need to develop and exercise a heightened sense of motion – their own and others' – in a variety of settings. Ethnographic studies of policing, for instance, draw attention to spatial components of officers' competence: place and time intersect, for instance, in police patrol officers' formulations of suspicious behaviour, of how they scan scenes for potential trouble, and how they plot their own routes through such environments. Equally, street dwellers and workers – sex workers, the homeless – have a highly developed sense of navigation through their urban settings. It is informed by self-interest, comprising economic gain and self-preservation. The urban landscape and the urban vision are mutually constitutive, while the city offers multiple versions of itself through maps and transport systems (Turnbull 2007).

Motion is managed locally, in the following sense. Social actors do not need to 'know' their environment in detail in order to navigate successfully within it. In other words, any individual actor does not need the equivalent of a complete plan of the city or of the neighbourhood in order to act successfully within it. Actors will have their own local, occasioned and habitual 'maps'. Psathas (1979) classically described the sort of ad hoc maps that social actors typically produce in order to give directions: obviously they do not contain all possible details and locations, but feature only places and directions that are relevant to the practical task at hand. Much practical navigation is of this kind: urban mobility may often rest on well-trodden routes that are marked by familiar landmarks (shops, churches, public buildings), and do not depend on extensive knowledge beyond those particulars. Kiddey and Schofield (2011) make reference to the navigational intelligence of homeless people in Bristol, which includes a knowledge of where security cameras are located. Such knowledge is not deployed merely to avoid surveillance, but also, selectively, to ensure surveillance: being on camera may make them safer, and may also provide evidence of one's whereabouts (in case of trouble). Knowles (2011) follows the urban journeys of contrasting dwellers – two homeless men in Montreal and privileged expatriate women in Hong Kong. The homeless men employ skilled navigation, knowing where to go and when in order to survive, from food handouts to warm-air vents. They have their own routes and their own stopping-places. The expat 'ladies that lunch' navigate the city, through 'restricted geographies', in ways that mean they remain insulated from the surrounding 'Chinese' social environment (while servants execute other journeys in the city on their behalf).

Crosnoe (2011) gives pertinent examples of contrasting uses of the same space. In his account of American High School life, he shows how two different young men, from different social backgrounds, can operate in 'the same' physical environment, but use it and navigate it quite differently, reflecting contrasting sub-cultural affiliations and identities, and broader differences in orientation to the multiple versions of school. Seyer-Ochi (2006) has provided an excellent exemplar of navigation, in her study of young people in the Fillmore district of San Francisco. She analyses a large corpus of situated maps of the neighbourhood, coupled with conversations and observations. Like other such studies, she demonstrates how extremely *local* such situated geographies are. *Place* is actively and selectively construed through boundaries, landmarks and routes. Such navigational and localised strategies are not, of course, confined to young or working-class actors, who are often closely tied to particular territories, and who express territorial loyalties. Cosmopolitans may traverse considerable distances, commuting, travelling on business, taking vacations, or moving between multiple homes. But they too do so by following familiar routes, using fixed points and defining highly personal identifications with local sites.

Movement implies transitions and boundaries. Key ideas that relate to these themes abound – not least in the literature of anthropology. The classic ideas surrounding *rites de passage* remind us that boundaries and the spaces between are physical as well as symbolic. As actors are moved from one social state to another theirs is often literally as well as metaphorically a passage. The familiar notion of liminality, that originates in the analysis of *rites de passage*, and has subsequently been extended to a wide variety of settings, is testimony to the pervasive quality of spatial locations and motions. In a similar vein, rituals remind us that just as spaces are symbolically segregated between *sacred* and *profane*, motion between them is ceremonially managed. Processions and similar kinds of gatherings are themselves mobile, and themselves consecrate participants. Pilgrimages are obvious cases in point. They are essentially mobile, and the ethnography of the pilgrimage is itself a mobile one (e.g. Dubisch 1990). Pilgrimage does not have to be defined strictly in accordance with traditional religious categories. The contemporary world provides many experiences that can be thought of as secular pilgrimages. The many forms of cultural tourism, for instance, combine holidays with collective movement to culturally segregated places and events. The escorted tours to the annual music festivals of Europe, the historical and archaeological holidays that are advertised in all the quality newspapers and magazines – these are all forms of secular pilgrimage. That is, they are secular in the sense that they are not aspects of any religion. At the same time, however, they construct the objects of devotion (operas, churches, museums) 'sacred' in the more general sense: they are marked out as special, significant and extra-ordinary. Such special or extraordinary status is managed and contrived. Places and objects of pilgrimage are not naturally special. They have to be marked as such in various ways. Thomas (2012) provides an apt and recent historical account of how such a place can be managed as a site of pilgrimage and devotion. The identification of Shakespeare's house in Stratford as a site of veneration and a place to visit was managed after the house's purchase by the Royal Shakespeare Club in 1847. It was then re-modelled in order that it should reflect the desired image: half-timbered, free-standing, embodying a Victorian and nostalgic ideal of the family. In managing the house, the town was also framed as a 'mecca' for tourists and visitors. It became part of a wider cultural phenomenon. Today we are totally familiar with birthplaces, writers' studies, artists' studios and the like being so framed as pilgrimage sites. Hence the ethnography of place also needs to take some account of how *destinations* are produced and managed.

Site-sensitive analysis need not be confined to anthropological fieldwork conducted among people who are closely aligned with a 'natural' environment. The same is true for the urban and organisational settings that are more often associated with sociological ethnography. Goffman's work is, throughout his publications, intensely sensitive to spaces and places. His ideal-typical social actor is constantly aware of his or her surroundings. The surrounding environment is simultaneously physical and interpersonal. The self-conscious social actor can be acutely aware of the presence of others, and of the security or insecurity of place. Being a person who is self-conscious and who is able to exercise a degree of self-control, implies a site-specific performance. Equally, therefore, Goffman's social actor is a navigator. She or he has, metaphorically speaking, a radar that scans others persons who are within the interactional space. Likewise, movement is guided by a sense of place: familiar and safe places contrast with the strange and the potentially threatening.

It is clear that an ethnographic attention to space and place means much more than simply mapping the physical environment within which organised social activity takes place. We need to be especially alert to social actors' *sense* of place. Place is intensely meaningful to social actors – from the most local of settings to broader physical and symbolic locations. Benson and Jackson (2013) provide a pertinent example, in the context of a study of middle-class constructions of place and belonging. From within a comparative study of London and Paris, they compare two London neighbourhoods – one a mixed urban location, the other a commuter-village. Middle-class inhabitants of the former (Peckham) perform discursive work to re-create Peckham as an imagined place, in contrast to popular images of a dangerous and run-down neighbourhood: they help to construct it on an everyday basis (by shopping and so on) but actively and practically engage in re-shaping it. In contrast, residents of the commuter villages of Horsley and Effingham, work at *maintaining* place, which is constructed in terms of a rural idyll. The respective places are constructed in contrasting ways (and are indeed very different environments) and in turn are used to create and sustain contrasting middle-class identities. In a setting like Peckham, of course, the middle-class construction (conservation area, artists' studios, gentrified 'village' enclaves) will also be very different from lower-class residents, and in turn will be gendered and differentiated by generation.

Analyses of space must be permeated by analyses of time. As I have suggested already, attention to time gives us analytic purchase on some of the most significant structuring principles of everyday life. Timetables and timescapes – whether formally defined in organisational terms, or developed more informally – structure multiple rounds of shared social activity. Time and space intersect in defining occasions, legitimate participation, and identity. When I conducted my research on the Welsh National Opera company, my own fieldwork patterns necessarily reflected the temporal flow of the organisation itself. Each new production, each revival of a previous production was allocated precisely the same amount of rehearsal time – six weeks. Each new production or revival had its place within a 'season' (the normal arrangement for most opera houses whereby a series of operas are presented in rotation for a limited period). Within the rehearsal period there is a routine, a relentless round that is observed. The first series of rehearsals take place within the rehearsal studio, and are accompanied by piano. Meanwhile the orchestra are rehearsing in *their* studio. These earlier rehearsals are for the performers and the director. Each working day has rehearsal periods of three hours – morning and afternoon. Sometimes an evening period can also be specified by the director. Each rehearsal period has a distinctive shape to it. The singers can often 'run through' the scene that is to be rehearsed, singing (not always at full voice) without any 'acting'. Then they and the director go through the scene, 'blocking' the action (as it is known in all theatrical settings). This is thoroughly repetitious work, as the director and the performers work together to negotiate the staged action, realise the narrative of the opera, create plausible characters and motives, and co-ordinate those actions to the inexorable needs of the music (Atkinson 2010).

The rehearsal cycle moves inexorably through time: towards the end of the six-week period, the singers and the orchestra come together for the first time. To begin with, they participate in the *Sitzproben* (seated rehearsals), and then move into the theatre, where technical and dress-rehearsals take place on the stage, on the set of the production. The rehearsal cycle culminates in the final dress rehearsal, and then the production moves towards the first night – which is clearly a key event that brings with it its own rituals. The first night party for new productions is a key juncture in the unfolding opera season.

Within this cycle, each individual performer has her or his own schedule. In addition to rehearsals, there are individual 'music calls', where singers are rehearsed individually by a member of the music staff. Music staff thus have their own working timetable that is shaped by the same organisational requirements. The overall result is a complex array of interlocking individual and collective schedules. This of course needs scheduling, as it cannot happen without careful planning. It also means that the opera company operates with its own very distinctive rhythms. It follows cycles of varying duration – the annual round of seasons, the same trajectory for each production, the relentless schedule for each production and rehearsal period. These are, needless to say, embedded in yet longer planning cycles: operas have to be planned many years ahead, production teams contracted and performers engaged. As I documented from my operatic ethnography (Atkinson 2006), *repetition* characterises this artistic work. Within the rehearsal period, scenes are rehearsed several times over, and within each rehearsal period, the same actions are repeated. Each rehearsal activity informs the next attempt. Performers and directors repeatedly try to 'find a way' to make the action work. The *repetiteur*, who provides the music at the piano, repeats the music over and over again. The music itself provides its own rhythms, while the opera's dramatic narrative also projects a temporal unfolding of the action. All of this calls for particular forms of temporal work: scheduling work and co-ordinating work among them. Within these temporal frames, aesthetic and emotional labour are enacted.

This is no more than a particular example of a general phenomenon. Organisational and work settings are regulated by temporal frames. As Zerubavel has pointed out in a number of publications (e.g. Zerubavel 1979), one can develop a formal analysis of organisations through a detailed examination of their timetables. Shifts, weekly rosters, training rotations, or annual cycles shape organised work. Hospitals, schools, prisons and similar kinds of organisations display similar features. Indeed, one of the defining characteristics of Goffman's ideal-type of the *total institution* is a common timetable, and the processing of inmates according to a common round of scheduled activities. At the other end of the scale, Goffman's discussion of encounters, situations and units of analysis suggested that a neglected, egocentric one was the individual 'daily round'. There is no doubt that irrespective of the precise content of the activities, the routine of daily tasks, domestic, industrial, bureaucratic or artistic, is a major organising principle for many people. In the absence of organisational or collective work routines, the craft-artists I have observed have a daily round of activities that depend on the self-discipline of the lone worker, rather than the collective discipline of the organisational timetable. Materials have to be prepared, and artefacts made through successive rounds of tasks. The daily round of routine activities is not necessarily a solitary succession of actions. Series of duties often need to be co-ordinated temporally and interpersonally. The daily round is also keyed to externally imposed timetables: the domestic routine is keyed to school hours, opening hours of shops, workplaces and public buildings, public transport timings. The artistic round is keyed to deadlines for commissions, major shows, galleries' timetables and the seasons.

Timescapes are important not solely from the point of view of schedules and co-ordination, however. The relationships between ethnography and history have been treated as problematic by many authors. There is one thoroughly fruitful way in which they intersect, however. That is, what we might call ethnohistory or ethno-archaeology. More simply put, many social settings are permeated by images and versions of their past.

The past may be used as a reference-point against which present states of affairs are evaluated. Likewise, the future is projected, in terms of shared hopes, fears and aspirations. We are familiar with the fact that 'traditions' are invoked to justify the present, while at the same time, those self-same traditions often have very shallow roots, and are themselves 'invented'. Nonetheless, they can exercise considerable symbolic force. Consequently, the ethnographic present always includes reference to the ethnographic past. Moreover, social actors can construct the past through individual or collective archives and collections. Physical artefacts serve as memorabilia, repositories of past experiences and past relationships, symbolic of past selves. The past is brought into the present through acts of memorialisation that use artefacts and mementos, stories and fantasies. These imagined pasts are significant in many ethnographic settings, whether they deal with the collective memories and local mythologies of an organisation, the shared culture of an informal grouping, or the imagined pasts and mythological charters of an entire nation. Personal biographies and collective pasts are interwoven, while key events are stored and narrated in providing an interpretative framework for such memorialising.

As we have seen already, memories and past events are enshrined in stories. Collectivities circulate cherished stories – often well rehearsed and frequently shared – that express membership and loyalty, to socialise new members, and to inscribe collective values. These are themselves among the narrative resources that members use to express membership. Shared stocks of stories create a past that enters into the restricted mythology of a given group. They celebrate culture-heroes, they enshrine shared privations and triumphs. They can be plundered for justifications of past, present and projected actions. They provide a counterpoint to current activities.

Ethnographies that are attentive to such structuring principles will be equally attentive to the multiple sensory dimensions that organise everyday life and its conduct. Many classic ethnographic studies have been oddly lacking in sensory dimensions. This reflects the extent to which many studies have implicitly been disembodied, and have also lacked their material circumstances. In the past, perhaps, too many ethnographic accounts have reconstructed social action in a vacuum – devoid of sensory context, lacking in the embodied experiences of sound, vision, smell or taste. It is clearly not necessary to gather data of this sort without good reason – but there are equally many research settings where a fuller sensory response can be called for. In any event, we know that the absence of any sensory data can leave a research setting denuded, and stripped of several possible domains of cultural significance. Luckily, that situation is being remedied in many contexts. Sensory ethnography (Pink 2009) has become something of a speciality in its own right, and attention to sensory orders informs many anthropological and sociological studies. This is not, then, an appeal to sensory ethnography merely in the interest of providing something that is 'richer' in background or detail. No doubt descriptive writing about sight, smell, sound and the like can render ethnographic texts more fully evocative of particular settings, and there is merit in that. But we must not lose sight of the fact that sociologically or anthropologically significant phenomena may be enacted through multiple modalities, and they include sensory modes of representation and encoding. Our focus remains on social and cultural organisation. Here I focus specifically on the soundscapes of everyday life.

Consider, for instance, the significance of sound. Self-evidently the traditional ethnographer has been a listener, and often a sound-recorder too. But attention to sound itself has too often been relegated to the background. We have been keen to record speech, such as interviews. But wider forms of sound have much more rarely featured as research topics in their own right. Indeed, as a number of commentators have pointed out, much methodological advice has stressed the desirability of minimising 'background' noise. Field researchers have been encouraged to find *quiet* opportunities for the conduct of extended conversations and interviews. This can often have the effect of decontextualising that speech, not just in terms of its physical setting, but also in terms of its sonic characteristics too. Moreover, it is characteristic of a great deal of normal research practice to edit out or to cut out the sounds of research settings. We strain to capture the details of interaction in order to transcribe them, and in transcribing them we often render them much more legible than they were originally audible – precisely because we edit out 'background noise'. And yet in many busy, interactionally dense, settings, social encounters take place within a social environment that have their own sonic features.

Let us start with something obvious. Many social settings and occasions have their own sounds expressed as music. Music pervades many social settings and social worlds. Music can be an everyday phenomenon, or it can mark out 'special' occasions, such as collective rituals. Music can evoke culturally and personally specific meanings – such as feelings of nostalgia, romance, ecstatic and religious responses. In contemporary social settings music is a background accompaniment in many social settings. Background music in shops, restaurants and other buildings is pervasive. Such music creates soundscapes in its own right, as well as contributing to a more general ambience, encouraging shopping or sociality. There is, moreover, the more 'accidental' musical accompaniment that 'leaks' from MP3 players, tablets and other personal devices. Settings such as public transport have their own soundscapes as a consequence.

DeNora (2000, 2003) has made a sustained and systematic contribution to 'sonic' sociology, which she approaches through the study of music. Having started with the historical sociology of Beethoven's artistic persona, she has subsequently developed a more generic approach to the place of music in everyday life. She draws attention to the pervasiveness of music in contemporary societies. Soundscapes are to be identified in the background music of shops, restaurants and similar settings. They help to configure the 'atmosphere' of such places, and hence contribute to the consumers' experiences. Such soundscapes can set the tone for their environments, signalling the sort of clientele they wish to attract and so on. Such sonic accompaniment can help to shape and co-ordinate collective activity in the setting, providing a form of rhythmic direction to the choreography of, say, shopping. More generally, therefore, the documentation and analysis of soundscapes feeds directly into a generic analysis of the temporal rhythms of everyday life and of their material markers. In a comparable vein, Kassabian's study suggests that virtually no musical genre is immune from incorporation into a pervasive aural culture (Kassabian 2013). Much music is 'heard', rather than being consciously listened to, but it helps to constitute what Kassabian calls a 'distributed subjectivity': the subject constituted through networks of relationships in which music plays a major role. Unlike DeNora's work, however, Kassabian's reflections (e.g. on video-art, film or Armenian jazz) or are not based on ethnographic fieldwork, although they are suggestive of ways in which soundscapes might be incorporated within sustained fieldwork in a multitude of everyday settings.

My own early fieldwork experience included a musical element. As a student I went to Crete in the company of fellow undergraduates Michael Herzfeld and Gregg Eaves in order to collect recordings of folk music and take photographs. The music in question was a distinctive Cretan genre known as *rizitika tragoudhia* (songs of the foothills). In a number of villages of the White Mountains of Western Crete, we persuaded individuals and groups to sing for our tape recorder. Nowadays we could buy commercial recordings of such songs but at the time there was little available. Very early on in our 'expedition' we came across the spontaneous performance of such songs. We arrived in one of our villages (which I call Topos) on the day before a funeral was to take place. As part of the funeral observances a group of male singers had been brought in from a village on the south coast of the island. They were singing *rizitika* songs in the street long after the funeral proper, and they paused long enough for me to take some photographs (cautiously, for they had a fearsome reputation). The episode and the village funeral that preceded it reminded us that the 'traditional' songs had a contemporary life and vigour, and that they were embedded in the round of everyday rituals. It also helped to highlight the extent to which these songs were also expressive of singers' identities, collective and individual. They were implicated in what Michael Herzfeld himself went on to call the 'poetics of manhood', when he went back to conduct extended fieldwork on Crete (Herzfeld 1985). Musical forms embed folk memories and recurrent expressions of Cretan identity: the songs express the desire for Cretan liberation from successive occupying powers. They were recycled to include the German occupation of the island, and no doubt were understood to have similar connotations during the military junta of the 1970s. The performance of the songs, therefore, constitutes a performance of collective identity and memorialisation.

More recently, my ethnographic fieldwork in an opera company (Atkinson 2006) inevitably brought music and ethnographic fieldwork into alignment, although my interest was more dramaturgical than musicological. In such overtly musical environments, the ethnography is of necessity multi-modal, in that music, embodied gesture, language and material goods are all equally enrolled in the rehearsal and performance of an opera. The enactment of operatic action also emphasises the way in which music generates its own temporal framing of action. The dramaturgical contrast between operatic performance and the 'straight' theatre lies in the tight framing of operatic acting. However the director and the performers may conceptualise and motivate a particular scene, the action must take as long or as little as the music allows. What can be spoken 'naturally' in a few moments, can be extended into many minutes by the score. A baroque *da capo* aria, moreover, demands that the performer must express 'the same' emotion repeatedly. In other words, there is a distinctive manner of action that music both enables and constrains. Moreover, music and singing elicit affective responses. Even in the rehearsal studio, in mundane – even scruffy – surroundings, the participants can be moved by the musical expression of emotion in arias and duets. The collective performance of music, by the singers with the orchestra or with a piano accompanist (repetiteur), is also an example of an intensely focused form of social interaction and collaborative work. The period of rehearsals constitutes what I have described as a 'bubble' of mutual commitment in the shared effort of making the opera 'work'. Each performance, moreover, is predicated on the close co-ordination of action, mutual attention and intersubjectivity. Music is one (not the only) means whereby such focused work is co-ordinated. In that sense, music is both the topic and the resource for shared attention.

Musical settings, or ubiquitous music in everyday surroundings, emphasise the extent to which sound and noise are more than background, heard but unnoticed, features of social worlds. We can take noise and sound to the foreground of many other ethnographic studies too. In contrast to artificially quietened research settings are studies that are explicitly addressed to the soundscapes of given social worlds. Historical and ethnographic studies can furnish richly textured sound-pictures that emphasise the extent to which noise, sound and music can mingle to generate rhythmic accompaniments to everyday life. There are, of course, specialists in the study of music in cultural contexts. They include *ethnomusicologists*. Historically, they have studied the musical forms and performances of non-Western cultures, or the folk music of European and American peoples. Strictly speaking, of course, all musicology is ethnomusicology, as Western art music is but one array of genres located within specific historical and cultural contexts. In any event, it is not necessary to try to become an ethnomusicologist in order to pay serious attention to the work of music in everyday life. Music obviously furnishes a major element in many ceremonials – religious, military and civil. They have their own musical genres: solemn religious music, stirring military music, romantic airs and so on. While music may not have any intrinsic 'meanings', it has multiple connotations, associations and functions. These are, of course, culturally specific.

Rice (2013) has demonstrated some of the fruitfulness of documenting soundscapes, in his case a soundscape ethnography of two major hospitals. The distribution and enactment of sound has pervasive influence in the hospital. As Rice describes, the panopticist surveillance exercised within the hospital has an auditory component, from the persistent bleeping of monitoring equipment to nurses' monitoring of noise levels on the ward. (Sudden loud noise can betoken trouble.) The acoustic techniques of 'stethoscopic listening' are among the key methods whereby the patient's body is inspected, and are key skills transmitted to medical students. The auditory culture of the hospital is a rich one. But Rice's monograph also illustrates a potential shortcoming in such sensory ethnography. In concentrating on just one sensory dimension, Rice denies himself the opportunity fully to explore the full range of techniques that are in play. Medical students certainly learn to hear heart or bowel sounds through their stethoscope, but they also have to learn how to read the body visually, from the direct gaze of the bedside to scans and microscopic examination of specimens such as blood smears or frozen sections (cf. Atkinson 1995). Equally, one might make a case for an ethnography of light and darkness, or of colour, or indeed smell (another pervasive feature of hospital settings), and the landscapes of pain and distress, fear and relief demand attention.

If sound and noise are virtually ubiquitous, then silence is striking, and culturally often significant. Silence contrasts with mundane sound. It is often a part of the wider symbolic reversals that mark occasions as special or sacred. Indeed, loud noises and profound silence are often combined to encourage collective attention and participation in religious devotions or other collective observances. Sound, silence and music combine with colour (such as colourful ceremonial robes, uniforms and decorations) in the construction of formal and celebratory events. Sonic and visual codes thus combine in contributing to the *mise-en-scène* and the definition of the situation.

Urban settings are very often noisy places, and the level and nature of the noise can help define the character of a neighbourhood, following and shaping the rhythms of the unfolding day. The noise of traffic, of commerce, of conversations and raised voices provides an obbligato accompaniment to the dramas of everyday life. Yet if we read the great majority of urban ethnographies, encounters and actions seem to take place in an atmosphere of quiet calm. Street-corners and bars seem oddly peaceful places. The 'voices' of participants seem rarely raised, as we read the reconstructions and transcripts of talk, and conversations or disputes all take place in even-toned terms: there seems to be little shouting or whispering. Viewed from a historical perspective, we can appreciate how noise can contribute to the distinctive ambience of urban settings.

Cockayne's study of England in the seventeenth and eighteenth centuries refers evocatively to 'hubbub' (Cockayne 2007). Noise, dirt and smell all contributed to distinctive urban scenes: traffic noise, animals, craft workers, street musicians, hawkers' cries – these all contributed to a rich mixture of urban confusion. But it was not without organisation. Trades, for instance, were often locally segregated. The temporal patterns of the days could be marked by changing patterns and volume of noise. Sounds punctuate the texture of everyday life. A cultural history of bells in nineteenth-century France (Corbin 1998) provides a fascinating case in point. Church bells ring and town clocks chime – obviously to mark the passage of time, but also to announce special occasions, such as *rites de passage* – and festivals. The post-revolutionary suppression of ecclesiastical bells in France was one episode in the trajectory of village bells in a sensory landscape of French rural life.

The relative 'silence' of many ethnographic accounts contrasts with many observers' accounts of urban life in general. Classics of early urban sociology and contemporary accounts of early modern cities emphasised the extent to which streets were thronged and noisy. Wirth's early account of urbanism as a way of life, for instance, stressed the sensory intrusion and stimulation characteristic of the modern city. 'Urbanism' is characterised in terms of sensory overload and stimulation, as well as the co-presence of strangers within increasingly complex spatial arrangements, and a specialised division of labour. When the early urban ethnographers of the Chicago School studied the city around them, an increasingly industrialised and modern conurbation, they would have been under no illusion concerning the dense soundscapes of their surroundings. Their studies were firmly located in specific streets and neighbourhoods where urban noise would have been a constant feature of the landscape. Yet those soundscapes rarely seem to be legibly present in the published work – and indeed, the smells and dirt of the new city were not at the forefront. Considering the reported noise and stink of the Chicago stockyards this is, perhaps, surprising.

The temporal flow of social life is susceptible to *rhythmanalysis* (Lefebvre 2004). Lefebvre outlines an intellectual project that makes time, tempo, rhythm and temporal patterns a series of analytic topics in their own right, together with their intersections with spatial arrangements. The sounds of everyday life also mark out the temporal rhythms. All city-dwellers will be familiar with the diurnal rhythms of traffic – from the early morning delivery lorries and garbage trucks to the constant background noise of traffic, to the punctuations of emergency vehicles. The normal rumbles are punctuated by locally specific sounds and noises. Cities have their distinctive sounds: San Francisco punctuated by the slap-slap of the cable-cars, or the doleful fog-horns out in the Bay; Venice punctuated by the sirens announcing *aqua alta*, interrupting the constant background of water. Again, the point of such observations is not merely to add local colour to the ethnography, but to incorporate notions of social and cultural order into the ethnographic analysis. The rhythms of everyday cycles, marked by changing soundscapes, are among the modes of organisation that ethnographers can and should remain attentive to.

Soundscapes are significant in many workplaces. Industrial settings can, of course, be extremely noisy, and that alone can help to constrain and shape the forms of sociability. To take just one example: the cotton mills of Lancashire were extremely noisy. The workers there developed their own system of sign-language through which basic, everyday forms of interaction could be sustained even when it was impossible to hear spoken interaction. In such circumstances, both the evolved sign-language *and* the industrial soundscape would be of equal cultural significance: each informs the other.

Contemporary recording devices mean that it is now possible to capture soundscapes in a way that it never has been before. Indeed, given the contemporary emphasis on multi-modal ethnography, we should expect such sensory mapping to be an almost routine aspect of field research (Pink 2011). Key research questions would, therefore, include:

- How does sound punctuate and order everyday life?
- How is sound (including music) used to impart rhythm to social action?
- How do soundscapes reflect social organisation?
- What are the cultural conventions of noise and silence?
- What are the ceremonial orders of sound?

9

Representations

The ethnographic enterprise is not complete until it has been transformed into representations of the social world, including doctoral theses and monographs, or journal papers (in many cases, all three). One of the most significant and contentious interventions concerns the proper and productive modes of writing that might generate ethnographic reconstructions. I recognise that there are other forms of reconstruction, such as ethnographic film, but they require further specialist treatment that lies beyond the scope of this book. In the course of this chapter I shall outline some of the relevant debates. In keeping with the general tenor of this book, I want to suggest the following. It is right to pay critical attention to the textual forms and conventions of ethnographic writing. The conventions of textual representation are among the obvious examples of reflexivity at work. That is, there is no escape from some form of conventional representation, from textual forms, in the reconstruction of social worlds. There is no perfectly neutral medium of expression that is devoid of such conventions. We can certainly make choices about *how* we use those conventions, or how we subvert them. We cannot avoid them. I shall, however, argue from a critical stance that some forms of contemporary writing fall into what I have referred to as the Romantic fallacy, emphasising personal expression and experiential responses, rather than a sustained representation of social action and social organisation. My general argument is a bit tricky. I want to argue that some degree of textual variation is possible and even desirable in some cases, but that too many contemporary forms of ethnographic and qualitative writing are a departure from that, and are ultimately self-defeating.

In recent years, those textual conventions have become especially prominent in debates about ethnography and its implications. As with a number of other debates in the social sciences, much of it is over-heated. It has led, however, to a number of innovations and experiments that deserve attention. In keeping with the general arguments of this book, I shall remain somewhat sceptical about some of the claims and some of the alleged innovations, while endorsing the need for critical reflection. The textual self-awareness of ethnography has various sources of inspiration, and has taken several turns. It has also looked different in different national and disciplinary contexts. It is my contention that self-conscious attention to textual and other conventions is productive, but some recent trends are unhelpful. Most significantly, an emphasis on textual forms and representational devices has led to a number of departures from the mainstream forms of writing and representation.

Ethnographic writing is inescapably rhetorical, in the sense that it relies on conventions of writing that help to define it as a genre in its own right, drawing on a variety of literary forms. Sociologists have commented on the rhetorical and textual character of their own discipline for some time. Characteristically, this has taken the form of close readings of texts of the discipline, and this in turn has impinged on our collective sensibilities concerning ethnographic texts. For instance, Brown (1977) argued that an understanding of sociological argumentation rests on an analysis of its rhetorical forms. He examined the characteristic use of figures of speech and metaphors, such as sociological irony. This proceeds by way of incongruity and contrast, whereby conventional morality is exposed as corrupt or self-interested, or deviance as rational. The tragic irony of good intentions leading to deleterious and unintended consequences is a prime example.

In a similar vein, Edmondson's analysis is based on a close reading of sociological texts (Edmondson 1984) and explores a number of recurrent rhetorical devices. Of particular relevance to ethnographic representation is her account of *rhetorical induction*. By that she means the deployment of examples and instances from which the reader can interpret generic aspects of social situations. One way of accomplishing this, Edmondson suggests, is through the use of the *actual-type*. Unlike the sociological device of the ideal-type, actual-types are reports of concrete events, spoken utterances and so on, that are characteristic (not necessarily representative in the statistical sense) of a broader analytic category.

The actual-type is in fact a recurrent trope in the presentation of ethnographic material. Its use is often described in terms of *vignettes*. That is, extracts of ethnographic materials – such as fieldnotes or extended quotes from interviews – are used to anchor generic statements about the social world, social process or cultural domain under discussion. The textual format is pervasive. It mirrors the underlying logic of ethnographic inquiry as I have presented it in this book. The textual format consists of a repeated series of interactions between the general and the particular. The local details (vignettes and gobbets) are embedded in discussions of generic social processes, so that the text implicitly answers my analytic proposition: What might this be a case of? Cases (examples) are constantly juxtaposed with categories of broader analytic significance. Such a textual convention thus mirrors what I referred to as *ethnographic abduction.*

Such presentational devices are embedded in what we know as *realist* forms of ethnographic writing. This is the closest the ethnography gets to a 'neutral' tone of voice. It reflects and inscribes a perspective that appears relatively detached from the scenes and actions it describes and analyses. Because of the interaction of generic ideas and specific exemplars, such texts can be quite busy, populated by dense illustrations and series of analytic ideas. It was this style of ethnographic reportage that I examined in a series of publications (Atkinson 1982, 1990, 1992, 1996) which specifically addressed the textual conventions of sociological ethnography. In doing so, I examined a number of textual conventions that ethnographers have deployed in constructing plausible and credible accounts of their chosen research settings and their ethnographic understandings of them. My own textual analysis (Atkinson 1982) stemmed from the irony that although interactionism was founded on a recognition of how language is constitutive of social reality, interactionists seemed to pay insufficient attention to their own written language. There seemed to be a disjuncture between the sensitivities of ethnographic fieldwork and the relative insensitivity of interactionist writing. While the influences of literary and other genres were apparent, they were implicit. I went on to examine ethnographic writing more closely in subsequent analyses (Atkinson 1990, 1992), where I explored just how ethnographic authors – especially those working on urban and organisational settings – re-created social actors and social worlds. This included not just the textual construction of social scenes, but also of social actors. Like their counterparts in fiction, the personae of ethnography are characteristically revealed through telling glimpses, assembled through fragmentary clues and anecdotal examples. A strong sense of *place* – so significant in anchoring the ethnography in its own location – is conveyed through tropes of highly vivid descriptive writing, rich in concrete detail, in a style strongly redolent of travel writing and similar genres. Ethnographic writing in this vein may have little by way of 'literary' invention in the artistic sense, but it owes much to genres that include literary realism.

There has been an affinity between realist fiction and realist ethnography in sociology since the latter's earliest years. As Carey (1975) pointed out, there were clear and acknowledged literary influences on the earliest sociological work of the Chicago School. In Chicago, which was itself a major influence on the development of ethnographic research, the sociological and literary imaginations were mutually informed, and the distinctive modes of ethnographic writing were directly influenced by literary forms. Cappetti (1993) has traced some of these convergences between the literary and the sociological imaginations in Chicago, the city and the university. We have, of course, become so used to the conventions of realist fiction that they seem 'natural', and so we readily overlook their conventional nature. Equally, it was easy to overlook the conventional nature of ethnographic reportage. In my own work I wanted to fracture the taken-for-granted nature of such textual forms, if only to confront ethnographers with their own implicit practices.

Of course, realist writing and reportage were not the only genres that ethnographers used. Van Maanen (1988) authored an incisive analysis of the different genres of ethnographic writing. He identified, amongst other things, the contrast between conventional, realist ethnographic texts, and the 'confessional' mode of autobiographical narrative. In the classic genres of urban ethnography, these two modes of writing were normally kept separate. The difference created a kind of textual cordon sanitaire between the personal and the scholarly. As we shall see, this is a distinction that has become increasingly blurred. The confessional is a popular form of writing on the part of social scientists, and ethnographic research lends itself particularly well to such personal reflection. Van Maanen's title of *Tales of the Field* captures very precisely the ways in which ethnographers' field experiences lend themselves to autobiographical accounts. Proverbially, we 'confess' the second-worst thing we did or that happened to us, keeping private the most discreditable aspects.

It comes as no surprise, of course, that confessions are just as conventionally contrived as any other textual genre. Sincerity, honesty and revelation are managed through culturally shared formats and narrative resources. We should not expect ethnographers' narratives to be much different from those of any other social actors. Just as I described earlier in this book, personal narratives follow culturally shared formats, and those of ethnographers are no different. Consequently we can identify a distinctive kind of confessional account that follows a form of 'quest' (cf. Atkinson 1996), from stranger and outsider to member and insider; from puzzlement to enlightenment; pursued through troubles and privations; aided by true friends and mentors; sometimes led astray by false expectations and poor advice. And so on. They follow many of the recognisable forms of the folk-tale (Propp 1958). The confessional genre understandably highlighted the *personal* side of ethnographic and similar styles of research. It placed the person of the ethnographer firmly in the text, and equally in the social processes of fieldwork itself. As I have suggested already, however, it also created the textual space for a romanticised image of the ethnographer. The personal struggle for comprehension, the vicissitudes experienced and overcome, the suspicion or hostility of one's hosts and informants: these helped to establish a sense of the lone researcher struggling in an alien environment. As I have acknowledged, the conventionally confessional account had the function of *separating* the personal and the analytic. It steadily became a widespread genre in its own right, often enshrined in edited collections of first-hand accounts of the fieldwork experience. It also helped to create the possibility of yet more impressionistic and experiential writing that has culminated in the move to *autoethnography*. This is a topic to which I shall return later in this chapter.

For a number of authors and commentators it is not enough to make sense of the styles of ethnographic writing. They go further in seeking to promote styles of writing as analytic methods in their own right. This has led to a number of textual experiments. In the work of authors such as Richardson, *writing* has been placed at the core of ethnographic research (see Richardson 1994a, 2000; Richardson and St Pierre 2005). The act of textual construction is regarded as constitutive of the work of the analyst. This approach has not merely heightened social scientists' self-consciousness about the conventions they employ, it has also led an increasing number of scholars to explore 'new' forms of writing, taking to various logical conclusions the overt appeal to a literary imagination to convey sociological or anthropological insights. (I have qualified 'new' here because the novelty of such approaches is not all that it seems.) One of the consequences of a reflective attention to the literary and rhetorical forms of scientific and social-scientific writing has been an overt willingness on the part of social scientists themselves to experiment with alternative modes of textual representation. If the conventions of factual writing and of realist fiction could be shown to be just that – conventions – then it was clearly open to scholarly authors to try different modes of writing. A number of 'experimental' approaches were advocated and tried from the 1980s onwards, as a direct acknowledgement of the reflexive character of ethnographic writing. That is, the recognition that textual organisations and genres do not merely *report* social phenomena in a transparent way, but shape and help to construct ethnographic arguments. See, amongst many others: Angrosino 1998; Banks and Banks 1998; Bochner and Ellis 2002; Church 1995; Ellis and Bochner 1996; Ellis and Flaherty 1992; Goodall 2000; Hecht 2006; Kirklighter et al. 1997).

One of the earlier sites of literary experimentation was to be found in Science and Technology Studies. The sociological analysis of scientific discourse, spoken and written, revealed that even the most 'hard' of sciences depended on rhetorical devices, and the spirit of reflexive analysis thus turned attention back on the textual practices of sociological analysts themselves. In making rhetoric problematic, therefore, some authors explicitly used 'alternative' literary forms to convey the nature of scientific persuasion, legitimation and authority. Mulkay (1985) experimented with dialogues, plays and so forth to present his own research about science and scientists. In developing these literary forms, Mulkay 'shows' rather than simply 'tells' some of the paradoxes, ironies and rituals of academic scientific discourse. There are elements of playfulness – with a very serious purpose – in this style of work. Parody and pastiche, for instance, can be used to throw into relief some of the conventions, and humorous interventions can (satirically) illuminate serious analytic themes. There is, therefore, an ironic contrast between the spare, degree-zero writing of the scientific text and the self-consciously playful explorations of the sociologist-author. On the other hand, similar analytic purchase might have been gained from a close rhetorical analysis of prize-winners' speeches, and indeed other acceptance speeches by award-winners. The latter clearly embody a variety of cultural conventions, not least the expectation that recipients will enact surprise and extreme emotion, coupled with expressions of extreme modesty tempered with barely controlled elation.

It is one of the features of many literary experiments that they are populated by multiple 'voices'. In contrast to the single authorial voice of the ethnographer, interspersed by fragments of reported speech and observed actions, the experimental forms allowed for different actors to be present in the text, without being subordinated to a single narrative scheme. The use of ethnographic data, and the writing of dialogues facilitated such a 'polyvocal' text. This could also accommodate a more deliberately shifting perspective. Rather than a culture or a group being represented from a single viewpoint, the author's and the reader's perspectives could be shifted. This also reflected the desire for more 'messy' texts. The traditional ethnographic genre, it had been claimed from various standpoints, tended to subordinate the multiple perspectives and constructions of complex social situations to a single, unifying narrative. While some people might think it was the intellectual task of the social scientist to create just such a unified text, others believe that it perpetrated a kind of symbolic violence on the realities of social life itself. If research dissolves the privilege of the observer/author, then it also implies that there should be multiple voices identifiable in the analysis. This goes well beyond the perfectly ordinary practice of quoting informants or including extracts from fieldnotes in order to illustrate ethnographic texts. The polyvocal text – and hence the analytic strategy that underlies it – does not subordinate the voices and press them into the service of a single narrative. Rather, there are multiple and shifting narratives. The point of view of the 'analysis' is a shifting one. There is no single implied narrator occupying a privileged interpretative position. A relatively early example of such a text is Krieger's (1983) account of a lesbian community. Krieger, as author/analyst, constructs a collage or palimpsest of narratives, juxtaposed in the style of stream-of-consciousness literary work. Her analysis of the community is implicit in those textual arrangements, which are not superseded or supplemented by a dominant authorial commentary. The expression of voices has become a major preoccupation of many qualitative researchers in recent years, and to some extent, the force of polyvocality has become blunted: in some contexts it can seem to mean little more than 'letting the informants speak for themselves', with little or no theoretical sophistication. On the other hand, it can give rise to complex and dense representations (see Atkinson 1996 for a review of different kinds of contribution). Equally, the celebration of voices can allow the author to find her or his 'voice' in a way that differs from the canons of conventional academic writing: it provides permission for first-person narratives that insert the author in her or his texts, rather than suppressing the personal in the analytic. However, the presence of multiple or alternating 'voices' in the text is no guarantee of adequate analysis. The fact that we can read or hear texts that express the multiple viewpoints of different actors or social categories does not absolve us from *analysing* those perspectives, their expression, the structures of their accounts and the cultural resources they employ in doing so. The mere juxtaposition is different accounts does not perform analysis in an adequate fashion. Ultimately, it is intellectually lazy (even though it may satisfy certain ideologically rooted intentions).

Increased textual awareness has also led many scholars in anthropology and sociology to address the textual nature of their own data. For many years the ethnographic fieldnote was the staple of field research. For an almost equally long period of time, fieldnotes have been taken for granted. This is partly because most researchers tended to treat their field data as private, and sharing data and its secondary analysis were alien to most researchers. Recent developments in analysis, research-methods training, data-archiving and so on have made fieldnotes and other ethnographic data more visible. Moreover, the textual turn has made ethnographers acutely self-conscious of the fact that in making fieldnotes they are already engaged in textual reconstructions of reality, long before they compose their monographs or journal papers. In the collection edited by Sanjek (1990) anthropologists reflected upon fieldnotes – how they are constructed, used and managed. We come to understand that fieldnotes are not a closed, completed, final text: rather they are indeterminate, subject to reading, rereading, coding, recording, interpreting, reinterpreting. The literary turn has encouraged (or insisted) on the revisiting, or reopening, of ethnographer's accounts and analyses of their fieldwork. From a sociological perspective, Emerson and his colleagues also explored the production of fieldnotes (Emerson et al. 2001), while Atkinson (1992) and Mishler (1991) among others discussed the textual production of both fieldnotes and transcripts. It is clear that we cannot exempt such data from the 'textual turn'. They are not merely 'givens'. Ethnographers actively create accounts of social phenomena as soon as they start to create such materials. Undoubtedly, when they come to 'write up' their field data, they more overtly and self-consciously have to think of themselves as 'authors'. A case in point is Wolf (1992), who revisited her fieldnotes, her journal and a short story she had written while she was doing fieldwork in a Taiwanese village and explicitly reflected on the different textual versions she created. More recently, Taussig (2012) has revisited fieldnotes, treating them as liminal texts, and excavating from them insights that go well beyond what is written (or drawn) in the notebooks themselves. Indeed, reflection on ethnographic notebooks leads us to speculate further on the nature of writing itself, and the relationships between personal texts and memory. It is not simply a matter of how accurate our notes may be, or indeed how accurately they trigger or recall. Rather, such exercises in textual reflection remind us that our ethnographic 'data' are never inert collections of information, to be stored and manipulated mechanistically, but things to think with. The process of inference is more like what Lévi-Strauss (1966) called *the science of the concrete*, in that we think through objects, images, textual fragments and memories.

As a consequence of some of these developments, ethnographic writing has often become more self-consciously artful in its textual organisation and style. There has now developed a much more 'literary' approach to writing ethnography in many quarters – in sociology, in anthropology and in other disciplines as well. Moreover, the presence of the ethnographer/author in the text has become more overt. If the traditional ethnographic text effaced the author in favour of an impersonally factual and authoritative account, in more recent years, that has been transgressed. This has been accompanied by a yet more general tendency for ethnographers to insert themselves into the research and the results of research. As Coffey (1999) has demonstrated, 'the ethnographic self' has become a prominent feature of academic discourse. The conduct of ethnography, the analysis of ethnographic data and the construction of ethnographic representations are all conveyed in more personal terms.

The genre of the anthropological monograph has been equally subject to critical scrutiny. The collection of papers edited by Clifford and Marcus (1986) was certainly influential, and its influence spread beyond the confines of anthropology alone. Behar and Gordon (1995) provided a feminist contribution, arguing that many women anthropologists had rejected the canonical textual styles of their contemporaries and experimented with 'other' literary forms. A collection of responses by British social anthropology was edited by James, Hockey and Dawson (1997). The issues are also taken up explicitly in the collection edited by Zenker and Kumoll (2010). Collectively, these and other interventions were greeted as heralding a *crisis of representation*. The classic monograph, relatively impersonal, embodying a single authorial perspective, had been the bedrock of anthropological ethnography. Its stability in time and space meant that while theoretical debates and competing interpretations could take place, the ethnographic monograph could provide enduring evidence. The textual critique of the genre itself, however, nibbled away at the very foundations of the discipline. The 'crisis' was, however, overblown, although the visibility of the contributions edited by Clifford and Marcus did fuel debates and experiments concerning textual forms (see also Spencer 1989, 2001).

In fact, there were plenty of examples of anthropologists analysing their own and others' textual practices independently of Clifford, Marcus and their authors. For instance, Boon (1982, 1983) produced an important body of work in which he examined just how the styles of anthropological work reflected and in turn shaped distinctive forms of anthropological thought. Boon elegantly displayed how the form as well as the content of functionalist anthropologies reinforced basic tenets of functionalism itself. Functionalist anthropology, taken as a genre rather than just individual texts, constructed a standardised form of society within its pages, with predictable institutional forms, predictable internal and external boundaries and equally predictable types of social organisation. Geertz (1983) published a detailed and prophetic analysis of the authorial style of Evans-Pritchard – one of the classic, archetypal British anthropologists. Geertz identified aspects of Evans-Pritchard's written style emphasising its 'transparent' quality, and hence how the anthropologist presents himself as a disinterested and reliable *witness* to the events described in his written work. Geertz was one of the most significant of cultural anthropologists to reflect on the textual conventions of his own discipline, in a way that reflected his own approach to cultural anthropology more generally. His meta-analytic perspective stressed the notion of a culture-as-text, and the role of the anthropologist as an interpretative one. It was, therefore, entirely congruent with his general anthropology that Geertz should treat styles of ethnographic reporting as significant features of the discipline itself, and that he should recognise textual conventions as constitutive of anthropological reconstructions of cultural forms (Geertz 1988).

As a consequence of all this activity it has become far more common for ethnographers and other qualitative scholars to embrace a self-conscious approach to their own textual productions. This has been associated with various calls for textual experimentation, the use of different genres, the blending of genres and the adoption of explicitly literary forms. These have included:

- A greater propensity to write the author 'into' the ethnographic text, so that the processes of inquiry and authorship are simultaneously available to the reader.

- An acknowledgement of the analytic opportunities afforded by 'messy texts' that challenge the smoothly realist surfaces of more traditional texts.

- A willingness to adopt more overtly 'literary' forms of text in order to create distinctive representational effects.

These have included various forms of autobiographically based writing, generically referred to as *autoethnography*, as well as the production of ethnographic fictions, the authoring of ethnodrama, the use of verse forms, and indeed a wide variety of textual forms. In recent years, however, the main ethnographic monograph itself has become a site of explicitly personalised research. We are now accustomed to reading ethnographies, by anthropologists and sociologists, in which the ethnographer/author is explicitly visible. The research itself is reported in such a way as to reflect the fieldworker's personal engagements with the social world. This is paralleled by styles of reporting in which the ethnographer appears, as it were, as a character in the action, rather than just an invisible but omniscient narrator of the more traditional ethnography. The author is an engaged one, a personal one and, sometimes, a passionate one.

Personal, sometimes transgressive, writing has become associated with various appeals to *postmodernism* in qualitative, ethnographic research. Many advocates for postmodernism are also keen on textual innovation. It is possible – even likely – that postmodern work will be written in an innovative and stylistically self-conscious way. The postmodern work is likely to be couched in terms of an open, 'messy' text, rather than a monograph or paper that conforms to all the conventions of scholarly factual writing. This text may well incorporate a mixture of different literary styles and genres. It may, for instance, include highly impressionistic, introspective and autobiographical passages of prose which are transgressive of the normal canons of academic discourse. Different kinds of prose may be interspersed with poetry, resulting in a more promiscuous mix of styles and genres. The exploration of personal, evocative forms of writing has led a surprisingly large number of ethnographic authors to write poetry as a way of constructing a personal response to their experiences in the field, or as a form of autoethnographic reflection. This form of personal poetry needs to be distinguished from other explorations of 'poetics'. Dell Hymes, the leading anthropologist of language, amongst others, documented the ethnopoetics of everyday language-use (Hymes 1981). This involved the demonstration of poetic forms and devices that are intrinsic to language-use – such as narrative forms. Here the analysis seeks to uncover the poetics of ordinary language. Some ethnographic poem-making derives from a similar inspiration, although further towards the 'literary' end of the spectrum. For instance, Laurel Richardson famously took the words of an informant and shaped them to construct a poem (Richardson 1993). It is clearly possible to use techniques of linguistic and narrative analysis to draw out the intrinsic, indigenous forms of linguistic performance. Clearly, there are forms of spoken language that have highly developed rhetorical forms – traditional narratives, riddles, jokes and the like – where an ethnopoetic analysis does not change the flow of recorded speech, but pays close attention to its rhetorical devices. Experiments like Richardson's go one stage beyond that, by editing the original words to create a new speech act (Richardson 1994b). This latter approach preserves the sense and much of the structure of the original language-in-use but re-forms it. Many examples of poetry are composed entirely *de novo*, however, and reflect on the author's personal feelings and experiences. Insofar as these are divorced entirely from data of any sort, it is not clear in what sense they count as ethnographic, or have any sustained claim to be part of a scholarly canon. There is, moreover, an irony at the heart of much experimental ethnographic writing that is exemplified by the use of poetry. That is, the expression of the poetic and authorial voice of the ethnographer–poet can pay insufficient attention to the intrinsically ethnopoetic sensibilities of others. It is the particular contribution of Dell Hymes (1981, 1996) among others, to demonstrate the *indigenous* forms of spoken performance. The imposition of an authorial style, in the form of a poem, may inadvertently do symbolic violence to the original forms of expression. The inherent, indigenous structuring of spoken action can thus be obscured by the imposition of the author's own individual voice.

The adoption of a poetic voice is but one way in which novel genres can be used. They also include *ethnodrama* (Mienczakowski 2001). Here the essential feature is that selected aspects of everyday life are reconstructed not through a conventional realist ethnographic text, but are re-presented in dramatic form. The methods and compositional techniques for such exercises can vary. The ethnographer may undertake more-or-less traditional field research and draw on those data – observations, interviews, transcribed talk – and choose to write the results in a dramatic form. Such dramas may therefore be constructed in such a way as to reflect the dramaturgical character of everyday life and social interaction. On the other hand, the author may use a more 'impressionistic' approach, more distinctly removed from field data, constructing what is essentially a new dramatic enactment on the basis of her or his understanding of a given setting. Different again is the form of ethnodrama that is not simply 'authored' by the ethnographer–observer, but is a collective project, produced collaboratively with chosen social actors. In other words, the ethnodrama is a form of social activity in its own right. It may be a way of mobilising a particular group, so as to give them voices that might otherwise go unheard. Here the dramatic reconstruction is a form of action-research in its own right. There is a potential criticism of any or all ethnodrama that parallels the criticism of ethnopoetry. There is no doubt that everyday life is intensely performative. The work of major authors like Erving Goffman has repeatedly shown forms of social life that are intrinsically dramaturgical. Arguably, it is the task of the social analyst to *examine* those dramaturgical forms, rather than imposing extrinsic dramatic reconstructions. The contrived writing of an invented ethnodrama can readily overwhelm the inherent dramaturgical complexity of everyday life, and the dramaturgical skills of everyday actors. To put it crudely: if everyday social life is so performative, do we really need social scientists to script it afresh? Again, we ought not to become quite so enamoured of our own skill as authors as to neglect the skills of others in authoring their own everyday lives.

Contrasts between evocative and realist ethnographic writing are easy to exaggerate. This is particularly true when advocates of the former try to summarise key differences. In an Appendix to her 'ethnographic novel', Ellis (2004) creates a list of binary oppositions between 'impressionist' and 'realist' ethnographies. Unfortunately, her characterisation of 'realist' research and realist texts is a caricature, implying that all such work is informed by a relentless quest for abstract concepts, generalisability and reliability. Equally, she implies that the 'impressionist' work that she herself practices is alone interested in the local, the specific, or the emotional. Of course, these contrasts are based on ideal-types, and are intended to be heuristic rather than definitive, but there is a false dichotomy at their heart, and a violence is done to the ethnographic tradition. Sociologists, anthropologists and others who have practised ethnographic research over many decades have been interested in the generic and the local, the concrete and the abstract, the evocative and the analytic. Ethnographic texts have explored the relationships between those different analytic moments (which do not stand in opposition). It is my contention that the 'impressionist' (a term I do not particularly like) and the 'realist' (a term I like even less) should go hand-in-hand. The desire to create evocative texts does not absolve us, collectively, from an analytic stance towards the social world.

Amongst the practitioners of autoethnography are those who use introspection, memory, autobiography and other constructions of 'self' as the subject-matter of their own research. The genres of research text here blur with those of biographical work. Reflexivity and first-person narratives lead directly to the possibilities of autoethnography. The term itself has several connotations. I focus on analyses that are based substantially or even exclusively on the writer's personal experiences, memories and actions. This, therefore, moves the personal from the marginal notes of the confessional tale to occupy the central place of sociological or anthropological analysis. Autoethnography and autobiography can be virtually indistinguishable. The resulting accounts can be highly charged emotionally for the author and reader alike (e.g. Tillmann-Healy 1996). Reed-Danahay's (1997) edited collection, and her overview (2001) showcase these developments. In these autoethnographic exercises, the ethnographer treats her/himself as the primary object of scrutiny, or at least a major part of it.

There is, however, good reason to be sceptical – analytically sceptical perhaps – about personal narratives and autobiographical accounts. As social scientists we know that such accounts in everyday life are always shaped and crafted in accordance with socially shared conventions and narrative forms. Even the most private of experiences is expressed in 'public' formats. I have already outlined such arguments in an earlier chapter on narratives and accounts. The expression of emotions is mediated by cultural and linguistic forms; memory is enacted through socially shared resources; personal identity is created through socially shared repertoires. We need, therefore, to be especially careful in thinking about recent directions in autoethnography. There is clearly a tendency for some contemporary authors, however, to present themselves as writing texts that offer especially personal documents that reflect and represent some sort of interior emotional life. In these accounts, experience is treated unproblematically, in the sense that it is *not* explicitly recognised as a matter of textual, narrative and cultural construction. Emotions need to be examined sociologically or anthropologically just as thoroughly as any other culturally shared forms of expression. They do not absolve us from methodical and sustained analysis. The personal emotions of authors are not exempt from this.

Contemporary autoethnographic and similar kinds of experiential writing, therefore, contain within them some quite serious dangers. In particular, they run the collective risk of obliterating some important sociological and anthropological principles, by appearing to grant a privileged status to the personal and the private, and treating them as if they were unmediated phenomena that can be revealed transparently in texts of experience. There is another danger too. The more we celebrate autoethnography, the greater the danger that we treat ourselves as being more interesting than the social worlds around us. The ethnographic imagination should be driven by an unswerving commitment to the view that whether we study familiar settings, or seek out strange social worlds, they are in principle interesting in their own right. They are not primarily vehicles for our own emotional responses, or blank canvases onto which we project our own anxieties and preoccupations. While reflexive understandings of the research process are important, they surely should not assume centre stage. We need to keep autoethnographic writing in its place. To return to one of my earlier contentions: there is nothing wrong in treating 'others' as endlessly rewarding topics of sustained inquiry, and strictures against negative 'othering' should not blind us to that.

We have recently witnessed not just autoethnographic writing and the production of poems but also ethnographic fiction. There have been several book-length works of fiction by ethnographers. Pfohl, for instance, conducted conventional sociological research, including work on the practical reasoning that psychiatrists undertake in order to predict 'dangerousness'. His *Death at the Parasite Café* is a very different exercise, mingling fictional texts in an exercise in political commentary (Pfohl 1992). Carolyn Ellis, who has championed many of the recent developments in new genres of ethnographic text has also composed an 'ethnographic novel', *The Ethnographic I* (Ellis 2004). This work takes ethnographic reflexivity to a particular extreme, through the construction of a fictionalised account of the conduct of ethnographic and autoethnographic work. Unlike some other fictional writing in this genre, it retains an explicitly pedagogic function, as well as taking ethnographic pedagogy as its subject-matter. It is constructed through a melange of true and composite, fictional episodes and characters. Its literary and pedagogic merits remain hard to discern amidst the detail of reconstructed dialogue and fictionalised encounters.

Here we come to the crux of my argument. It is my contention that too many contemporary authors who claim to endorse textual experimentation in effect display a failure of nerve. To put the argument in a nutshell, instead of a thoroughly modernist embrace of textual experimentation and multiple textual forms, in fact we have far too many texts that display what I have previously referred to as romantic or sentimental realism. That is, an undue emphasis on narratives of personal experience, that celebrate the personal, and that stress a storied, readerly textual form. This does not mean, of course, that there have been no significantly experimental texts. But I want to dwell on the contemporary genres of qualitative inquiry that include – but are not exhausted by – so-called autoethnographic writing.

Now it seems to me that the current vogue for certain styles of fictionalised or autoethnographic texts display a recurrent failure of nerve in this respect. They are, perhaps, 'experimental' in the sense that they do not present themselves as conventional forms of academic writing – as papers or monographs. But equally, the failure of nerve I allude to resides in the embrace of a restricted set of textual practices that are the reverse of modernist experimentation. They revert to conventionally realist or naturalistic writings, often based on personal experience and feelings, that do little justice to the potential of truly experimental texts. Moreover, these contemporary textual types often appeal to an emotional response in the reader, rather than inviting an intellectual, analytic engagement. To that extent, therefore, they are reductionist, in (literally) reducing social life to an experiential dimension. They embody what I term *sentimental realism* (see Atkinson 2013a). In other words, the apparently unconventional textual forms that are employed (autobiographical and emotional evocations) in effect create a new form of Romantic subject (the author–researcher) that traduces the sociological and anthropological understandings of selfhood and identity.

Goodall (2000) is a useful point of departure, in that he provides an accessible source that expresses some of the principles of the 'new' ethnographic writing in a lucid fashion. While he acknowledges the contributions of some predecessors, it is noticeable that – in confirmation of my own thesis – his book is more or less silent on the long tradition of anthropological writing; it would – yet again – be possible to infer that interest in such literary issues was a recent invention. More significantly, he clearly stresses the centrality of writing about the 'self' (that is, the ethnographer–author). Indeed, it is, apparently, an imperative: 'new ethnographers have an obligation to write *about* their lives' (p. 23, emphasis original). Now it is not at all clear to me that there is such an obligation, but there is a more fundamental issue: *how* that self is conceptualised and therefore how it is written into the text.

I return to the main burden of my argument. In contemporary autoethnography and cognate forms of 'new' writing, we are presented with a Romantic subject. The self that is implicitly inscribed in these texts of 'new ethnography' is not one conceived in sociological terms. On the one hand, sociological analysis implies that we must think in terms of a social actor, performative in character, constituted by a variety of practices – linguistic and otherwise. But in its emphasis on the writing of personal experience, the new ethnographic text posits a subject of interior subjectivity, a relatively stable 'self'. Now this is not the self of symbolic interactionism, or of Goffman's version of micro-sociology. It is certainly not a self of either modernism or postmodernism. Indeed, there is a paradox at the heart of too much contemporary ethnographic work. It pays lip-service to a plastic, fragmented, socially constituted view of the social self, but endorses a completely different view of the self of the ethnographer-as-author. For instance, Neumann (1996) gives a succinct justification for this view: '*autoethnography* renames a familiar story of divided selves longing for a sense of place and stability in the fragments and discontinuities of modernity. Writing and reading such stories has long been a means of collecting ourselves, of seeking order and meaning in a world that often conspires against continuity' (pp. 173–4, emphasis in original). Such a search for ontological security is antithetical to the sociological or anthropological imagination. In a quite different vein, but with an equivalent force, Richardson's autobiographical fragment in the same volume (Richardson 1996) suggests a recuperative move, in the reclamation of an authentic 'self' in contrast to various forms of dramaturgical enactment over the course of a life and academic career. Again, such a contrast is fundamentally at odds with a sociological understanding of everyday life and its performativity. Characteristic too is the programmatic, if personally expressed, statement by Quinney (1996), where he suggests that writing an ethnography about an early episode in your life 'will encompass your emotional and spiritual life, your very being' (p. 357). And he goes on in a very telling phrase, that: 'This is ethnography as the lived experience of the ethnographer' (p. 357). It may well be a deeply felt personal memoir, but whether it is ethnography, in the sense intended by sociologists and anthropologists, is a different matter. The resulting text, however, certainly satisfies my criterion for sentimental realism.

These are but fragmentary examples from a large and varied corpus. There are various textual strategies in play, and some texts are more transgressive or exploratory than others. For the most part, however, the texts, whether described as ethnography, autoethnography or performance pieces, stick fairly closely to the tropes of conventional creative writing. There is a considerable emphasis on personal recollection, on the evocation of feelings (often highly charged and painful), and the exploration of characters (often close to the narrator). A story rather than an analytic theme is also characteristic. Narrative coherence is valued over modernist ambiguity, and parallels the quest for authorial selfhood.

So far, then, I have argued that ethnographic texts of feelings, experience and autobiography are but an incomplete realisation of ethnography's textual possibilities. My argument is not that they are 'wrong' in any sense, indeed rightness and wrongness seem completely inappropriate criteria in any event. Rather, I suggest that they are restricted versions of what is possible. That is so for two reasons. First, the repeated emphasis on the experiential robs the texts of many other analytic possibilities. Second, the autobiographical (autoethnographic) mode reduces the potential scope of textual experimentation. The cumulative consequence is a paradoxical *lack* of textual experimentation. This is coupled with a further danger: that is a form of narrative or *rhetorical reductionism*. Texts of personal experience – whether factual or fictionalised – are too often constructed in terms of a naturalism that denies the potential complexities of the social self and of social encounters, and indeed of the multiple modalities of everyday life (Atkinson et al. 2008).

To put it another way, too much contemporary ethnographic fiction, and autobiographical reflection, is too rooted in its own mundane forms of reality-construction. Personal narrative is valuable up to a point, but it also has profound limitations. It does not allow us to explore the full *analytic* possibilities of ethnographic writing. Our task as social scientists is not merely to conjure up and evoke social worlds and situations. It is not enough to give our readers vicarious experiences, however vividly reconstructed. What I have referred to as sentimental realism carries a number of problems. Two main issues are: the failure of textual nerve, and the emphasis on the expression of experience. These are inter-related, but are not inseparable. Indeed, one could argue that modernism's various textual possibilities would be especially suited to the expression of personal experience. The internal dialogue of 'stream of consciousness' fiction (such as is to be found in the novels of Virginia Woolf) would, for example, provide ample exemplars for the exploration of interiority and subjective experience. The multiple timeframes of the modernist novel can also reflect the temporal as well as the spatial kaleidoscopes of everyday life. The modernist work of fiction reflects a distinctive fracturing of taken-for-granted experience, just as modernist visual art disturbs the visual codes of mundane looking. But too many of the contemporary exercises in ethnographic fiction and poetry restore a monological mode of expression, putting the author once more in the position of a privileged narrator: the all-knowing analyst is replaced by an all-feeling *auteur*.

It seems to me that far too much contemporary work is devoted to the recuperation of personal experience: sometimes the author's own (as in autoethnography), or the reported experiences of others (through the collection of interview materials). And yet, as I have argued throughout this book, that is not the sole – or even the principal – goal of social research. A focus on personal experience diverts attention from analytic focus on modes of social organisation, on social action, on the forms of representation, and indeed all of the forms and types of collective activity. In other words, we need to recognise and reinforce the analytic issue that social life is itself conducted through multiple modes of organisation and representation. It does not follow with absolute necessity that the analysis and representation of social life must itself always be multimodal. But it does mean that textual or narrative reductionism – the adoption of a single textual form – is not in itself adequate. Or at least, it means that the reduction of social life to a narrative expression of experience is severely limited. We need to do justice to the multiple modes of social action and social organisation that define any given social world. We ought, therefore, to avoid condensing the varieties of the social world into first-hand confessional modes, essentially realist in tone, based upon an un-sociological view of the interiority of the individual subjective self. We need to turn outwards to explore more systematically and more analytically the variety of representational and formal modes of organisation – textual, visual, sonic – that inhabit the social worlds we engage with.

Here, therefore, I find myself in agreement with Hammersley (1998), who insists that an evaluation of ethnographic research should by no means rest primarily on the rhetorical and persuasive power of the text. Evocative and literary writing, Hammersley argues, should not substitute for canons of rigour, or criteria of evidence. A recognition of textual conventions does not imply that the research enterprise should be thought of primarily in rhetorical or textual terms. As I have been trying to establish, textual experimentation and personal reflection certainly do not substitute for the detailed ethnographic exploration of social action and the forms of cultural life. I depart from Hammersley to the extent that I recognise the potential value of textual variation, *provided that it serves an analytic purpose*. A similar perspective is to be found in the discussion by Gay y Blasco and Wardle (2007) of anthropological texts, examining characteristic forms of narrative, argumentation and other recurrent textual features to be found in ethnographic monographs. This general perspective represents what we might call the more sober view of textual conventions. It is an extension of the recognition that social science is inescapably reflexive: that is, methods and representations necessarily shape the phenomena they report. But that does not mean that the social scientists need or ought to abandon normal canons of argumentation and evidence.

10
The Ethics of Ethnography

While I have ordered this book primarily in terms of analytic topics, current interest in the subject suggests a discussion of ethics. The ethics of social research – of all sorts – have become prominent, and potentially problematic, for a number of reasons. Among the most prominent of antecedents is the influence of institutional ethical reviews and regulations, and the increasing stringency with which *all* research is subject to ethical oversight. In this chapter I do not intend to rehearse all of the arguments *pro* and *contra* institutional review boards and ethics committees – but to underscore the extent to which the commitments of ethnography outlined in the foregoing chapters have direct consequences for research ethics. For a pungent view on ethics and social research see Dingwall (2008) and for an extended review of the complexities of ethics and qualitative research, see Hammersley and Traianou (2012); see also Ryen (2004) and Murphy and Dingwall (2007). While ethical commitments have always been central to the conduct of ethnographic research, contemporary ethical regulation is in danger of governing the research process itself, through a process that Haggerty (2004) refers to as 'ethics creep'.

At the outset, however, I want to make one thing clear, and to re-state something I have already implied. With a very small number of egregious exceptions, *ethnography is among the most ethical forms of research*. This assertion will be expanded upon. For the moment I base it on these two major issues. First, unlike any other research approach, ethnography derives from a very distinctive personal commitment on the part of the researcher. Fieldwork embodies a personal, intellectual and even emotional commitment to the lives of others that clearly surpasses virtually any other form of inquiry. While such an engagement and the trust it is based on can clearly be abused – and has been on occasion – the vast majority of field researchers have created a highly commendable attitude towards their research hosts and informants. The general orientation of ethnographic understanding is also, in itself, ethically commendable. The general methodological attitude of cultural relativism implies not merely a non-judgemental perspective, but – more positively – one within which the culture and social organisation of a given people are granted serious attention. While ethnographers are not required to *celebrate* the lives of others, they are committed to representing them in their full complexity, with due regard for the rationality of social action, and with respect for the social actors involved. This is not to deny that there are examples of field research that raise significant moral issues. Hammersley and Traianou (2012) list a number of them, some egregiously problematic, others perhaps less so (pp. 8–11).

In contrast, one can argue that several standard research strategies in the contemporary world are profoundly problematic from a methodological point of view. The 'gold standard' (which it is not) strategy of the randomised controlled trial (RCT) can be thoroughly dubious (see Timmermans and Berg 2003 for a series of studies questioning gold standards in biomedical knowledge). It is highly manipulative. In many clinical trials, for instance, participants are told that if they agree to participate then they have a fifty-fifty chance of receiving a novel treatment that the researchers have reason to believe might be superior to the current treatment of choice. The use of a placebo in such a trial is even more dubious. What could be *less* ethical than determining a person's medical treatment not on need but on the basis of a random-number generator? The very principle of the RCT is ethically flawed, although it is rarely criticised on those grounds. The fact that in practice – ethnographically speaking – we know that informed consent is sometimes managed in a perfunctory way, that consent is therefore far from fully informed, and that the attitudes of clinical staff administering the research can be less than admirable does nothing to mitigate the ethically flawed procedure of the trial. The fact that RCTs are more methodologically problematic than their advocates often acknowledge makes their ethical status even more questionable.

Equally, the ethnographer's commitments surely place her or his chosen approach well above the run of social science methods. The question here is not just one of intellectual superiority, but of the ethical shakiness of the hit-and-run approach of far too much social investigation. The postal survey, the telephone interview and the like are not merely shallow forms of data collection, but imply no commitment to the complexity of social actors' lives, no long-term engagement with them, and can do nothing to respect the particularities of given social worlds. To that extent, they are not merely limited in terms of their ability to tell us about the social world, but are ethically impoverished too. Life-history and similar biographical research, on the other hand, can share with ethnographic research the sort of interpersonal and long-term commitment I am invoking here. The two perspectives (and their respective forms of publication) represent a style of social investigation that conveys an adequate respect for social actors. I really do mean life-history work here. Series of de-contextualised, one-off individual interviews with informants do *not* qualify. Much social science research approximates the cynical collection of personal information that is the stock-in-trade of contemporary commercial interests. Wistful reflections that commerce has more digital information than social scientists, as if that were a problem for the social scientists, are unfortunate in this regard. Insofar as it fails to capture the social and cultural nature of social life, a great deal of conventional social research is scientifically flawed, as well as being jejune.

The relationship between ethics, qualitative research more widely, and ethnography more narrowly, is not a new topic. Indeed, there have been numerous commentaries on the conduct of research and the contemporary practice of ethical oversight (cf. Denzin and Giardina 2007), and these debates are in turn embedded in much wider frameworks of political dispute, feminist debate and postcolonial discourse; in some quarters, qualitative research is explicitly directed towards resistance against American neo-conservatism (e.g. Denzin and Giardina 2009). These are all contentious issues that impinge on the politics and ethics of ethnographic research, but in this chapter I focus on a more restricted range of issues that remain pressing for practical researchers and that demand collective responses on their part, as well as personal reflection by individual researchers.

Ethical regulation has been largely inspired by biomedical research. This point has been made sufficiently often that it does not in itself require further elaboration. The models that are implicitly developed in the social sciences are fundamentally based on those that have been developed for the management of medical research activities, such as clinical trials. Here the primary, though by no means sole, interest has been on the informed consent of individuals who agree to take part in a trial. The significance of informed consent was enshrined in post-Nuremberg codes of ethics from their inception. In one sense it is hard to quarrel with the general principle. Clearly, one would not want human subjects to participate in experiments or trials unwillingly. Coercion would seem wrong and contrary to our most cherished beliefs. Likewise, it seems incontrovertible that participants should not merely consent, but should do so with knowledge and understanding of what risks might be involved, if any. There is, therefore, a form of contract between the researcher(s) and the participants that establishes an appropriate balance of rights and obligations, freely entered into, and fully understood on both sides. In biomedical research such a contract is a thoroughly skewed one, while ethnography approximates a much more equal set of relationships. Research-based critiques of persuasion to participate in clinical trials include Barton (2007) and Barton and Eggly (2009); for research on participants' limited understandings of RCT participation, see Featherstone and Donovan 1996; 2002.

The biomedical model has been widened to apply to many other forms of research involving human subjects. Given their nature, the social sciences are involved in ethical review and approval more than any other field of research outside of biomedicine. Yet the models and their implicit assumptions about the nature of research are themselves sociologically or anthropologically deficient, and they rarely apply in any satisfactory way to the conduct of ethnographic research. This is not merely a technical issue of research design, nor is it simply a narrowly sectarian issue, based on differences in disciplinary cultures. This certainly does not derive from any inherent lack of ethical principles on the part of ethnographers; it does demonstrate how poorly research of all sorts is served by the culture of biomedicine.

Let us consider things a little more concretely. A cursory inspection of most ethics committees' protocols will demonstrate how problematic they can be. It is common for applicants for ethical approval to have to answer a check-list of closed questions, and to amplify on any of the answers if any of them is the dispreferred response (usually 'no'). Most ethnographers will, however, know that the answers they give will be at best half-truths, and that they are often at risk of misrepresentation (at least, in the eyes of an unsympathetic and literal-minded investigator). Consider, for instance, the seemingly innocuous question 'Will participants be informed of their right to withdraw from the research at any stage?', some version of which is enshrined in most protocols. At first sight it seems impossible to quibble with the basic right of a research participant to withdraw, and to do so at any stage of the research process. The participant's right to do so would seem self-evidently to over-ride the interests and convenience of the researcher. From the ethnographer's point of the view, however, such an issue is far more complex. It goes back one stage to the nature of 'participation' and 'participants'. For the right to withdraw from a research project is predicated on the assumption that one participates on an individualistic basis, and that any participant is, in principle, equivalent to any other. But the reality of fieldwork suggests that a quite different form of social contract must underpin it. In simple terms, an individual cannot withdraw from an ethnographic project if he or she is a member of a collectivity, without in effect vetoing the participation of all others who are willing, even enthusiastic, research hosts. The ethnography of, say, a research laboratory cannot proceed if just one scientist withdraws completely and denies the anthropologist the opportunity to be present in the laboratory, to observe research group meetings and so on. He or she can, of course, decline to be interviewed or otherwise be involved on an individual basis. The difference between the individual interview and membership of the research group is precisely the crux that renders most ethical protocols anthropologically naïve at best. My own ethnography of the Welsh National Opera Company (Atkinson 2006) could have been rendered quite impossible had one member of the company withdrawn her or his 'participation', while all had the opportunity to talk to me or not on a purely voluntary basis.

As we know, the great majority of ethnographic research projects depend on the successful negotiation and maintenance of *access*. Access covers a number of embedded issues. It means far more than simply physical access to a given research site. It means that social actors grant the researcher access to their everyday lives: they grant licence to witness, participate in and converse about issues that might otherwise reach a more restricted social circle. It means having privileged access to the everyday activities of organisations, associations and networks that are based on some sense of *membership*. They do not have to be especially secret or esoteric; merely they have to be settings or groupings that are not perfectly open and public. (I recognise that this glosses over the fact that many 'public' settings are by no means unrestricted, as many photographers, skateboarders, rough-sleepers and other potential users of space know to their cost.) The idea of *membership* in this context is very different from the idea of *participation* that is enshrined in most codes of ethics. The reason for this is simple. As I have already noted, most of these codes are based on biomedical models. And most of those are based on individualistic modes of enrolment. The individual patient agrees to be allocated randomly to the experimental or control arm of a clinical trial. The paid volunteer enters upon a drugs trial on her or his own account. Each participant is equivalent to any other. If there is randomisation involved, each has an equal chance of allocation to one or other arm of a study. In the analysis of the data, each participant is treated separately as a data point.

Since each participant is a separate monad within standard biomedical research, it makes perfect sense to treat her or him on this individualistic basis. Individual actors 'enter' or 'enrol' on the research, and they can 'withdraw' on an equally individual, voluntaristic basis. Thought of in this light, the question from the hypothetical ethics-committee protocol I used as a starting-point makes perfect sense. But why does it not make perfect sense for the ethnographer? For the reasons we have already alluded to. We normally do not enrol a series of individual participants for our research. We are normally dealing with social actors because they are members of an organisation, or are privy to some activity that we wish to study. Membership is very different from simple individual participation.

Obviously, our access negotiations involve ethical issues. Discussions of access have for a long time dealt with the kinds of bargains that researchers enter into with their hosts. But again it needs to be understood that these are largely about the collective rights and interests of the members of the social setting. We guarantee individual anonymity, certainly. But we also give undertakings not to harm the organisation, or indeed to divulge its identity in some (not all) cases. But access must imply a commitment that is more than merely individual. In concrete terms, how can it make sense for the would-be ethnographer, who has carefully negotiated access to, say, a research laboratory, with all the reasonable undertakings and assurances that might be expected, to say that the research can be brought to a complete halt if one individual person seeks to withdraw? For that is what it would probably mean. It is not possible to study an organisation on the basis that one or more individuals has withdrawn consent. Can it make sense for one school pupil to change her or his mind, and so exclude the researcher from observing all the other pupils in a class? Does it make sense for the researcher studying the laboratory to agree to abort the study if one laboratory technician decides to withdraw goodwill? In some contexts, of course, one disaffected or unwilling member can render the research intolerable or impossible, but it is not clear that the regulation of research makes sense if the assumption is built in from the outset that this is part-and-parcel of the research design.

As may be envisaged, the ethnographer – confronted with the ethics committee's questionnaire with its deceptively simple item – needs to answer 'Yes, but ...', or 'No, but ...' and expand on the responses at considerable length. Now this is not simply a matter of filling forms, for what is illustrated in a concrete fashion is the profoundly mistaken view of social research enshrined in such protocols. Let us, for instance, consider further the elementary and foundational issue of 'informed consent'. It seems like the sort of ethical principle that we would all want to subscribe to. But in reality it is far from clear what informed consent actually means in most research, and certainly far from clear what it can mean for the conduct of ethnographic research. We need the sort of analysis of ethics protocols that Cicourel (1964) famously performed for the survey interview. In the context of real-world research, all such questions require considerable interpretative work to render them sensible. But it is precisely that background understanding that most ethics protocols transform into a 'check-list' form of anticipatory audit. It therefore becomes all but impossible to respond in good faith.

One may, after all, consent to take part in a research project in the conventional way. It is not clear, however, how far beyond data collection most informed consent procedures go in practice, or can go in principle. I may agree to be interviewed about my consumption preferences. I may give consent on the basis that my personal information will not be divulged. But to what extent do I give consent for my data to be pooled with that derived from others, and then subjected to statistical manipulation? Should my consent be sought to manipulate the data in accordance with basic demographic, face-sheet data? Should I give my consent to have my personal information aggregated and cross-tabulated in order to generate, say, gender differences, or ethnic differences in consumption? Should I be asked if I consent to having the information transformed into ideal-typical models of taste and *habitus*, in the style of Pierre Bourdieu? The answer to these questions is that most researchers would find it bizarre to have to predict every possible analytic *outcome* and every unanticipated *finding* of the analysis. And in reality, most researchers are asked about the collection of data and the protection of individual subjects' identity: they are rarely called upon to anticipate the findings of research. As a consequence, most 'informed consent' is so minimally informed as to be virtually worthless. Hammersley has recently argued that certain forms of analysis may be thought of as unethical. If I have interviewed an informant about some substantive topic – their state of health for instance – they have probably not given informed consent to have their words subjected to discourse analysis or narrative analysis (Hammersley 2014). Returning to a theme in the previous chapter, one might also ask to what extent people may give their informed consent to having their words transformed into poems or one-act plays. Of course, most researchers are not expected or required to go back to their survey informants to ask their consent to publish the result that many people with their particular characteristic score highly on a scale of authoritarian attitudes (for example). Equally, we do not normally require ethnographers to return to the field and re-negotiate permissions because they have come up with a completely unforeseen line of analysis. But perhaps one should if informed consent were to be taken literally and to its logical conclusion. Of course, one can turn such arguments round somewhat, by suggesting that most informed consent is nugatory, since informants, participants and hosts can never be given accurate predictions of all that might be done with data and precisely what kinds of findings are likely to emerge.

Ethnographers would find it especially difficult to establish the boundaries of informed consent in any case. This case has been argued persuasively by a number of authors, including Murphy and Dingwall (2007). This is not because we wish, in most cases, to engage in covert research, but because the nature of the research itself is so profoundly an emergent property of the processes of data collection and research design, that are themselves emergent, unfolding processes, that it becomes all but impossible to solicit consent to the research that is 'informed' in the sense of being predictable and explicable before the research itself is carried out. If the outcomes of an ethnography were entirely predictable, then there would be virtually no point in conducting the research at all. It is, after all, possible to discover issues that are critical of the institution or association studied, quite unpredictably, that cannot be incorporated into undertakings before the event. It may, for instance, be a research outcome that educational institutions have practices that have deleterious consequences for students, based on gender, ethnicity or social class. One may document similar sources of bias among the police or other agencies of social control. A clinic may implicitly ration health care on the basis of social characteristics. It is hard to guarantee – for the purposes of informed consent – that nothing will be discovered to the disadvantage of the institution, even if individual members' identities are not to be divulged. Admittedly, we often have to persuade potential research hosts that we are *not* in search of the discreditable or the scurrilous, and in most cases we are more interested in the humdrum routines of everyday life than most people give us credit for. But however much we may stress that for ethical and analytic purposes, it is still hard to ensure that no possible criticism of an institution or association will be implied by our findings. As Murphy and Dingwall (2007) point out, the iterative nature of ethnographic inquiry means that access is always tentative and conditional, that 'consent' is always relational and sequential, rather than based on a one-off contractual agreement, and that ethnographic researchers will never find it possible to specify at the outset all that their research will involve. Covert research can, of course, uncover phenomena that would otherwise remain inscrutable – see Prokos and Padavic (2002) for an example documenting sexism in a police academy – but my argument is not about that. The problem is, rather, the anthropological impossibility of 'informed consent' to any meaningful extent.

A good example of unanticipated research, that incidentally reflects back on the status of the clinical trial as the 'gold standard', is furnished from my own research on haematologists (Atkinson 1995). I attended many clinical conferences and meetings at which cases were 'presented'. My main interest was in the rhetoric and performance of such clinical work. But in the course of those case conferences, it became apparent that the precise diagnosis and classification of some patients was being contested by professional colleagues. The description and staging of some tumours by at least one clinician were being queried. The strong suspicion was that these particular patients, who were being enrolled into a multi-site clinical trial, were being described in such a way as to make them conform to the particular clinical requirements of that trial. This was not a matter of wholesale professional misconduct. But at the margins, where diagnostic criteria were not clear-cut, the patients were being included in the trial in accordance with the clinician's interests, rather than in terms of the collegial consensus expressed by clinical pathologists and other specialists. Now this was not a central part of the research, and the detail of that aspect of the ethnography has never been published, there being no pressing reason to do so. But it illustrates quite vividly the sort of ethical dilemmas that can arise in the course of conducting and analysing ethnographic work. Incidentally, of course, it illustrates some of the problematic issues of the clinical trial itself as the model of research. The diagnostic criteria for inclusion or exclusion depend upon the practical judgements of medical practitioners, and while the allocation of patients to one or other arm of the trial may be based on chance, and be double-blinded, the diagnostic work that determines their eligibility for participation is not and cannot be. This is indeed a classic case of an apparently 'hard' research design depending on much 'softer' personal judgements.

I have illustrated just some ways in which features of contemporary ethics discourse and practice are poorly suited to the ethnographic enterprise. This is not because I am proposing a form of ethnographic work that is covert, or unethical. Rather, the individualistic assumptions built into contemporary practice, and derived from unsuitable models, do not fit the purposes and practical conduct of ethnographic research. This is, incidentally, one way in which the conduct of ethnographic fieldwork differs from much of what is currently done under the rubric of qualitative research. As I have rehearsed more than once in this book, much of the latter is in fact based on interviewing series of individual informants (Atkinson and Silverman 1997). While there remain significant ethical issues about the proper representation of such informants' interview talk, the general models of informed consent approximate much more closely when one is conducting one-off informant interviews. Genuine *field* research, on the other hand, escapes the assumptions that inform current regulatory practice.

It is instructive to reflect on the extent to which social scientists are hindering their own research, and the existence of double standards in public life. The world is full of intellectual and popular work that would never pass muster with the average research ethics committee, but it is not governed by such committees, nor does anybody seem to call its practitioners to account. There have been several recent publications based on various forms of deceptive, surreptitious and covert research. In one case, the act of deception was absolutely central to the theme of the book. In her first book, *Self-Made Man*, Norah Vincent (2006) describes a protracted period in which she dressed as male, made herself up to look male (including the creation of reasonably convincing stubble) and learned to act as a male in contemporary America. But the acquisition of personal experience was completely unethical, judged by the standards of academic research. Likewise, Ehrenreich's undercover study of corporate recruitment is a classic exposé based on procedures that would be regarded as ethnographically unethical (Ehrenreich 2006). Popular works of this sort can be justified in terms of the extent to which the author disguises individual identities, and muddies the water by fictionalising individuals and reported events. This is, quite explicitly, the approach taken by Julian Baggini (2007), who set up house in the English town of Rotherham, in order to discover at first hand the 'facts' of everyday life in the most representative postcode neighbourhood in England. He provides a sort of classic 'community study' account. He acknowledges, however, that his acquaintances had not given permission to be quoted or identified, and so he mixes identities and creates composite characters. The crucial point, of course, is that no social scientist would be allowed to behave ethically *post hoc* in the absence of explicit informed consent. Popular works escape such constraints.

There is a long, and perfectly honourable tradition of exploratory and investigative work by journalists and other authors. It overlaps with a similar genre of autobiographical writing in which the author embarks on a personal quest or adventure, writes about her or his experiences, and in the process writes about a variety of other people as well as providing graphic descriptions of distinctive social settings and locales. Recent examples include an account of a young English man learning the martial art *aikido* in Japan (Twigger 1999), an unmusical Englishman following up the quixotic decision to play Cuban music in Cuba and to find *la bomba*, the spirit of Cuban soul (Neill 2005), a man's quest for authentic flamenco guitar and its spirit of *duende* (Webster 2004), and the quest for expertise in blues guitar (Hodgkinson 2006), and other quests to engage with martial arts (Polly 2007; Preston 2007). Clearly these and similar works constitute a genre in their own right, and are predicated on the twin themes of personal discovery and the search for authentic experience. But they have the common property of being silent as to whether the many people who have taught and helped the author granted explicit permission for the author's activities to be turned into a book.

At the other end of the spectrum from the professional social scientist is the work of the author of fiction or the professional actor. Sebastian Faulks researched a novel (*Human Traces*) by interviewing psychiatrists and patients in order to inform his account of mental illness. One of his key informants is acknowledged by name; a mental-health media volunteer, she no doubt helped the novelist in the full knowledge of what she was doing, but social scientists would normally be reluctant to name their gatekeepers, sponsors or informants. Siri Hustvedt taught as a volunteer in the Payne Whitney Psychiatric Clinic in order to research one of her novels, *The Sorrows of an American*. Now I do not mention these examples in order to say 'Look at what journalists and fiction authors get away with' in order to justify a free-for-all. But these examples – that could be repeated many times over – help to illustrate a number of things. First, social scientists are in danger of handicapping themselves, for no very good reason, and leaving it to others who are not so obsessively regulated to produce the equivalent of ethnographic insight. Second, journalists, playwrights and other investigators could reasonably ask 'What harm has been done to anybody?'. Indeed, one can point to the value of researching books and articles, in order to ensure their accuracy, and propose that – in the absence of any harm – there is every justification for doing such work. Once you designate something as professional research, however, you are immediately drawn into the nexus of ethics committees and similar institutional bodies. Social scientists seem to be in danger of hobbling themselves while others gain an advantage.

It is puzzling that social scientists have found themselves on the back foot in recent years. It is doubly ironic that ethnographers should sometimes find themselves especially wrong-footed by ethics committees and similar review boards. There is singularly little evidence to be found that the conduct of ethnographic research has actually led to any harm whatsoever. Even field research that might be viewed as contravening current standards of ethical approval rarely seems to have been *harmful*. On the other hand, the technicalities of medical ethics committees have *not* prevented actual (in some cases, grievous) harm to trial participants. Such egregious errors and failures are not routinely treated as reasons to abandon the entire enterprise of biomedical research.

My examples from the world of literature and journalism also help to remind us of the sheer complexity of the social world and the multiplicity of ways in which we can engage with and document it. We are in danger of allowing the quite proper concerns for research ethics in general to transform the entire research process into a formulaic one, such that there are only a very limited number of permissible research designs, determined not by their general epistemology, nor by their validity, but by their capacity to yield simple research protocols that can be checked against a set of simple (but often inappropriate) criteria. Anticipatory audit is the tail that wags the research dog.

So far I have not even considered the very limited view of 'ethics' that is enshrined in the procedures of committees. As we have seen, they seek to enforce a model based on individual participants, and are concerned primarily about their informed consent. There is singularly little attention granted in the written codes and guidelines to other – arguably more important – issues. The following are some issues that might well be thought to be significant: giving adequate analytic attention to muted, marginal or subaltern social categories; ensuring that the rhetoric of publications does justice to the reported actions and actors; ensuring that research promotes the interests of social justice. There are many such 'ethics' that can be derived from critical, feminist, postcolonialist and other standpoints. But ethics regulation is all too often predicated on a model of positive science, with no regard for more general cultural and political considerations.

In contrast, the conduct of ethnographic research has been predicated on a set of commitments and values that arguably render it much more sensitive to the interests of 'participants', and make the personal values of the researcher(s) more central than most other forms of research. Ethnographic research calls for a greater personal commitment to the field and its members than virtually any other mode of research. Ethnographers spend months and years of their lives working closely with social actors as they go about their own daily lives. The commitment of ethnographers to engage with forms of social life is one that goes beyond virtually any other research strategy. Indeed, it is noticeable in the examples cited above that when authors such as novelists want to explore the authenticity of a given cultural form, they find themselves engaging in participant observation, even though they do not grace it with the term. Of course, they do not and cannot commit the sort of time and analytic effort that social scientists do and should devote to the exercise.

In the ideal world, the ethics of social research would be predicated on a different set of approaches. It is worth reminding ourselves that the word *protocol* can have different connotations. In the sense most used in today's research communities, it means a prescriptive set of injunctions and prohibitions that regulates research. It captures the sense in which research and its proper management have been treated in *procedural* terms, reducible to check-lists and formulae. On the other hand, protocol can also refer to proper conduct. And we ought to think of research conduct in this more general – and indeed more social – sense. We need to work to refine the collective sense of research protocols in terms that are driven by *values* rather than by *procedures*. For instance, many ethnographers spend a good deal of time developing trust with their hosts and informants. The promotion and development of such a positive interpersonal working relationship might provide a more anthropologically and sociologically informed basis for proper conduct than the jejune notion of informed consent based on a single paper-based transaction. Likewise, the establishment of social relationships in the field should be recognised for what it is – a *process* rather than an event that can be predetermined and inscribed within a single document. This would recognise that research projects have a trajectory, rather than a fixed, linear design. It would also take account of the fact that social relations in the field are of different sorts, from the most intimate to merely fleeting encounters and acquaintanceships. They cannot be subsumed under a single category of research participants, and the degree of consent or disclosure simply cannot be the same for all the individuals who might be present in and pass through a research site. Likewise, we need to assess the proper ways of treating persons who are observed in public places, when no social relationships are developed on the part of the ethnographer. Again, informed consent is an unhelpful approach in such contexts.

The extent of indeterminacy and unpredictability in field research ought to be appreciated in the course of research planning, and hence in the process of ethical approval. This is not tantamount to *carte blanche* based on a claim that nothing can be foreseen. But if research is guided by values and general principles, and their general application outlined, rather than enshrined in highly specific and prescriptive check-lists, then research can be carried out humanely, sensibly and in accordance with positive values. The big problem that arises in contemporary practice reflects the fact that it is not congruent with general sociological or anthropological imagination. Because of its individualistic emphases on informed consent, it does not map well onto the realities of ethnographic research, as we have seen. As a consequence, ethical regulation by contemporary ethics committees can have very undesirable unintended consequences. It can force scholars who have a very thorough commitment to working well with their research hosts into a form of deviance. Because ethics protocols are sometimes half-baked, they force the researchers into half-truths. It is clearly undesirable if ethical issues in general are perceived as something to be worked around, rather than providing a positive framework for practical research conduct.

Equally, requirements for formal documentation of informed consent can radically transform emergent (or even established) social relations in the field, by imposing an inappropriate degree of formality on otherwise informal relations that are embedded in the ordinary give-and-take of social life. It transforms the pre-contractual and mutual nature of everyday life into the contractual obligations of individual self-interest and protection. Moreover, there is every temptation towards deviance. There is certainly anecdotal evidence to suggest that ethnographers feel constrained to represent their research as if it were merely a series of extended interviews, accompanied by individual consent by the informants. Any fieldwork is quietly relegated to the background, so that the letter of ethical approval can be sustained while the more bone-headed aspects of regulation can be circumvented. This, in turn, helps to fuel that unwarranted reliance on interview data rather than the observation and recording of social action *in situ*.

Does all this mean that there is no place for ethical considerations? By no means, but we must start from our anthropological, sociological understandings of the research process and the social worlds we work with. We need to remind ourselves that a research contract between researcher and hosts inescapably rests on pre-contractual bases of mutual trust. We need to ensure that social research is underpinned by practices and understandings that are in accordance with such research itself, and do not run counter to them. This will not be achieved by trying to fit ethnographical fieldwork to the procrustean bed of current procedure; nor will it be achieved simply by tinkering with current paperwork. Meanwhile, as social scientists contrive to tie themselves in knots over the ethical approval of their research projects, large areas of everyday life go reported with minimal ethical regulation. In the face of massive failures of data protection by financial institutions, government departments and other public agencies, it is hard to take seriously the need for committees to devote much of their time, and by doing so delay research activities, to micro-managing the detailed wording of consent forms and assurances of anonymity before a social scientist can interview another social actor who is entirely *compos mentis* and capable of consenting to granting an interview. It is, of course, hard to imagine just how one might coerce an informant to grant an ethnographic interview or to narrate a life-history lasting several hours if he or she did not consent to such an activity.

The burden of my comments is not to advocate wholesale rejection of or resistance to the general principles of ethical oversight of research. My argument is this: If the general oversight of research is to be taken seriously, rather than regarded as a nuisance that invites rule-breaking, then it needs to be grounded in an expert understanding of the complexities of everyday social life and of the contingencies of real-life social research. The imposition of ill-informed frameworks does nothing to enhance the quality of research, the credibility of research, or the uses to which it is put. Indeed, the danger is that the manifest inadequacy of current ethical guidelines will lead social scientists into half-truths, if not outright deception. The translation of 'ethics' into box-ticking exercises, based on a threadbare conception of the research process itself, is liable to be self-defeating, by encouraging procedural deviance rather than research informed by the best available values and standards of conduct that are derived from and inform research about everyday social conduct.

It is incumbent upon sociologists, anthropologists and others to insist to multiple audiences that the intellectual commitments of ethnographic research are profoundly ethical, in ways that are not even approximated by bureaucratic protocols. Such commitments do not, however, necessarily entail the sort of rhetoric of 'social justice' promoted by Norman Denzin and his colleagues (e.g. Denzin and Giardina 2007). While the social sciences are often, and in principle, exercises in the service of social justice, I do not share the view that the particular perspectives of postmodernism, alternative literary forms, the conduct of autoethnography or personal testimony, or so-called qualitative inquiry in general are inherently aimed at the promotion of social justice. My comments on research ethics and the particularities of ethnographic fieldwork are predicated on a much more conventional view of scholarship and its commitments. Ethnographic research has its distinctive ethical issues and perspectives. That does not entail a wholesale re-casting of the scholarly enterprise, however. The highest ethical imperative is, from my own point of view, a fidelity to everyday life and its complex, detailed processes. This end is not served by a form of ethical reductionism that simply equates qualitative research with a higher good, without an adequate exploration of how such qualitative research actually represents and reconstructs everyday life.

Indeed, we have to recognise another moral imperative, which is actually shared with conventional biomedical research ethics. If research activities are scientifically flawed, then their intrusion on people's everyday lives is not justified. Hence ethical, moral research must be methodical, well-informed, well-grounded in previous research evidence. The self-indulgence of experiential and autoethnographic writing rarely match up to such elementary requirements. Consequently, their ethical status – insofar as they involve people other than the author – is often questionable. Furthermore, as Delamont (2009) has pointed out, some autoethnographic writing, such as the misery-memoir genre of writing about one's family-members (e.g. Ronai 1996) can be distinctly unethical.

Although I have suggested that ethnographic fieldwork is inherently ethical, I do not want to conclude by suggesting that any research strategy is justified primarily by moral or personal commitments alone. Like Hammersley and Traianou (2012), I do not subscribe to the sort of 'moralism' that insists that any form of research is inherently personally or politically justified. The commitments of ethnographic fieldwork do not in themselves confer sainthood. Ethnographers – or qualitative researchers more generally – too often claim to be special and different. We are, of course, used to the image of the anthropologist as hero. In earlier generations, the anthropologist could portray her- or himself as heroic in a traditional manner: an explorer in a strange land; among strangers; making sense of the unknown; facing physical and moral danger (Atkinson 1996). In more recent years, perhaps, that heroic mould has changed somewhat. While fieldworkers undoubtedly face issues of personal safety in a wide variety of settings, the heroism is likely to take more of a *moral* heroism. The anthropologist in particular is now more inclined to claim a distinctive form of authenticity – not merely of knowledge, but also of personal virtue and experience. The undeniable element of *participation* in the field, and of the consequently *dialogic* nature of the field experience all too often are used as the basis for claims to a kind of moral superiority.

The anthropologist-as-hero occupies a special place in the moral discourse of the disciplines. He or she, first of all, attributes none of these personal virtues to any other practitioner of the social sciences. Anthropologists repeatedly deny that others also practise ethnographic fieldwork, and collectively they cannot conceive of anyone else laying claim to such a methodological commitment. This is because it is not a methodological issue for them, it is a personal one. Ineffable, mysterious in its essence, ethnography in this academic world escapes any methodological precepts and training (especially among British practitioners). It is in that sense, therefore, that heroism is claimed. The Promethean ethnographer snatches understanding from her or his personal commitment to the field, and from a commitment to a form of life. Now one does not want to caricature the position unduly, but I think plenty of social scientists will recognise this picture. It is one of the things that gives anthropology – British anthropology in particular – its distinctive strength. It ensures a community of initiates who – whatever their doctrinal differences and petty jealousies – share an unshakable confidence in their own superiority. They do not acknowledge any ethnography beyond their own circles, and completely fail to recognise that others have been conducting it for as long as they have. No matter. We must continue to co-exist, and to take the best from a variety of different disciplinary and national traditions in the interests of careful, well-informed field research.

When I assert that ethnographic fieldwork is an inherently ethical undertaking by virtue of its fidelity to everyday sociality, therefore, that does not mean that it justifies self-righteousness. The latter is to be found among too many *soi-disant* qualitative researchers, who seem to believe that there is a moral superiority in being postmodern, and eschewing nasty positivist tendencies, such as a commitment to getting things right (since 'truth' is an outlawed term in their worldview). There is nothing inherently moral or ethical, however, about sloppy research, self-indulgent writing, or the rejection of ordinary criteria for the adequacy of research (or indeed any investigation). Indeed, I would suggest that work in this vein includes too much activity of dubious value for it to be regarded as inherently praiseworthy. In contrast, it is possible to have research that respects the fluidity and unpredictability of everyday life without that research itself lacking systematic method. It is possible – imperative, even – to accompany fieldwork with the hard intellectual work of analysis, not just impressionistic evocation. In that sense, therefore, I find myself in almost complete agreement with Hammersley and Traianou (2012) when they propose that the researcher's most important commitment is to conduct research in the interest of producing knowledge.

11

Conclusions

This book has been something of a manifesto, a personal statement of commitment and of enthusiasm. On the way I have inevitably been critical of a number of trends and tendencies. My own personal and intellectual commitment to the conduct of ethnographic fieldwork is not without caution. We need to conclude, therefore, with a stock-taking: Where are we collectively and what are the prospects for ethnography – as a research method and as a genre?

To begin with, I need to repeat myself a little. In the first place, the dissemination and reception of qualitative research have an odd position in the social sciences. On the one hand, they enjoy unprecedented popularity. Among the social sciences, qualitative methods continue to be widespread. They are no longer confined to anthropology or sociology. Cultural geographers and discursive psychologists also make major contributions, methodological and substantive. The applied fields (health, nursing, education, criminology, social work) have substantial bodies of research that show no sign of flagging. There are some quarters where qualitative research seems under attack. In the United Kingdom we have witnessed a discourse of derision concerning qualitative research and its evidential value in educational research. In the United States, qualitative work has been perceived to be under threat, excluded from key funding opportunities. There is no doubt that in some quarters – academic and political – quantitative evidence takes precedence.

In the United Kingdom and elsewhere we periodically witness a form of academic moral panic focused on a supposed quantitative deficit. Cyclically, we are told that there is a desperate shortage of social scientists who are trained to an adequate level in social statistics. The implication is often that quantitative skills are the proper stuff of research, while qualitative research is the easy option. The imagery of hard and soft approaches is easily adopted, and stereotyped views often prevail. But the popularity of qualitative research does not mean that it is always well done. In many quarters we suffer a form of qualitative deficit, because too many students and practitioners seem to think that it really *is* a soft option. We have far too many poorly conducted and under-analysed studies, and qualitative researchers can too often be their own worst enemies, confirming those damaging stereotypes. I shall not repeat myself yet again here: it is clear in the preceding chapters where my reservations lie.

So to some extent, criticisms of generic qualitative research can be well founded. We have to combat poor quality research wherever it is found, irrespective of whether it is quantitative or qualitative in nature. The other side of the argument is clear, however. We need collectively to encourage and to celebrate the methodical and thorough conduct of ethnographic research, with all the skills and effort that it implies. In the course of this book, I have outlined just some of the analytic issues that need to be incorporated into such an approach.

But is ethnography being weakened or under threat? I think not, although there are challenges that affect ethnographic research (and similar undertakings) in the current academic field. There are, almost always, funding pressures. Ethnographic fieldwork is demanding not only of the researcher's personal commitment and imagination, but also of time. And time is expensive. For many scholars, the doctoral years are a precious and rare opportunity to undertake ethnographic fieldwork and to analyse their materials thoroughly. Pressures to complete the doctorate and have it examined as speedily as possible can squeeze even that precious period. Moreover, as any experienced practitioner will attest, it takes time to write up ethnographic work for publication. Unlike, say, the experimentalist, we ethnographers cannot readily publish interim results, or write up a series of self-contained studies relatively quickly. Consequently, pressures for rapid publication (for employment, tenure, promotion and for grant applications) can prove difficult for those committed to fieldwork. Such pressures can readily lead us to take a line of least resistance: a series of focus-groups or a small number of in-depth interviews can lend themselves to a much quicker turn-round and publication schedule. Consequently, we need research directors and research funders to recognise the return on investment in research time.

Equally, we need to ensure that research methods are adequately taught, also with sufficient investments of time. We shall not ensure ethnographic work of the highest quality if it is technically limited. This means much more than superficial courses in 'qualitative research' as if that were enough to develop all of the necessary knowledge and skills. If we are going to be faithful to the social and cultural complexity I have been referring to, then we need graduate students who are adept at collecting and analysing interactional data, narrative and discursive data, visual and sonic materials and sensory data. They need to have a decent acquaintance with the full range of sociological, anthropological and other perspectives that should inform their work. They need to know enough about a range of published work that allows them to make informed and disciplined comparisons. Above all, they need practical apprenticeship in the conduct of research. Again, this takes time.

In return, we need to maintain ethnographic research that is directed at the production of sustained, disciplined knowledge about social worlds and social processes. We cannot and will not justify investment in research that is self-indulgent, such as the stream of autoethnography and sentimental writing that is disproportionately influential in some quarters. There are currently plenty of examples of published ethnographic research that amply justify themselves, and they continue in the best traditions that have informed ethnographic research for decades. They address major issues in contemporary social life, and they do so in ways that no other style of social research can emulate: Alice Goffman (2014) on the margins of American urban life; May Joseph (2013) on contemporary urbanism in New York City; Karen Ho (2009) on working lives and cultures on Wall Street; Adriana Petryna (2009) on the international trade in biomedical experiments and human subjects; Daniel Briggs (2012) on crack cocaine users in London. The potential list is, if not endless, extensive. These and many monographs like them are not works that, as it were, just *happen* to be ethnographic in their inspiration and their method. In their intimate engagement with their subject-matter, and in the recurrent dialogue between the local and the generic, these studies could have been enacted and written in no other way. Incidentally, inspection of those selected texts – and again the list could be extremely long – shows that they owe little or nothing to pettifogging 'methods' issues. They do not concern themselves with this or that version of grounded theory, or the niceties of the extended-case method. What they do contain is the result of detailed fieldwork, attentive to local organisation and cultural forms, reported without recourse to fancy textual footwork.

At the time of writing, sectors in the United Kingdom and the United States have also introduced an academic policy that may prove antipathetic to ethnographic work. It concerns *open access* publishing. In essence it derives from the belief that research that has been funded by public money should be freely available. It is made possible by virtue of digital, on-line publishing. It also means that the researcher (her or his funding body or university) pays for the publication costs, while the publications are free to all readers. Now this policy has been very poorly thought through (a frequent enough phenomenon) and derives mainly from the physical and biomedical sciences (equally frequent in their influence). The great majority of research on the sciences is externally funded, and publication in journals is the norm. But when we turn to the humanities and social sciences, there is a different picture. A good deal of research is not externally funded, and it remains unclear who will pay for publication. Moreover, the *monograph* is the life-blood of many disciplines, and the ethnographic monograph remains the desirable outcome for many an ethnographic project. It remains far from clear just how 'open access' monographs are to be managed. That might not matter were it not for the fact that UK academics (among others) face periodic national reviews of research excellence (the Research Assessment Exercise as was, the Research Excellence Framework as it currently is). And currently the threat is that only open access publications will 'count' in future exercises. Given that there is also talk of a co-ordinated international programme of research evaluation, such issues may become pressing beyond the national boundaries of the UK. A classic compromise or fudge will probably be the final outcome, but it is not a healthy environment for the publication of monographs.

There is, of course, pressure on the ethnographic monograph from elsewhere. Many publishers are simply not interested in such books. Commercial publishers often want books that can sell in large numbers – thousands or tens of thousands – mainly to students, while monographs sell a couple of hundred copies. This is not a totally glum picture. There remain publishers who are committed to monographs, but even they can find it hard. The University presses and some commercial publishers can certainly make ends meet, but that means that the cover price for each monograph can be considerable, and sale restricted to libraries. Meanwhile, library budgets are being squeezed (which contributes to a general reluctance to pay for expensive journal subscriptions) and libraries want to concentrate on providing 'resources' for students rather than acting as repositories of research for academics. It is a vicious circle that may endanger the academic monograph. Ultimately, of course, that will impoverish the disciplines that are fed by book-length research works. In the social sciences that could mean a monoculture comprising general textbooks, methods texts and works of general social theory. All will be deprived of much of the evidence-base that makes them and their disciplines worthwhile. We already have too much social 'theory' that is devoid of any direct evidence about the social world, and we should do all we can to resist such a culture of publishing. Ethnographic research is undoubtedly publishable in academic journals, and we are not totally dependent on the scholarly monograph. But the monograph remains the major outcome of sustained ethnographic fieldwork.

There will be ways to preserve the monograph, even if it is not quite in its current form. In some quarters, that will involve the production of e-books (or whatever embodies that principle in the foreseeable future) that offer more than the conventional printed book. We are starting to see examples of that kind of genre. Throughout this book I have made reference to the multiple modalities of social action and cultural forms. We therefore will potentially benefit from forms of publication that are faithful to those modes of organisation. Digital resources can thus be used to capture visual, audio and documentary materials in addition to the more conventional text.

A truly digital environment offers much more than simply links to websites or to other storage media through which illustrative examples can be accessed. The use of hypertext and then hypermedia software and the possibility of a digital ethnographic environment presented extended opportunities for ethnographic representation and authoring. Weaver and Atkinson (1994) explored the possibilities of hypertext for enhanced ethnographic analysis and writing. Hypertext dissolved the distinctions between data navigation on the one hand and authoring on the other. Analytic commentary could be hyperlinked to data-sets, to audio- and video-recordings, to background documents, to literature reviews and summaries. Indeed, the navigational possibilities were highly flexible. Most importantly, the hypertext strategy emphasised the extent to which an ethnography might be non-linear. The opportunity for an analyst or a reader to navigate by taking multiple pathways through multiple texts and representations suggested digital resources could be faithful to the intrinsic complexity of any given social world. Moreover, they would support simultaneous, multiple interpretative frames and pathways. They would also allow readers to engage with 'the ethnography' at different levels of sophistication and complexity. It could be explored at a relatively superficial level – perhaps suitable for a general public readership and for 'public engagement' exercises. Equally, it could be consumed at greater depth, exploring interpretations and theoretical analyses as well as 'the data'. Indeed, one possibility that was envisaged in this model was the possibility of the 'reader' also becoming an 'author', creating novel interactions with the data, providing her or his own commentary, and adding to the linkages within and beyond the ethnographic data-sets. The hypertext strategy was then extended in the development of a hypermedia environment. Obviously the crucial difference here is the addition of multi-media data and forms of representation. Where hypertext was based on multiple links and navigations between textual data and interpretations, hypermedia allowed the analyst to create navigational pathways that incorporated audio- and video-recordings, as well as still images and other forms of information. The hypermedia environment thus allows for the degree of flexibility of hypertext, plus the multiple modes of representation. One can therefore hear the informants' voices, see the video-recordings of embodied activity, explore physical spaces with virtual tours, and so forth. The hypermedia environment thus facilitates a complex exploration of complex social phenomena. Such hypermedia-based forms of representation are congruent with contemporary emphases on the multiple modalities of everyday social interaction, and consequent attempts to develop multi-modal forms of ethnographic analysis and representation. The practical construction of a hypermedia ethnographic environment has been demonstrated (Dicks et al. 2005). At the time of its construction, however, it was clear that it was labour-intensive. While the collection of digital data was relatively easy, given current technology, the complex tasks of editing video-materials proved to be greedy of both time and digital memory. More significantly, the lack of generic software meant that the hypermedia ethnography itself was not readily transportable from one research environment to another.

It now appears that information technology and the possibilities of digital ethnography have converged in such a way that ethnographies can be authored and published in ways that are robustly transferable. They do not permit the same degree of navigational flexibility and complexity, but they do permit the use of multi-media illustrative and supplementary materials. We have, perhaps, had to wait for the commercial success of the e-book for the needs of ethnographers and commercially viable technology to converge. It is now perfectly possible for e-books to embed links to illustrative and analytic materials in such a way that the reader can choose to 'click' on relevant icons, and to access materials of different degrees of density. The reader's navigational options are restricted. In essence he or she can choose only to click on an embedded link or not to bother. There is certainly no possibility of a creative engagement with the text. But the text itself is undoubtedly more complex than conventional hard-copy monographs, and the current technology provides a robust and universally available platform.

Vannini (2012) has authored just such a monograph, which is one of a series of such books. The research is focused on travel on the ferries that serve the communities in the Vancouver region. Life by the water and travel between the islands revolve around the comings and goings of the ferries. Vannini makes the ferries his main substantive focus, and therefore makes mobility the guiding analytic theme. Place, space and mobility are, perhaps, among the modalities of social activity that are hard to convey in linear, conventional texts, and the opportunities afforded by digital representation are potentially well suited to such phenomena. Moving images can, perhaps, convey what the printed word alone cannot.

The resulting monograph has embedded links to data in the form of recordings and visual records, providing a vividly memorable exemplar of how digital resources and e-book formats can be used productively. Similar ethnographies have also been produced using the resources of the e-book: see Mingé and Zimmerman (2013); Somerville (2013); Uimonen (2012). The results are perhaps variable in terms of their analytic quality, but the general direction taken in such publications suggests a viable way forward.

In this vein we can start to envisage publications that offer a package that is also more than the printed page: exemplars of research-in-action that provide conventional text (digitally or in print) with digital materials such as interviews and commentaries with the author(s), or textual materials and so on. One can even, perhaps, envisage digital monographs that can be read at different levels (just like levels of difficulty in games), so that one can have a fairly superficial reading, or a deeper one. One can get the 'story' at the elementary level, with more complex arguments and conceptual elaboration at another level. But this is speculative. What is definite is that ethnographers need to strive to maintain not only the integrity of the monograph, but also find ways – in collaboration with the right publishers – to refresh and renew the genre.

Finally, it is always worth asking ourselves just what endures in the social sciences. The answer(s) must include well-crafted ethnographies. It is no accident that the discipline of anthropology maintains a cumulative tradition based on decades of major ethnographic monographs. We still read the classic works in that vein, as well as the continuing numbers of contemporary monographs. We read the ethnographies of past generations not because of a nostalgia for disappeared cultures of the colonial epoch. We do so because they furnish well-turned, closely analysed accounts of the multiple ways of being human. They do what nothing else can, in documenting social life in its complexity and variety. Likewise, the classics of sociology are still read, and the ethnographic imagination informs our views of social life. Whether it be the classics of the Chicago School, or later works of urban sociology or criminology, or indeed detailed studies of work and institutions, we are nourished by their close readings of social organisation and cultural forms. The precise local details of institutions and locales change; the regimes of organisations change; the circumstances of deviance and social control change. But we continue to learn from the classic studies. The precise details of Erving Goffman's social environment may well have changed. In the era of the mobile phone we cannot assume that the person apparently shouting and gesticulating to themselves is deranged: it is now perfectly normal. Civil inattention is changed when social actors loudly discuss their intimate private lives in public (also on their mobile), in the full hearing of others around them. The boundaries of personal space are transformed somewhat when people play music loudly through headphones. But the generic perception of human conduct that Goffman initiated and documented retains its relevance. The same can be said of the ethnographic tradition in general.

Well-conducted ethnographic fieldwork will, therefore, continue to generate research of enduring value. It may not always serve the short-term needs of policy-makers, and it may sometimes be difficult to fit into the temporal and financial constraints of contemporary institutional life. It does not only take time to conduct and to write, it often takes time for it to inform the disciplines. But it will provide a stream of life-blood for the social sciences, providing as it does fundamental understanding of human conduct in its extraordinary variety, of everyday life in its local diversity, and of social actors endowed with remarkable skills and knowledge.

References

Angrosino, M. (1998) *Opportunity House: Ethnographic Stories of Mental Retardation*. Walnut Creek, CA: AltaMira.
Appadurai, A. (ed.) (1986) *The Social Life of Things*. Cambridge: Cambridge University Press.
Atkinson, J.M. and Drew, P. (1979) *Order in Court: The Organization of Verbal Interaction in Judicial Settings*. London: Macmillan.
Atkinson, P. (1982) Writing Ethnography, in H. J. Helle (ed.), *Kultur und Institution*. Berlin: Dunker and Humblot, pp. 77-105.
Atkinson, P. (1990) *The Ethnographic Imagination: Textual Constructions of Reality*. London: Routledge.
Atkinson, P. (1992) *Understanding Ethnographic Texts*. Thousand Oaks, CA: Sage.
Atkinson, P. (1995) *Medical Talk and Medical Work: The Liturgy of the Clinic*. London: Sage.
Atkinson, P. (1996) *Sociological Readings and Re-Readings*. Aldershot: Avebury.
Atkinson, P. (1997) *The Clinical Experience: The Construction and Reconstruction of Medical Reality*, 2nd edn. Aldershot: Ashgate.
Atkinson, P. (2005) Qualitative research: unity and diversity, *Forum Qualitative Forschung/Forum: Qualitative Research* (Germany), 6 (3), Art. 26. Available at: www.qualitative-research.net/fqs-texte/3-05/05-3-26-e.htm (accessed 10 May 2014).
Atkinson, P. (2006) *Everyday Arias: An Operatic Ethnography*. Lanham, MD: AltaMira.
Atkinson, P. (2010) Making opera work: bricolage and the management of dramaturgy, *Music and Arts in Action*, 3: 1. http://musicandartsinaction.net/index.php/maia/article/view/makingoperawork (accessed 10th May 2014).
Atkinson, P. (2013a) Ethnographic writing: the avant-garde and a failure of nerve, *International Review of Qualitative Inquiry*, 6 (1): 19–36.
Atkinson, P. (2013b) The mastersingers: language and practice in an operatic masterclass, *Ethnography and Education*, 8 (3): 355–70.
Atkinson, P. (2013c) Blowing hot: the ethnography of craft and the craft of ethnography, *Qualitative Inquiry*, 19 (3): 397–404.
Atkinson, P. and Delamont, S. (2004) Qualitative research and the postmodern turn, in M. Hardy and A. Bryman (eds), *Handbook of Data Analysis*. London: Sage, pp. 667–81.
Atkinson, P. and Housley, W. (2003) *Interactionism*. London: Sage.
Atkinson, P. and Silverman, D. (1997) Kundera's *Immortality*: the interview society and the invention of the self, *Qualitative Inquiry*, 3 (1): 104–25.
Atkinson, P., Coffey, A. and Delamont, S. (2003) *Key Themes in Qualitative Research: Continuities and Change*. Walnut Creek, CA: AltaMira.
Atkinson, P., Delamont, S. and Housley, W. (2008) *Contours of Culture: Ethnography for Complexity*. Lanham, MD: AltaMira.

Atkinson, P., Delamont, S. and Watermeyer, R. (2013) Expertise, authority and embodied pedagogy in operatic masterclasses, *British Journal of Sociology of Education*, 34 (4): 487–503.

Baggini, J. (2007) *Welcome to Everytown: A Journey into the English Mind*. London: Granta.

Banks, A. and Banks, S. (1998) *Fiction and Social Research: By Ice or Fire*. Walnut Creek, CA: AltaMira.

Barnes, J.A. (1994) *A Pack of Lies: Towards a Sociology of Lying*. Cambridge: Cambridge University Press.

Barton, E. (2007) Institutional and professional orders of ethics in the discourse practices of research recruitment in oncology, in R. Iedema (ed.), *The Discourse of Hospital Communication: Tracing Complexities in Contemporary Health Care Organizations*. New York: Palgrave Macmillan, pp. 18–38.

Barton, E. and Eggly, S. (2009) Ethical or unethical persuasion? The rhetoric of offers to participate in clinical trials, *Written Communication*, 26 (3): 295–319.

Becker, H.S. (1982) *Art Worlds*. Berkeley, CA: University of California Press.

Becker, H.S. and Geer, B. (1957) Participant observation and interviewing: a comparison, *Human Organization*, 16: 28–32. (Reprinted in *Qualitative Methodology*, ed. William J. Filstead. Chicago, IL: Markham, 1970, pp. 133–42.)

Becker, H.S., Faulkner, R.R. and Kirshenblatt-Ginblett, B. (eds) (2006) *Art from Start to Finish: Jazz, Painting, Writing and Other Improvisations*. Chicago, IL: University of Chicago Press.

Behar, R. and Gordon, D. (eds) (1995) *Women Writing Culture*. Berkeley, CA: University of California Press.

Benson, M. and Jackson, E. (2013) Place-making and place maintenance: performativity, place and belonging among the middle classes, *Sociology*, 47 (4): 793–809.

Benzecry, C.E. (2011) *The Opera Fanatic: Ethnography of an Obsession*. Chicago, IL: University of Chicago University.

Berger, P. and Luckman, T. (1967) *The Social Construction of Reality*. London: Allen Lane.

Bittner, E. (1967) The police on skid row, *American Sociological Review*, 2: 699–715.

Blenkinsop, H. (2013) Forgotten memories: silence, reason, truth and the carnival, in L. Stanley (ed.), *Documents of Life Revisited: Narrative and Biographical Methodology for a 21st Century Critical Humanism*. Farnham: Ashgate, pp. 121–32.

Blumer, H. (1954) What's wrong with social theory?, *American Sociological Review*, 19: 3–10.

Bochner, A. and Ellis, C. (eds) (2002) *Ethnographically Speaking: Autoethnography, Literature and Aesthetics*. Walnut Creek, CA: AltaMira.

Boellstorff, T., Nardi, B., Pearce, C. and Taylor, T.L. (2012) *Ethnography and Virtual Worlds: A Handbook of Method*. Princeton, NJ: Princeton University Press.

Boon, J.A. (1982) *Other Tribes, Other Scribes: Symbolic Anthropology in the Comparative Study of Cultures, Histories, Religions, and Texts*. Cambridge: Cambridge University Press.

Boon, J.A. (1983) Functionalists write too: Frazer/Malinowski and the semiotics of the monograph, *Semiotica*, 46 (2–4): 131–49.

Bourdieu, P. (1986) *Distinction*. London: Routledge.
Bourdieu, P. (1997) *The Logic of Practice*. Cambridge: Polity Press.
Briggs, D. (2012) *Crack Cocaine Users: High Society and Low Life in South London*. London: Routledge.
Brown, R.H. (1977) *A Poetic for Sociology*. Cambridge: Cambridge University Press.
Burawoy, M. (ed.) (1991) *Ethnography Unbound*. Berkeley, CA: University of California Press.
Burawoy, M. (1998) The extended case method, *Sociological Theory*, 16 (1): 4–33.
Cappetti, P. (1993) *Writing Chicago: Modernism, Ethnography and the Novel*. New York: Columbia University Press.
Carey, J.T. (1975) *Sociology and Public Affairs*. Beverly Hills, CA: Sage.
Charmaz, C. (2006) *Constructing Grounded Theory: A Practical Guide through Qualitative Analysis*. London: Sage.
Church, K. (1995) *Forbidden Narratives: Critical Autobiography as Social Science*. Luxembourg: Gordon and Breach.
Cicourel, A. (1964) *Method and Measurement in Sociology*. New York: Free Press.
Clifford, J. and Marcus, G.E. (eds) (1986) *Writing Culture*. Berkeley, CA: University of California Press.
Cockayne, E. (2007) *Hubbub: Filth, Noise and Stench in England, 1600–1770*. New Haven, CT: Yale University Press.
Coffey, A. (1999) *The Ethnographic Self*. London: Sage.
Coffey, A. and Atkinson, P. (1996) *Making Sense of Qualitative Data*. Thousand Oaks, CA: Sage.
Coffey, A., Holbrook, B. and Atkinson, P. (1996) Qualitative data analysis: technologies and representations, *Sociological Research Online*, 1, 1, www.socresonline. (Reprinted in A. Bryman and R.G. Burgess (eds), *Qualitative Research*, vol. 2. London: Sage, 1999, pp. 165–182.)
Corbin, A. (1998) *Village Bells: Sound and Meaning in the 19th-Century French Countryside* (trans. M. Thom). New York: Columbia University Press.
Cortazzi, M. (1993) *Narrative Analysis*. London: Falmer.
Cottrell, S. (2004) *Professional Music-Making in London: Ethnography and Experience*. Aldershot: Ashgate.
Crosnoe, R. (2011) *Fitting In, Standing Out: Navigating the Social Challenges of High School to Get an Education*. Cambridge: Cambridge University Press.
DeCoker, G. (1998) Seven characteristics of a traditional Japanese approach to learning, in J. Singleton (ed.) *Learning in Likely Places: Varieties of Apprenticeship in Japan*. Cambridge: Cambridge University Press, pp. 68–84.
Delamont, S. (2002) *Fieldwork in Educational Settings*, 2nd edn. London: Falmer.
Delamont, S. (2009) The only honest thing: autoethnography, reflexivity and small crises in fieldwork, *Ethnography and Education*, 4 (1): 51–63.
Delamont, S. (2014) *Key Themes in the Ethnography of Education*. London: Sage.
Delamont, S. and Atkinson, P. (1995) *Fighting Familiarity*. New York: Hampton Press.
Demetry, D. (2013) Regimes of meaning: the intersection of space and time in kitchen cultures, *Journal of Contemporary Ethnography*, 42 (5): 576–607.

DeNora, T. (2000) *Music in Everyday Life*. Cambridge: Cambridge University Press.
DeNora, T. (2003) *After Adorno: Rethinking Music Sociology*. Cambridge: Cambridge University Press.
Denzin, N. and Giardina, M. (eds) (2007) *Ethical Futures in Qualitative Research*. Walnut Creek, CA: Left Coast Press.
Denzin, N. and Giardina, M. (eds) (2009) *Qualitative Inquiry and Social Justice*. Walnut Creek, CA: Left Coast Press.
Denzin, N.K. and Lincoln, Y. (eds) (1994) *Handbook of Qualitative Research*. Thousand Oaks, CA: Sage.
Denzin, N.K. and Lincoln, Y. (eds) (2000) *Handbook of Qualitative Research*, 2nd edn. Thousand Oaks, CA: Sage.
Denzin, N.K. and Lincoln, Y. (eds) (2005) *Handbook of Qualitative Research*, 3rd edn. Thousand Oaks, CA: Sage.
Dicks, B., Mason, B., Coffey, A. and Atkinson, P. (2005) *Qualitative Research and Hypermedia: Ethnography for the Digital Age*. London: Sage.
Dingwall, R. (1977) Atrocity stories, *Work and Occupations*, 4 (4): 371–96.
Dingwall, R. (2008) The ethical case against ethical regulation in humanities and social science research, *21st Century Society: Journal of the Academy of Social Sciences*, 3 (1): 1–12.
Douglas, M. (1966) *Purity and Danger*. London: Routledge and Kegan Paul.
Dubisch, J. (1990) Pilgrimage and popular religion at a Greek holy shrine, in E. Badone (ed.), *Religious Orthodoxy and Popular Faith in European Society*. Princeton, NJ: Princeton University Press, pp. 113–139.
Edmondson, R. (1984) *Rhetoric in Sociology*. London: Macmillan.
Ehrenreich, B. (2006) *Bait and Switch: The Futile Pursuit of the Corporate Dream*. London: Granta Books.
Elias, N. (1978) *The Civilizing Process* (trans E. Jephcott). New York: Urizen Books.
Ellis, C. (2004) *The Ethnographic I: A Methodological Novel About Autoethnography*. Walnut Creek, CA: AltaMira.
Ellis, C. and Bochner, A. (eds) (1996) *Composing Ethnography: Alternative Forms of Qualitative Writing*. Walnut Creek, CA: AltaMira.
Ellis, C. and Flaherty, M.G. (1992) *Investigating Subjectivity: Research on Lived Experience*. Thousand Oaks, CA: Sage.
Emerson, R.M., Fretz, R.I. and Shaw, L.L. (1995) *Writing Ethnographic Fieldnotes*. Chicago, IL: University of Chicago Press.
Emerson, R.M., Fretz, R.I. and Shaw, L.L. (2001) Participant observation and fieldnotes, in P. Atkinson, A. Coffey, S. Delamont, J. Lofland and L. Lofland (eds), *Handbook of Ethnography*. London: Sage, pp. 352–68.
Entwistle, J. (2009) *The Aesthetic Economy of Fashion: Markets and Values in Clothing and Modelling*. Oxford: Berg.
Evans, B. (2005) *Before Culture: The Ethnographic Imagination in American Literature, 1865–1920*. Chicago, IL: University of Chicago Press.
Ewart, E. (2013) *Space and Society in Central Brazil: A Panará Ethnography*. London: Bloomsbury.
Featherstone, K. and Donovan, J.L. (1996) Random allocation or allocation at random? Patients' perspectives of participation in a randomised control trial, *British Medical Journal*, 317 (7167): 1177–80.
Featherstone, K. and Donovan, J. L. (2002) 'Why don't they just tell me straight, why allocate it?' The struggle to make sense of participating in a randomised controlled trial, *Social Science and Medicine*, 55 (5): 709–19.

Featherstone, K., Atkinson, P., Bharadwaj, A. and Clarke, A. (2005) *Risky Relations: Family, Kinship and the New Genetics*. Oxford: Berg.
Fine, G.A. (1985) Occupational aesthetics, *Urban Life*, 14 (1): 3–32.
Fine, G.A. (1990) Organizational time: temporal demands and the experience of work in restaurant kitchens, *Social Forces*, 69: 95–114.
Fine, G.A. (ed.) (1995) *A Second Chicago School?*. Chicago, IL: University of Chicago Press.
Fleck, L. (1979 [1937]) *The Genesis and Development of a Scientific Fact*. Chicago, IL: University of Chicago Press.
Foreman, K. M. (2008) *The Gei of Geisha: Music, Identity and Meaning*. Aldershot: Ashgate.
Foster, H. (1995) The artist as ethnographer? In G.E. Marcus and F.R. Myers (eds), *The Traffic in Culture: Refiguring Art and Anthropology*. Berkeley, CA: University of California Press.
Foucault, M. (1970) *The Order of Things: An Archaeology of the Human Sciences*. London: Tavistock.
Gabrys, J. (2012) Becoming urban: sitework from a moss-eye view, *Environment and Planning A*, 44: 2922–39.
Garfinkel, H. (1956) Conditions of successful degradation ceremonies, *American Journal of Sociology*, 61: 240–4.
Gathings, M.J. and Parrotta, K. (2013) The use of gendered narratives in the courtroom: constructing an identity worthy of leniency, *Journal of Contemporary Ethnography*, 42 (1): 668–89.
Gay y Blasco, P. and Wardle, H. (2007) *How to Read Ethnography*. London: Routledge.
Geertz, C. (1973) *The Interpretation of Cultures*. New York: Basic Books.
Geertz, C. (1983) Slide show: Evans-Pritchard's African transparencies, *Raritan*, 3 (Fall): 62–80.
Geertz, C. (1988) *Works and Lives: The Anthropologist as Author*. Cambridge: Polity.
Gilbert, N. and Mulkay, M. (1984) *Opening Pandora's Box: A Sociological Account of Scientists' Discourse*. Cambridge: Cambridge University Press.
Gimlin, D. (2012) *Cosmetic Surgery Narratives: A Cross-Cultural Analysis of Women's Accounts*. London: Palgrave.
Glaser, B. (1978) *Theoretical Sensitivity*. Mill Valley, CA: Sociology Press.
Glaser, B. (1992) *Emergence Versus Forcing*. Mill Valley, CA: Sociology Press.
Glaser, B. and Strauss, A.L. (1965) *Awareness of Dying*. Chicago, IL: Aldine.
Glaser, B. and Strauss, A.L. (1967) *The Discovery of Grounded Theory*. Chicago, IL: Aldine.
Goffman, A. (2014) *On the Run: Fugitive Life in an American City*. Chicago, IL: University of Chicago Press.
Goffman, E. (1961) *Asylums: Essays on the Social Situation of Mental Patients and Other Inmates*. New York: Doubleday Anchor.
Goffman, E. (1963) *Stigma: Notes on the Management of Spoiled Identity*. Englewood Cliffs, NJ: Prentice-Hall.
Goffman, E. (1964) The Neglected Situation, *American Anthropologist*, 66(6) (Part two, special issue): 133–36.
Goffman, E. (1967) *Interaction Ritual: Essays in Face-to-Face Behavior*. New York: Doubleday Anchor.
Goffman, E. (1983) The interaction order, *American Sociological Review*, 48: 1–17.

Goldman, L. (1983) *Talk Never Dies: The Language of Huli Dispute*. London: Tavistock.
Goodall, H.L. (2000) *Writing the New Ethnography*. Lanham, MD: AltaMira.
Gross, M. (2012) 'Objective culture' and the development of nonknowledge: Georg Simmel and the reverse side of knowing, *Cultural Sociology*, 6 (4): 422–37.
Haase, B. (1998) Learning to be an apprentice, in J. Singleton (ed.), *Learning in Likely Places: Varieties of Apprenticeship in Japan*. Cambridge: Cambridge University Press, pp. 107–21.
Hagedorn, K.J. (2002) Sacred secrets: lessons with Francisco, in R. Emoff and D. Henderson (eds), *Mementos, Artifacts and Hallucinations*. London: Routledge, pp. 31–44.
Haggerty, K. (2004) Ethics creep: governing social science research in the name of ethics, *Qualitative Sociology*, 27: 391–414.
Hall, T. and Smith, R. (2011) Walking, welfare and the good city, *Anthropology in Action*, 18 (3): 33–44.
Halstead, N., Hirsch, E. and Okely, J. (eds) (2008) *Knowing How to Know: Fieldwork and the Ethnographic Present*. Oxford: Berghahn.
Hamilton, L. (2013) The magic of mundane objects: culture, identity and power in a country vets' practice, *The Sociological Review*, 61 (2): 265–84.
Hammersley, M. (1998) *Reading Ethnographic Research: A Critical Guide*, 2nd edn. London: Longman.
Hammersley, M. (2014) On the ethics of interviewing for discourse analysis, *Qualitative Research*, 14 (5): 529–41.
Hammersley, M. and Atkinson, P. (1983) *Ethnography: Principles in Practice*. London: Tavistock.
Hammersley, M. and Atkinson, P. (2007) *Ethnography: Principles in Practice*, 3rd edn. London: Routledge.
Hammersley, M. and Traianou, A. (2012) *Ethics in Qualitative Research: Controversies and Contexts*. London: Sage.
Harper, D. (1987) *Working Knowledge: Skill and Community in a Small Shop*. Berkeley, CA: University of California Press.
Heath, C. (2013) *The Dynamics of Auction: Social Interaction and the Sale of Fine Art and Antiques*. Cambridge: Cambridge University Press.
Hecht, T. (2006) *After Life: An Ethnographic Novel*. Durham: Duke University Press.
Herzfeld, M. (1982) *Ours Once More*. Austin, TX: University of Texas Press.
Herzfeld, M. (1985) *The Poetics of Manhood*. Princeton, NJ: Princeton University Press.
Herzfeld, M. (2004) *The Body Impolitic: Artisans and Artifice in the Global Hierarchy of Value*. Chicago, IL: University of Chicago Press.
Ho, K. (2009) *Liquidated: An Ethnography of Wall Street*. Durham, NC: Duke University Press.
Hodgkinson, W. (2006) *Guitar Man*. London: Bloomsbury.
Holman Jones, S. (2007) *Torch Singing: Performing Resistance and Desire from Billie Holiday to Edith Piaf*. Lanham, MD: AltaMira.
Horodowich, E. (2008) *Language and Statecraft in Early Modern Venice*. Cambridge: Cambridge University Press.
Hughes, E.C. (1971) *The Sociological Eye: Selected Writings*. New York: Aldine–Atherton.
Hunter, K. (1991) *Doctors' Stories: The Narrative Structure of Medical Knowledge*. Princeton, NJ: Princeton University Press.

Hurdley, R. (2013) *Home, Materiality, Memory and Belonging: Keeping Culture*. London: Palgrave.
Hurdley, R. and Dicks, B. (2011) In-between practice: working in the 'thirdspace' of sensory and multimodal methodology, *Qualitative Research*, 11 (3): 277–92.
Hymes, D. (1981) *In Vain I Tried to Tell You: Essays in Native American Ethnopoetics*. Philadelphia, PA: University of Pennsylvania Press.
Hymes, D. (1996) *Ethnography, Linguistics, Narrative Inequality: Towards an Understanding of Voice*. London: Taylor and Francis.
James, A., Hockey, J. and Dawson, A. (eds) (1997) *After Writing Culture*. London: Routledge.
Jordan, B.G. and Weston, V. (eds) (2003) *Copying the Master and Stealing His Secrets: Talent and Training in Japanese Painting*. Honolulu: University of Hawai'i Press.
Joseph, M. (2013) *Fluid New York: Cosmopolitan Urbanism and the Green Imagination*. Durham, NC: Duke University Press.
Kassabian, A. (2013) *Ubiquitous Listening: Affect, Attention, and Distributed Subjectivity*. Berkeley, CA: University of California Press.
Kelly, J. (2007) *Art, Ethnography and the Life of Objects*. Manchester: Manchester University Press.
Kempton, W. (1981) *The Folk Classification of Ceramics: A Study of Cognitive Prototypes*. New York: Academic Press.
Kendon, A. (1990) *Conducting Interaction: Patterns of Behaviour in Focused Encounters*. Cambridge: Cambridge University Press.
Kiddey, R. and Schofield, J. (2011) Embrace the margins: adventures in archaeology and homelessness, *Public Archaeology*, 10 (1): 4–22.
Kirklighter, C., Vincent, C. and Moxley, J.M. (eds) (1997) *Voices and Visions: Refiguring Ethnography in Composition*. Portsmouth, NH: Boynton/Cook.
Knoblauch, H. (2013) *Powerpoint, Communication, and the Knowledge Society*. Cambridge: Cambridge University Press.
Knowles, C. (2011) Cities on the move: navigating urban life, *City*, 15 (2): 136–53.
Krieger, S. (1983) *The Mirror Dance*. Philadelphia, PA: Temple University Press.
Labov, W. (2013) *The Language of Life and Death: The Transformation of Experience in Oral Narrative*. New York: Cambridge University Press.
Laurier, E. (2010) Being there/seeing there: recording and analysing life in the car, in B. Fincham, M. McGuiness and L. Murray (eds), *Mobile Methodologies*. London: Palgrave Macmillan, pp. 103–17.
Leach, E.L. (1970) *Lévi-Strauss*. London: Fontana.
Lefebvre, H. (2004) *Rhythmanalysis: Space, Time and Everyday Life*. London: Continuum.
Lehrer, A. (2009) *Wine and Conversation*, 2nd edn. New York: Oxford University Press.
Lévi-Strauss, C. (1963) *Structural Anthropology*. New York: Basic Books.
Lévi-Strauss, C. (1966) *The Savage Mind*. London: Weidenfeld & Nicolson.
Lewis, O. (1959) *Five Families: Mexican Case Studies in the Culture of Poverty*. New York: Basic Books.
Lewis, O. (1968) *La Vida*. London: Panther.
Lewis, O. (1972) *A Death in the Sanchez Family*. Harmondsworth: Penguin.
Lyman, S. and Scott, M.B. (1968) Accounts, *American Sociological Review*, 33: 46–62.

Lyon, D. and Back, L. (2012) Fishmongers in a global economy: craft and social relations on a London market, *Sociological Research Online*, 17 (2): 23. www.socresonline.org.uk/17/2/23.html (accessed 10 May 2014).

Makagon, D. and Neumann, M. (2009) *Recording Culture: Audio Documentary and the Ethnographic Experience*. Thousand Oaks, CA: Sage.

Martens, L. (2012) Practice 'in talk' and talk 'as practice': dish washing and the reach of language, *Sociological Research on Line* 17(3): 22, http://www.socresonline.org.uk/17/3/22.html (accessed 10 May 2014).

Mauss, M. (2006) *Techniques, Technology and Civilisation* (trans. D. Lussier and J. Redding, ed. N. Schlagber). Oxford: Berghahn.

Mauss, M. (2007) *Manual of Ethnography* (trans. D. Lussier, ed. N.J. Allen). Oxford: Berghahn.

Melbin, M. (1987) *Night as Frontier: Colonizing the World After Dark*. New York: Free Press.

Mienczakowski, J. (2001) Ethnodrama: performed research – limitations and potential, in P. Atkinson, A. Coffey, S. Delamont, J. Lofland and L. Lofland (eds), *Handbook of Ethnography*. London: Sage, pp. 468–76.

Mills, C. Wright (1940) Situated actions and vocabularies of motive, *American Sociological Review*, 5: 439–52.

Mingé, J.M. and Zimmerman, A.L. (2013) *Concrete and Dust: Mapping the Sexual Terrains of Los Angeles*. New York: Routledge.

Mishler, E. (1984) *The Discourse of Medicine: Dialectics of Medical Interviews*. Norwood, NJ: Ablex.

Mishler, E. (1991) Representing discourse: the rhetoric of transcription, *Journal of Narrative and Life History*, 1 (4): 255–80.

Moeran, B. (1997) *Folk Art Potters of Japan: Beyond an Anthropology of Aesthetics*. London: Curzon.

Moeran, B. (2011) The book fair as a tournament of value, in B. Moeran and J.S. Pedersen (eds), *Negotiating Values in the Creative Industries: Fairs, Festivals and Competitive Events*. Cambridge: Cambridge University Press, pp. 119–44.

Moerman, M. (1988) *Talking Culture: Ethnography and Conversation Analysis*. Philadelphia, PA: University of Pennsylvania Press.

Moles, K. (2008) A walk in thirdspace: place, methods and walking, *Sociological Research Online*, 13 (4): 2. www.socresoline.org.uk/13/4/2.html (accessed 10 May 2014).

Morrow, C. (2013) Lies and truths: exploring the lie as a document of life, in L. Stanley (ed.), *Documents of Life Revisited: Narrative and Biographical Methodology for a 21st Century Critical Humanism*. Farnham: Ashgate, pp. 19–30.

Morse, J., Stern, P.N., Corbin, J., Bowers, B., Charmaz, K. and Clarke, A.E. (2009) *Developing Grounded Theory: The Second Generation*. Walnut Creek, CA: Left Coast Press.

Mosko, M.S. (2013) Omarakana revisited, or 'do dual organizations exist?' in the Trobriands, *Journal of the Royal Anthropological Institute*, 19 (3): 482–509.

Mulkay, M. (1985) *The Word and the World*. London: George Allen and Unwin.

Murphy, E. and Dingwall, R. (2007) Informed consent, anticipatory regulation and ethnographic practice, *Social Science and Medicine*, 65 (11): 2223–34.

Nakamura, F. (2007) Creating or performing words? Observations on contemporary Japanese calligraphy, in E. Hallam and T. Ingold (eds), *Creativity and Cultural Improvisation*. Oxford: Berg, pp. 79–98.

Neill, R. (2005) *Looking for La Bomba: The Adventures of a Musical Oaf*. London: Penguin.
Neumann, M. (1996) Collecting ourselves at the end of the century, in C. Ellis and A. Bochner (eds), *Composing Ethnography: Alternative Forms of Qualitative Writing*. Walnut Creek, CA: AltaMira, pp. 172–98.
O'Connor, E. (2005) Embodied knowledge: the experience and the struggle towards proficiency in glassblowing, *Ethnography*, 6 (2): 183–204.
O'Connor, E. (2006) Glassblowing tools: extending the body towards practical knowledge and informing a social world, *Qualitative Sociology*, 29: 177–93.
Petryna, A. (2009) *When Experiments Travel: Clinical Trials and the Search for Human Subjects*. Princeton, NJ: Princeton University Press.
Pfohl, J. (1992) *Death at the Parasite Café: Social Science (Fictions) and the Postmodern*. London: Macmillan.
Pinch, T. and Clark, C. (1986) The hard sell: 'patter marketing' and the strategic (re)production and local management of economic reasoning in the sales routines of market pitchers, *Sociology*, 20 (2): 169–91.
Pink, S. (2009) *Doing Sensory Ethnography*. London: Sage.
Pink, S. (2011) Multimodality, multisensoriality and ethnographic knowing: social semiotics and the phenomenology of perception, *Qualitative Research*, 11 (3): 261–76.
Plummer, K. (1995) *Telling Sexual Stories: Power, Change and Social Worlds*. London: Routledge.
Polly, M. (2007) *American Shaolin: One Man's Quest to Become a Kungfu Master*. London: Abacus.
Potter, J. (1996) *Representing Reality: Discourse, Rhetoric and Social Construction*. London: Sage.
Potter, J. and Wetherell, M. (1987) *Discourse and Social Psychology: Beyond Attitudes and Behaviour*. London: Sage.
Preston, B. (2007) *Bruce Lee and Me: A Martial Arts Adventure*. London: Atlantic.
Prokos, A. and Padavic, I. (2002) 'There oughtta be a law against bitches', *Gender, Work and Organization*, 9: 439–459.
Propp, V. (1958) *Morphology of the Folktale*. Bloomington, IN: Indiana Research Center in Anthropology.
Psathas, G. (1979) Organizational features of direction maps, in G. Psathas (ed.), *Everyday Language: Studies in Ethnomethodology*. New York: Irvington, pp. 203–25.
Quinney, R. (1996) Once my father travelled West to California, in C. Ellis and A. Bochner (eds), *Composing Ethnography: Alternative Forms of Qualitative Writing*. Walnut Creek, CA: AltaMira, pp. 357–82.
Reed-Danahay, D. (2001) Autobiography, intimacy and ethnography, in P. Atkinson, A. Coffey, S. Delamont, J. Lofland and L. Lofland (eds), *Handbook of Ethnography*. London: Sage, pp. 407–25.
Reed-Danahay, D. (ed.) (1997) *Auto/Ethnography: Rewriting the Self and the Social*. Oxford: Berg.
Rice, T. (2013) *Hearing and the Hospital: Sound, Listening, Knowledge and Experience*. Canon Pyon: Sean Kingston Publishing.
Richardson, L. (1993) Poetics, dramatics, and transgressive validity: The case of the skipped line, *The Sociological Quarterly*, 34(4): 695–710.

Richardson, L. (1994a) Writing: a method of inquiry, in N. Denzin and Y. Lincoln (eds), *Handbook of Qualitative Research*. Thousand Oaks, CA: Sage, pp. 516–529.

Richardson, L. (1994b) Nine poems: marriage and the family, *Journal of Contemporary Ethnography*, 23 (1): 3–13.

Richardson, L. (1996) Speech lessons, in C. Ellis and A. Bochner (eds), *Composing Ethnography: Alternative Forms of Qualitative Writing*. Walnut Creek, CA: AltaMira, pp. 231–9.

Richardson, L. (2000) Writing: a method of inquiry, in N. Denzin and Y. Lincoln (eds), *Handbook of Qualitative Research*, 2nd edn. Thousand Oaks, CA: Sage, pp. 923–48.

Richardson, L. and St Pierre, E.A. (2005) Writing: a method of inquiry, in N. Denzin and Y. Lincoln (eds), *Handbook of Qualitative Research*, 3rd edn. Thousand Oaks, CA: Sage, pp. 959–78.

Riessman, C.K. (1993) *Narrative Analysis*. Newbury Park, CA: Sage.

Riessman, C.K. (2002) Analysis of personal narratives, in J.F. Gubrium and J.A. Holstein (eds), *Handbook of Interview Research*. Thousand Oaks, CA: Sage.

Rimer, J.T. (1998) The search for mastery never ceases: Zeami's classic treatises on transmitting the traditions of the *nō* theatre, in J. Singleton (ed.), *Learning in Likely Places: Varieties of Apprenticeship in Japan*. Cambridge: Cambridge University Press, pp. 35–44.

Rock, P. (1979) *The Making of Symbolic Interactionism*. London: Macmillan.

Ronai, C.R. (1996) My mother is mentally retarded, in C. Ellis and A. Bochner (eds), *Composing Ethnography: Alternative Forms of Qualitative Writing*. Walnut Creek, CA: AltaMira, pp. 109–31.

Roth, J. (1963) *Timetables*. New York: Bobbs–Merrill.

Ruchti, L.C. (2012) *Catheters, Slurs and Pickup Lines: Professional Intimacy in Hospital Nursing*. Philadelphia, PA: Temple University Press.

Ryen, A. (2004) Ethical issues, in C. Seale, G. Gobo, J.F. Gubrium and D. Silverman (eds), *Qualitative Research Practice*. London: Sage, pp. 230–47.

Sacks, H. (1992) *Lectures on Conversation* (ed. G. Jefferson). Oxford: Blackwell.

Said, E. (1978) *Orientalism*. New York: Pantheon.

Sanjek, R. (ed.) (1990) *Fieldnotes*. Ithaca, NY: Cornell University Press.

Saunders, B.F. (2008) *CT Suite: The Work of Diagnosis in the Age of Noninvasive Cutting*. Durham, NC: Duke University Press.

Schütz, A. (1967) *The Phenomenology of the Social World*. Chicago, IL: Northwestern University Press.

Seyer-Ochi, I. (2006) Lived landscapes of the Fillmore, in G. Spindler and Lorie Hamond (eds), *Innovations in Educational Ethnography*. Mahwah, NJ: Lawrence Erlbaum.

Silverman, D. (1985) *Qualitative Methodology and Sociology*. Aldershot: Gower.

Silverman, D. (1993) *Interpreting Qualitative Data: Methods for Analysing Talk, Text and Interaction*. London: Sage.

Simpson, P. (2011) Street performance and the city: public space, sociality, and intervening in the everyday, *Space and Culture*, 14 (4): 415–30.

Singleton, J. (1998) Craft and art education in Mashiko pottery workshops, in J. Singleton (ed.), *Learning in Likely Places: Varieties of Apprenticeship in Japan*. Cambridge: Cambridge University Press, pp. 122–33.

Smith, R. (2010) Whose method is it anyway? Researching space, setting and practice, Working Paper 135, Cardiff: Cardiff University School of Social Sciences.

Somerville, M. (2013) *Water in a Dry Land: Place-Learning Through Art and Story*. New York: Routledge.

Spencer, J. (1989) Anthropology as a kind of writing, *Man*, 24 (1): 145–64.

Spencer, J. (2001) Ethnography after post-modernism, in P. Atkinson, A. Coffey, S. Delamont, J. Lofland and L. Lofland (eds), *Handbook of Ethnography*. London: Sage, pp. 443–52.

Spooner, B. (1986) Weavers and dealers: the authenticity of an oriental carpet, in A. Appadurai, A. (ed.), *The Social Life of Things*. Cambridge: Cambridge University Press, pp. 195–235.

Spradley, J.P. (1979) *The Ethnographic Interview*. New York: Holt, Rinehart and Winston.

Stephens, N., Atkinson, P. and Glasner, P. (2008) The UK Stem Cell Bank as performative architecture, *New Genetics and Society*, 27 (2): 87–98.

Strauss, A.L. and Corbin, J. (1998) *Basics of Qualitative Research: Grounded Theory Procedures and Techniques*. 2nd edn. Thousand Oaks, CA: Sage.

Taussig, M. (2012) *I Swear I Saw This: Drawings in Fieldwork Notebooks, Namely My Own*. Chicago, IL: University of Chicago Press.

Tavory, I. and Timmermans, S. (2009) Two cases of ethnography: grounded theory and the extended case method, *Ethnography*, 10 (3): 243–63.

Taylor, S. and Littleton, K. (2012) *Contemporary Identities of Creativity and Creative Work*. Farnham: Ashgate.

Tesch, R. (1990) *Qualitative Research: Analysis Types and Software Tools*. London: Falmer.

Thomas, J. (2012) *Shakespeare's Shrine: The Bard's Birthplace and the Invention of Stratford-upon-Avon*. Philadelphia, PA: University of Pennsylvania Press.

Thrift, Nigel (2006) Re-inventing invention: new tendencies in capitalist commodification, *Economy and Society*, 35: 279–306.

Tillman-Healy, L.M. (1996) A secret life in a culture of thinness, in C. Ellis and A. Bochner (eds) *Composing Ethnography: Alternative Forms of Qualitative Writing*. Walnut Creek, CA: AltaMira, pp. 76–108.

Tilly, C. (2006) *Why?*.Princeton, NJ: Princeton University Press.

Timmermans, S. and Berg, M. (2003) *The Gold Standard: The Challenge of Evidence-Based Medicine and Standardization in Health Care*. Philadelphia: Temple University Press.

Todorova, M. (2009) *Imagining the Balkans*, rev. edn. Oxford: Oxford University Press.

Turnbull, D. (2007) Maps and plans in 'learning to see': the London Underground and Chartres Cathedral as examples of performing design, in Grasseni, C. (ed.), *Skilled Visions: Between Apprenticeship and Standards*. Oxford: Berghahn, pp. 125–41.

Twigger, R. (1999) *Angry White Pyjamas*. London: Phoenix.

Uimonen, P. (2012) *Digital Drama: Teaching and Learning Art and Media in Tanzania*. New York: Routledge.

Vail, D.A. (1999) The commodification of time in two art worlds, *Symbolic Interaction*, 22 (4): 325–44.

Van Maanen, J. (1988) *Tales of the Field*. Chicago, IL: University of Chicago Press.

Vannini, P. (2012) *Ferry Tales: Mobility, Place, and Time on Canada's West Coast*. New York: Routledge.
Villette, S.M. and Hardill, I. (2010) Paris and fashion: reflections on the role of the Parisian fashion industry in the cultural economy, *International Journal of Sociology and Social Policy*, 30 (9/10): 461–71.
Vincent, N. (2006) *Self-Made Man: My Year Disguised as a Man*. New York: Viking.
Voysey Paun, M. (2006) *A Constant Burden*, rev. edn. Aldershot: Ashgate.
Weaver, A. and Atkinson, P. (1994) *Microcomputing Strategies for Qualitative Data Analysis*. Aldershot: Avebury.
Webster, J. (2004) *Duende: A Journey in Search of Flamenco*. London: Black Swan (new edition).
West, C. (1984) *Routine Complications*. Bloomington, IN: Indiana University Press.
Whyton, T. (2013) *Beyond 'A Love Supreme': John Coltrane and the Legacy of an Album*. Oxford: Oxford University Press.
Wirth, L. (1938) Urbanism as a Way of Life, *American Journal of Sociology*, 44(1): 1–24.
Wolf, M. (1992) *The Thrice Told Tale*. Stanford, CA: Stanford University Press.
Woolf, G. (2011) *Tales of the Barbarians: Ethnography and Empire in the Roman West*. London: Wiley–Blackwell.
Zenker, O. and Kumoll, K.(eds) (2010) *Beyond Writing Culture*. New York: Berghahn.
Zerubavel, E. (1979) *Patterns of Time in Hospital Life*. Chicago, IL: University of Chicago Press.

Index

abduction, ethnographic, 57, 155
abduction stories, 101, 102, 103
abductive logic, 56–7, 61, 68
abstraction, 56, 68
access issues, research projects, 176, 177
accounts and narratives *see* narratives/narrative analysis
actual-types, 154
aesthetics, 109–28
  aesthetic criteria, 30, 116, 117
  aesthetic judgements, 20, 111, 123
  aesthetic order, 20
  art galleries, 131–2
  art works, 109, 110, 111, 115, 119, 131, 133
  art worlds, 110, 116, 132
  embodied skills, 124, 126
  ethno-aesthetics, 109, 111, 113, 117
  ethnographic and aesthetic, points of confluence between, 109
  ethnographic collecting, 117–18
  evaluation, 23, 111, 113, 114, 116, 117, 123
  interpretation, 112
  knowledge, 120–1
  material culture, 117, 118, 120
  multi-modality, 117, 119
  opera performance/opera singers, 111, 112, 113, 114, 115
  performance/performativity, 110, 112–13, 122
  social actors, 116, 117
  social worlds, 110
  techniques, 112, 121, 122, 123, 124, 125
  tools, 119–20, 127
  'work itself,' 111
  see also singers
analytic induction, 66
analytic perspectives, 11, 55–72, 97, 101
  coding of data, 59–60, 61, 62
  extended case method, 55, 63–6
  grounded theory, 55–64
  heuristic methods, 56, 57–8
  interviews, 92–3
  local and generic distinction, 65, 66, 69, 70
  representations, 158–9

analytic perspectives, *cont.*
  research process, 9–10, 11
  sensitising concepts, 9, 57–8
  theory-building, 61–2, 70, 71
  vulgar versions, 61, 67
anthropology, 36, 48, 63, 109, 133, 161
  British social anthropology, 161, 187
  classic, 63, 69, 122
  ethical issues, 187–8
  Manchester School, 63
  places and spaces, 133, 136
  social and cultural, 12, 24, 47, 49–50, 161, 187
  structuralist, 47–8
Appadurai, A., 69, 84, 122
architecture, urban, 131
art, sociology of, 109, 110
art galleries, 131–2
art nouveau architecture, 131, 133
art works
  aesthetics, 109, 110, 111, 115, 119
  places and spaces, 131, 133, 135
art worlds, 110, 116, 132
artefacts, 1, 2, 7, 11, 97, 108, 109, 130, 144, 145
  aesthetics, 117, 118, 119, 122
  material *see* material artefacts/goods
Atkinson, Paul, 60, 79, 94, 112, 193
  accounts and narratives, 96, 107
  ethical issues, 176, 180, 187
  ethnography perspectives, 10, 19, 21, 25, 26, 32
  fieldwork, 38, 39, 45, 46
  places and spaces, 134, 143, 149
  textual representations and ethnographic writing, 155, 156, 159, 167, 169
Atlas/ti (analytic software), 138
atrocity stories, 104
auction TV channels, 83–4
auctioneers, 122, 123
audiences, 83, 113–14, 115
authenticity, 99, 111, 115, 183, 187

autobiographical/biographical narratives, 95, 98, 105, 124, 156, 159, 181
  need for scepticism, 165–6
  see also narratives/narrative analysis; representations, textual; writing, ethnographic
autoethnography, 157, 162, 165, 166, 168
  ethical issues, 186, 187
avant-garde artists, French, 109
awareness contexts, 88, 90, 91

Back, L., 123
Baggini, Julian, 181
Barton, E., 175
Becker, Howard, 15, 99, 110, 111
Beethoven, Ludwig Van, 147
Behar, R., 161
bel canto tradition, in aesthetics and voice production, 111, 112, 113
Benson, M., 142
Benzecry, C. E., 114
Berg, M., 173
Berger, P., 25, 46
Bilbao (Spain), art gallery at, 132
biographies, 95, 98, 105
  ethical issues, 173–4
  see also autobiographical/biographical narratives
biomedical research, 174–5, 176
  see also clinical trials; randomised controlled trials (RCTs)
Bittner, E., 135, 136
Blenkinsop, H., 105
Blumer, Herbert, 9, 57
body-art, 114
book fairs, 69
Boon, J.A., 161
boundaries
  disciplinary, 49, 50
  national/cultural, 30, 41, 192
  physical, 130, 134
  places and spaces, 20, 29, 130, 139, 140, 196
  symbolic, 68, 70, 130, 134
boundary work, 50
Bourdieu, Pierre, 2, 47, 50, 85, 115, 125, 178
Brazil, Panará people of, 136
bricolage, 118–19, 120
Briggs, Daniel, 191
British social anthropology, 161, 187
Brown, R.H., 154
buildings, 132, 134–5
Burawoy, M., 64, 66

calligraphy, 124, 125
camcorders, 42

cameras, digital, 42
capacities, human, 35
Cappetti, P., 156
CAQDAS software package, 59, 60, 61
Cardiff University, International Academy of Voice, 111
career-narratives, 96, 98
Carey, J. T., 155
carpets, aesthetics, 114–15
case studies, 36, 38
cassette recorders, 42
cautionary tales, 104
ceremonies, 41, 65, 122
  and interaction, 75, 76, 83, 86, 87
Charmaz, C., 63
Chicago School, 45, 64, 65, 151, 195
  ethnographic writing, 155–6
  Second Chicago School, 110
Chicago urban sociology, 133, 138
Chihuly, Dale, 115
Cicourel, A., 177
cinematography, film-based, 42
city neighbourhoods, 129, 151
Clark, C., 83
classroom encounters, 77
Clifford, J., 161
clinical encounters *see* medical encounters
clinical trials, 174, 175, 176, 179–80
  see also randomised controlled trials (RCTs)
closed awareness, 89
Cockayne, E., 150
codes of behaviour, adherence to, 62
coding of data, 59–60, 61, 62
Coffey, A., 10, 60, 160
collecting, ethnographic, 117–18, 145
Colòn opera house, Buenos Aires, 113
Coltrane, John, 102–3
commitments, ethnographic work, 23, 25
  ethical issues, 172, 173–4, 183, 187
  fieldwork, 34–54, 187, 190
communities of practice, 39
community studies, 133, 181
complexity of everyday life, 19, 38, 52, 61, 68
Complication, in narrative, 102
compositional work, 41–2
computer software, 42–3, 52, 59, 60, 138
conduct of ethnographic work, 3, 5, 6, 12, 34, 37, 38, 41, 51, 76, 196
  ethical issues, 180, 182, 183, 184
  see also ethics of ethnography
conferences, 83, 85
  clinical, 179, 180
confessions, 156–7

confidentiality, 179
consent *see* informed consent
constant, principle of, 66
constructivism, 74–5, 93
  see also social constructions
conversation analysis, 43, 48
  interaction research, 73, 76, 78, 79, 80, 82
  see also discourse; interaction; language; speech acts; speech events; speech-exchange
conversion stories, 103
Cooley, Charles Horton, 39
Corbin, J., 57–8, 63
Cortazzi, M., 49
cosmetic surgery, 98
Cottrell, S., 114
courtroom narratives, 107
courtroom settings, formality, 77
covert research, 179, 181
craft artists/workers, 90, 118, 119, 120, 123, 124, 144
craft materials, 119, 120
credibility, 101
Crete, music in, 147–8
Crosnoe, R., 140
cultural anthropology, 12, 24, 47, 49–50
cultural codings, places, 132, 133, 134–5
cultural competence, 22, 115, 138
cultural conventions, 29, 48, 96, 108, 130, 152, 158
  aesthetics, 114, 116
cultural relativism, 173
cultural studies, 49
cultural tourism, 141
culture(s), 44, 82, 109, 131
  enculturation, 39, 105, 121, 122, 128
  of fragmentation, 59, 63
  material *see* material culture

Dakar–Djibouti expedition, French, 109
data analysis and collection, 2, 57, 173, 179
  coding of data, 59–60, 61, 62
  de-contextualising and re-contextualising of data, 60
  ethnography perspectives, 9–10, 11, 15, 30–1
  fieldwork, 38, 43, 51, 52
  interviews, 92, 94, 95–6
  one-dimensional data, 60
  setting data aside, 71
  software, 42–3, 52
  see also research practice
data-management software, 42–3
Dawson, A., 161

death and dying, studies, 88–9, 91
Death at the Parasite Café (Pfohl), 166
deception, 90, 96, 101, 186
de-contextualising of data, 60
deductive research, 35, 56
degradation ceremonies, 87
Delamont, Sara, 32, 186–7
Demetry, D., 139
DeNora, T., 147
Denzin, Norman K., 24, 25, 174, 186
department stores, 131
destination management, 141
developmental logic, 36
Dicks, B., 42
digital recording/technologies 42, 43, 52, 73, 78, 121, 194, 195
  see also technologies, multiple
Dingwall, R., 104, 172, 179
disciplinary boundaries, 49, 50
discourse/discourse-analysis, 29, 41, 43, 48, 65, 73, 74, 78
  adversarial discourse, 81
  scientific discourse, 158
  see also conversation analysis; interaction; language; speech acts; speech-exchange
discursive psychology, 24
distributed subjectivity, 147
Donovan, J.L., 175
Douglas, Mary, 47
dramatic performance, 84–5
dramaturgy/dramaturgical metaphor, 46, 76, 82, 84, 85
  textual representations, 164, 168
dualism, 99, 103
Durheim, Emile, 2, 47

Eaves, Gregg, 147
e-books, 194, 195
Edmondson, R., 154
educational settings, 37
Eggly, S., 175
Ehrenreich, B., 181
Elias, C., 88
Ellis, Carolyn, 164, 166
embodiment/embodied skill, 17, 46, 124, 126
Emerson, R.M., 41, 160
emic analysis, 138
emotions, expression of, 165–6
empiricism, 56
encounters, 7, 73, 76, 79, 92, 95
  focused, 79, 84
  formal, 77–9, 85
  informal, 79–80

encounters, *cont.*
  medical, 75, 78, 80, 82, 85
  pedagogic, 77, 79, 80
  professional, 77, 78
  professional status, and gender, 82
enculturation, 39, 105, 121, 122, 128
engagement, 21–2, 34, 39
Entwistle, J., 116
environmental settings *see* places and spaces
esoteric knowledge, 115, 121
Estates Theatre, Prague, 133
estrangement, 33
'ethics creep,' 172
ethics of ethnography, 172–88
  access issues, 176, 177
  anonymity, 177
  check-lists and box-ticking, dangers of, 184, 186
  clinical trials, 174, 175, 176, 179–80
  commitment, 172, 173–4, 183
  conduct of research, 180, 182, 183, 184
  confidentiality, 179
  contract between researcher and participants, 174–5
  covert research, 179, 180, 181
  deviance, procedural, 184, 185, 186
  ethics committee protocols, 175, 176, 177, 178, 184
  ethnography as ethical form of research, 172–3
  exploratory and investigative work, 181–2
  harm avoidance, 182
  informed consent, 173, 174, 177, 178, 179, 184, 185
  interests of researcher, 180
  inter-personal working relationships, 184
  membership concept, and ethical issues, 176, 177
  participation, 175, 176, 177, 187
  qualitative research, 174, 180, 186, 188
  questionnaires, ethics committee, 177
  randomised controlled trials (RCTs), 174
  regulation, 174–5, 184
  trust, 172, 184
  unethical practices, 178, 180, 181, 187
  withdrawal rights, 175–6, 177
  see also conduct of ethnographic work
ethno-aesthetics, 109, 111, 113, 117
ethno-archaeology, 144
ethnodrama, 163–4
ethnographic abduction, 57, 155
Ethnographic I, The (Ellis), 166
'ethnographic self,' 160, 167, 168
ethnographic writing *see* representations, textual; writing, ethnographic

ethnography
  classic studies, 15, 129, 136–7, 145, 195
  conduct of work *see* conduct of ethnographic work
  depending on observation, 40–1
  depending on participation, 39–40
  ethics *see* ethics of ethnography
  everyday life, 16–33
  generalisability, 36–7
  goals, 28, 55
  and history, 116, 144–5
  meaning, 25
  multi-modality *see* multi-modality
  multiple skills requirement, 43–4
  perspectives, 9–33
  textual self-awareness, 154
  theoretical nature, 44–54
  see also fieldwork, ethnographic
ethnohistory, 144
ethnomedicine, 121
ethnomethodology, 24, 46–7, 76, 93
  aesthetics, 121, 122, 123
ethnomusicology, 109, 149
ethnopoetics, 163, 164
ethnoscience, 47, 121, 122
Evans-Pritchard, Edward, 161
events, 84, 99, 106, 112
  speech events, 60, 95, 100, 107
everyday life, 88, 122, 181
  complexity, 19, 38, 52, 61, 68, 164, 173, 182, 193
  conducted through material artefacts, 18–20
  dialectical, 20–1
  and ethical issues in research, 185, 186
  language, 18, 19, 163
  as locally enacted, 14, 17–18
  music, place in, 147
  navigational properties, 139, 140
  performed, 18, 86
    see also performance/performativity
  physical, 17
  places and spaces, 130, 131, 135, 139, 140
  procedures and processes, 27
  skilful, 16–17
  socially constructed, 14, 21, 28
  symbolic, 17
  taken-for-granted features, 73
  taking place in specific locations, 18
  unfolding over time, 18
evocative ethnographic writing, 164, 165
exchange, 78, 122
  speech-exchange, 79, 80, 81

exotic cultures, 109
expatriates, 140
experience, 13, 22, 23, 105, 132, 165, 170
　see also personal experience
experimental writing, 157–8, 162, 163, 167
exploratory and investigative work, 181–2
extended case method, 63–4
　and grounded theory, 55, 65–6
　limitations, 64–5

face-work, 78, 81
fashion industry, 114, 116
Faulkner, R.R., 111
Faulks, Sebastian, 182
Featherstone, K., 89, 175
felicity, in performance, 113
female anthropologists, 161
fictional works, 14, 155, 166, 169–70, 182
fieldnotes, 41, 42, 51–2, 71, 86
　textual representations, 154, 158, 159–60
fieldwork, ethnographic, 2, 3–4, 14, 15, 36, 118, 129
　accounts and narratives, 104, 108
　commitments, 34–54, 187, 190
　conduct see conduct of ethnographic work
　cyclical nature, 11, 35
　ethical issues, 172, 175
　'fields' of, 4, 11, 12, 25–6, 68
　key features, 11–12
　as multi-modal see multi-modality
　as participatory, 34–5
　as pragmatic, 35–6
　representations, 156, 162
　substance, 10–11
　see also ethnography
figures of speech, 154
Fillmore, San Francisco, 140
fine-art auctioneers, 122, 123
first-person narratives, 159, 165
fishmongers, multi-sensory ethnographic study, 123–4
Fleck, Ludwick, 58
flexible fieldwork, 35
focus groups, 12
Foreman, K.M., 124
formal encounters, 77
Formalism, 23
Foucault, Michel, 69, 70
fragmentation, analytic culture of, 59, 63
'frontstage' and 'backstage' regions, 130
functionalist anthropology, 161

Gabrys, J., 138
Garfinkel, H., 87

Gathings, M.J., 107
Gay y Blasco, P., 171
gaze, 79, 121
Geer, Blanche, 15, 99
Geertz, Clifford, 14, 48, 67, 161–2
Gehry, Frank, 131
geisha, 124
generalisability, 36–7
genetic conditions, 89
gesture, 19, 79, 112
Giardina, M., 174, 186
Gilbert, Nigel, 96
Gimlin, D., 98
Glaser, Barney, 56, 57, 70, 88–9, 90, 91
Glasner, P., 134
glassblowing, 126–8
globalisation, 64, 66
Goffman, Alice, 191
Goffman, Erving, 14, 19, 46, 117, 164, 195–6
　interaction research, 73, 74, 75, 76, 78, 82, 83, 86, 87, 90
　mental health institutions, analysis, 68, 69, 87
　places and spaces, 141–2
　total institution, 68, 70, 91, 144
Goldman, L., 81
Goodall, H.L., 167
Google Earth, 138
Gordon, D., 161
grand theory, 55, 63, 66
grounded theory, 55–64
　and extended case method, 55, 64–5, 65–6
　limitations, 64–5
　and 'qualitative' research, 57, 58

Haase, B., 124
habitus, 85, 86, 125, 178
　see also self-presentation
Haggerty, K., 172
Hall, T., 137–8
Hamilton, L., 119
Hammersley, Martin, 10, 26, 39, 170, 172, 173, 178, 187, 188
Harper, D., 118, 119
hearing, 40
Heath, C., 122, 123
Herzfeld, Michael, 48, 91, 147, 148
heuristic methods, 56, 57–8, 62, 65
historical ethnography, 116, 144–5
Ho, Karen, 191
Hockey, J., 161
Holman Jones, S., 113
homeless people, 140

homosexuality, and 'coming-out' as gay, 89, 90
Horodowich, E., 87–8
hospitals, 68, 69, 85, 88, 107, 149
hotels, 131
Housley, William, 45, 46
Hughes, Everett, 45, 110, 111
Huli people, Papua New Guinea, 81
Human Traces (Faulks), 182
Hunter, K., 107
Husserl, Edmund, 24–5
Hustvedt, Siri, 182
Hymes, Dell, 163
hypermedia, 193–4
hypertext, 193, 194
hypothesis testing, 35, 45, 56, 58

ideal-types, 37, 68, 69, 70, 144, 154
ideas, 55–6, 58, 61, 66, 67, 82
  preliminary, 35, 41
idiographic research, 36
images, 42, 44, 71, 85, 118, 133, 194, 195
imagination, 67, 78
impressionism, 164, 165
in situ, activity in, 4, 17, 61, 86, 92, 129, 185
'in-depth' interviews, 94
indexing of data, 59
individuals, excessive research focused on, 12–13, 108, 139, 177, 180
  accounts and narratives, 98, 105
  and interaction, 75, 76
  see also interviews
inductive logic, 56, 58, 61, 70
information management, 90, 91
informed consent, 173, 174, 177, 178, 179, 184, 185
  see also ethics of ethnography
interaction, 6, 73–91
  ceremonies, 75, 76, 83, 86, 87
  conversation analysis, 73, 76, 78, 79, 80, 82
  and discourse, 73, 74, 78
  encounters *see* encounters
  generic forms, 80
  grammar of, 74
  patterns, 73
  performance, 73, 76, 77, 79, 82, 83–4
  repair (correction of an utterance), 80–1
  rituals, 41, 86, 87
  self-presentation, 77, 81, 83, 84, 85
  situations, 74, 75, 77, 79, 87
  speech-exchange, 78, 80, 81
  strategic, 88, 89–90
  symbolic interactionism, 24, 45–6, 50

interaction order, 6, 19, 67, 73, 74–6, 81, 85, 88, 89, 91
  fieldwork, 46, 48
  Goffman on, 74, 75
  overlooking in conduct of general ethnographic analysis, 76
  studies, 78
interactionist sociology, 39, 45, 51, 66, 73, 74, 78
International Academy of Voice, Cardiff University, 111
interpretive anthropology, 48
interpretivism, 16
interruption, analysis, 81
'interview society,' 94
interviews
  analytic perspectives, 92–3
  correct treatment of data, 95–6
  'in-depth,' 94
  and ethical issues, 176
  life-history, 95, 105, 173–4
  'open-ended,' 94
  over-reliance on/limitations of, 12, 54, 55, 60, 73, 92, 93–4, 95, 185
  and participant observation, 92, 93
  recorded, 38, 76, 93
  rhetoric, 94, 95, 98, 107
  talk, performative action, 99–100
  see also accounts and narratives; individuals, excessive research focused on; 'qualitative' research/inquiry; transcription
intimacy, in nurse–patient relationship, 75
irony, sociological, 154

Jackson, E., 142
James, A., 161
Japanese calligraphy, 124
Japanese painting, 116
Japanese tea-bowl analogy, 29–30
jewellery TV channels, 83–4
Jordan, B.G., 91
Joseph, May, 191

Kassabian, A., 147
Kelly, J., 109
Kendon, A., 79
Kiddey, R., 140
Kirshenblatt-Ginblett, B., 111
Knoblauch, H., 85
knowledge
  aesthetics, 120–1
  distribution of, 89, 91
  embodied, 46

knowledge *cont.*
  esoteric, 115, 121
  local, 47, 124
  medical, 107, 173
  navigational, 140
  scientific, 15, 26, 58
  specialised, 53
  tacit, 116, 121
  taken-for-granted, 58, 64
  working, 119
knowledge-in-action, 47, 121
knowledge-systems, 47, 121–2
Knowles, C., 140
Krieger, S., 159
kula, 69, 122
Kwalitan (software package), 59

laboratory ethnography, 37
Labov, William, 49, 100–1, 102
language/language-use, 26, 29, 73, 92–3, 94, 155
  everyday, 17, 19, 163
  forms and functions, 93
  spoken *see* conversation analysis; discourse
Laurier, E., 138
Leach, Bernard, 115
Lefebvre, Henri, 151
legal proceedings, formality, 77
Lehrer, A., 115
Lévi-Strauss, Claude, 2, 47, 118, 136, 160
Lewis, Oscar, 71
life-history interviews/research, 95, 105, 173–4
liminality, 141
Lincoln, Y., 24, 25
listening, 40
literary turn, 160
lithographs, 110
Littleton, K., 98
localism
  everyday life as locally enacted, 14, 17–18
  local and generic distinction, 65, 66, 69, 70
  local knowledge, 47, 124
  places and spaces, 4, 129, 133, 140
locations, 18, 20, 29
London, comparative study, 142
'Love Supreme, A' (Coltrane), 103
Luckman, T., 25, 46
lying, 89, 90, 91, 101
Lyman, S., 98
Lyon, D., 123

Mackerras, Sir Charles, 104
macro-level perspective, 56, 64, 66

Makagon, D., 42
Malinowski, Bronislaw, 136
Manchester School of anthropology, 63
Manual of Ethnography (Mauss), 117
Marcus, G.E., 161
market-traders, performance, 83
Martens, L., 78
martial arts events, 84
master-classes, 79, 111, 112
material artefacts/goods, 18–20, 21, 29, 38, 44, 49
  aesthetics, 119, 120
material culture, 3, 49, 97
  aesthetics, 117, 118, 120
  ethnography perspectives, 20, 29, 30
  fieldwork, 38, 44, 49
material order, 20, 38, 49, 52
Mauss, Marcel, 1–2, 3, 30, 47, 117–18, 121, 125
Mead, George Herbert, 1, 23, 39
medical encounters, 75, 78, 80, 82, 85
medical institutions, 37
medical knowledge, 107, 173
medicine, voice of, 80, 81
Meek, Barrie, 90
Melbin, M., 136
memory, 97, 145, 165
mental health institutions, analysis (Goffman), 68, 69, 87
metaphors, 71, 154
methodological relativism, 22
micro-ethnography, 117, 121
micro-level perspective, 64, 66, 74, 168
  social interaction, 75–6
'middle-range' theory, 64
middle-range theory, 64
Mills, C. Wright, 97–8
mini-disk recorders, 42
Mishler, E., 80, 81
mobile methods, 137, 138
  see also motion
mobile phone technology, 42
modernism, 15, 27
Moeran, B., 69
Moerman, M., 81, 82
monographs and papers, ethnographic, 36, 37, 41–2, 102–3, 118, 191, 192, 193, 195
  textual representations and ethnographic writing, 153, 159, 161, 162, 171
  see also publishing considerations; representations, textual; writing, ethnographic
moral calculus, 89
moral order, 78

mortification of the self (Goffman), 69, 87
Mosko, M.S., 136
motion, 129, 137–9, 140
   see also mobile methods
motive, 97–8
movement/mobility see motion
Mozart, Wolfgang Amadeus, 133
Mulkay, Michael, 96, 158
multi-modality, 30–1, 37–8, 42
   aesthetics, 117, 119
   places and spaces, 148, 151
Murphy, E., 172, 179
museums, 130
music festivals, 141
musical performance, 79, 84, 96
   see also opera performance/opera singers
musical settings, 146–7, 149
mythic structures, in narratives, 102–3

Nakamura, F., 124
narratives/narrative analysis, 6, 43, 48, 49, 53–4, 101, 138
   autobiographical/biographical narratives, 95, 98, 105, 106, 124, 156, 165–6, 181
   career-narratives, 96, 98
   events/speech events, 60, 95, 99, 100, 106, 107
   fieldwork, 104, 108
   first-person narratives, 159, 165
   genres of narrative, 103
   making a case, 107
   mythic structures in narratives, 102–3
   personal experience, 87, 94, 95, 97, 99–100, 102, 105
   plausibility, 96, 97, 101
   representations, 156, 163
   rhetoric, 94, 95, 98, 107
   speech acts, 93, 94, 95, 105, 108
   stories, 100–1, 102, 103, 104
   structural properties, 100–1, 102
   truth, in accounts of informants, 91, 96–7, 101
natural science, 15, 26, 82–3
   Western science versus other knowledge-systems, 121–2
naturalistic writing, 167
navigation, 139, 140
neglected situation, 74
neo-conservatism, American, 174
Neumann, M., 42, 168
noise, ubiquitous, 146, 149, 150
non-verbal communication, 19
novelty, 4, 6, 116, 157

numerical analysis, 12
nurse–patient relationship, intimacy in, 75

observation, 53, 54, 82
   absence of truly observational analysis, 75, 76
   analytic perspectives, 56, 57
   ethnography depending on, 40–1
   interaction, 75, 76, 85–6
   see also participant observation
Omarakana, Trobriand village of, 136
O'Neill, Dennis, 111
open access publishing, 191–2
'open-ended' interviews, 94
open-mindedness, 35
opera performance/opera singers, 79, 96, 132
   accounts and narratives, 103, 104
   aesthetics, 111, 112, 113, 114, 115
   rehearsals, 143–4
   schedules, 143
   'straight' theatre versus opera performance, 148
   Welsh National Opera (WNO) company, 96, 103, 142–3
organisational encounters, 77
orientalism, 31
Orientation phases, of stories, 102
othering, 31, 32
   'taking role of the other,' 23, 28, 33, 35, 39, 78
other-initiated repair, 80

Padavic, I., 179
pageants of performance, 69, 84
Panará people, of Brazil, 136
panopticon (Foucault), 69
paradigms, 49, 50
Park, Robert, 138
Parrotta, K., 107
participant observation, 12, 25, 35, 51, 79, 86, 183
   and interviews, 92, 93
   observer-as-participant and participant-as-observer, 39–40
participation
   ethical issues, 175, 176, 177, 187
   ethnography depending on, 39–40
   fieldwork, 34–5
Paulme, Denise, 1
Payne Whitney Psychiatric Clinic, 182
Peckham, London, 142

pedagogic encounters, 77, 79, 80
performance/performativity, 82, 93
　aesthetics, 110, 112, 112–13, 122
　clinical trials, 179–80
　collective, 148
　competences, 86
　cultural performance, 104–5
　dramatic, 84–5
　in everyday life, 18, 86, 104–5
　felicity in performance, 113
　interaction, 73, 76, 77, 79, 83–4, 86
　interview talk, performative action, 99–100
　musical, 79, 84, 96
　pageants of performance, 69, 84
　see also opera performance/opera singers
performative architecture, 134
personal experience, 7, 54, 167, 168, 169, 170, 181
　accounts and narratives, 87, 94, 95, 97, 99–100, 102, 105
　analytic perspectives, 68, 70–1
　see also experience
Petryna, Adriana, 191
Pfohl, J., 166
phenomenology, 24, 25, 46, 93
pilgrimages, 141
Pinch, T., 83
placebos, in clinical trials, 173
places and spaces, 18, 20, 29, 129–52, 155
　architecture, 131, 133
　art galleries, 131–2
　boundaries, 20, 29, 130, 139, 140, 196
　buildings, 132, 134–5
　Chicago urban sociology, 133, 138
　colour, 135, 136
　cultural codings, 132, 133, 134–5
　cultural significance, 131
　everyday life, 130, 131, 135, 139, 140
　Goffman on, 141–2
　light and dark, 134, 136
　localism, 4, 129, 133, 140
　motion, 129, 137–9
　multiple uses of space, 135
　public spaces, 130, 135
　shopping centres/shops, 131, 135
　social class, 142
　soundscapes, 40, 42, 70, 146–7, 149, 151
　streets, 130, 135, 136, 150
　time and timescapes, 129, 130, 136, 142, 144
　tourism, 132–3
　work settings, 130, 135, 144
　see also research settings
plausibility, of accounts, 96, 97, 101

Plummer, Ken, 90, 97
poetry, 163
police work, 135–6, 139
politeness, in encounters, 78, 88
polyvocal text, 158–9
positivism, 14–15, 24, 25
postmodernism, 13, 14, 15, 27, 64, 162–3
potlatch, 69
Potter, J., 48
pottery, 114, 124
Powell, H.A., 136
pragmatism
　American pragmatist philosophy of science, 55
　analytic perspectives, 55, 61, 65, 70
　and Chicago School, 65
　pragmatic nature of fieldwork, 35–6
Prague, 133
predictability, 14, 41
　unpredictability, 184, 188
preliminary ideas, 35, 41
presentations, 84–5
Primitive Classification (Durkheim), 2
procedural approaches, 72
processions, 141
professional encounters, 77, 78
Prokos, A., 179
Propp, V., 156
prose, 163
Psathas, G., 140
public spaces, 130, 135
publishing considerations, 12, 58, 62, 83, 108, 151, 178, 190, 194, 195
　open access publishing, 191–2
　see also monographs and papers, ethnographic; representations, textual; writing, ethnographic
pure theory, 56

qualitative GIS, 138
qualitative research/inquiry, 2, 9, 25, 54
　accounts and narratives, 92, 93
　coding of data, 59–60, 61, 62
　ethical issues, 174, 180, 186, 188
　and grounded theory, 57, 58
　popularity, 3, 76, 189
　shortcomings/limitations, 12–13, 14, 15, 22, 28, 37–8, 48, 76, 93, 189–90
　see also interviews
quantitative research, 38
Quinney, R., 168

radiology, ethnography of, 85
randomised controlled trials (RCTs), 173, 175
　see also clinical trials

RCTs (randomised controlled trials), 173, 175
  see also clinical trials
realist writing, 155, 156, 164, 165, 167
re-contextualisation of data, 60
recorded interviews, 38
recording devices, 151–2
  see also digital recording
reductionism, 68
Reed-Danahay, D., 165
reflective practice, 27
reflexivity, 4–5, 26, 27, 158, 165, 166
relativism, 26
Renaissance Venetian Republic, speech management, 87–8
repair-work (correction of an utterance), 80–1
representations, textual, 7, 153–71, 193
  autoethnography, 157, 162, 165, 166, 168, 186
  conventional, 153
  crisis of representation, 161
  ethnodrama, 163–4
  fieldnotes see fieldnotes
  literary turn, 160
  monographs see monographs and papers, ethnographic
  polyvocal text, 158–9
  textual conventions, 153–4, 155
  textual turn, 159, 160
  textual variation, 153, 170–1
  see also monographs and papers, ethnographic; writing, ethnographic
reputational stories, 104
research
  analytic perspectives, 9–10, 11, 55–6
  biomedical, 174–5, 176
  correct teaching of methods, 190–1
  covert, 179, 180, 181
  deductive, 35, 56
  ethnography perspectives, 15–16
  evaluation of ethnographic research, 170
  goals, 22, 23
  hypothesis testing, 35, 45, 56, 58
  inductive, 56
  origins of ideas, 55–6
  procedures, 183–4
  self-indulgent, 188, 191
  settings see research settings
  social world, engagement with, 21–2
  unanticipated, 179–80
  see also data analysis and collection; qualitative research/inquiry; social research; social science

Research Assessment Exercise/Research Excellence Framework, UK, 192
research ethics see ethics of ethnography
research settings, 109, 132, 155
  analytic perspectives, 57, 65, 69
  fieldwork, 36, 37
  places and spaces, 145, 146, 149
  see also places and spaces
research-in-action, 195
restaurants, 131, 139
rhetoric, 94, 95, 98, 107, 154
  clinical trials, 179–80
rhetorical devices, 158
rhetorical induction, 154
rhetorical reductionism, 169
rhythmanalysis, 151
Rice, T., 149
Richardson, Laurel, 157, 163, 168
Riessman, C.K., 49
rites of passage, 87, 134, 141, 150
rituals, 41, 86, 87, 141
rizitika tragoudhia (Cretan musical genre), 147–8
Romanticism, 7, 23, 100, 157
  Romantic fallacy, 153
Roth, Julius, 69, 70
Ryen, A., 172

Sacks, Harvey, 14, 41, 47, 88, 90
Said, Edward, 31
Sanjek, R., 159–60
Saunders, B.F., 85
Schofield, J., 140
schools, 37
Schültz, Alfred, 24–5, 39, 46
science
  American pragmatist philosophy of, 55
  ethnoscience, 47, 121, 122
  natural see natural science
  social worlds, 82–3
  see also social sciences
Science and Technology Studies, 157–8
science of the concrete, 160
Scott, M. B., 98
screenprints, 110
sculptors, 110
Second Chicago School, 110
self-correction, 80–1
self-initiated repair, 80
Self-Made Man (Vincent), 181
self-presentation, 77, 81, 83, 84, 85, 117
semiotic order, 19
semiotics, 24
sensitising concepts, 9, 57–8

sensory ethnography, 146
sensory mapping, 151–2
sentimental realism, 167, 168, 169
settings, ethnographic *see* places and spaces; research settings
Seyer-Ochi, I., 140
shopping centres/shops, 131, 135
signs/signification, 19
silence, 150
Silverman, D., 94, 95, 180
Simmel, Georg, 74, 88
singers *see* opera performance/opera singers
single-method designs, 38
Singleton, J., 124
situations, 74, 75, 77, 79, 87
skill, 16–17, 22, 126
  multiple skills requirement of ethnography, 43–4
Smith, Dorothy, 14
Smith, R., 137–8
social action, 72, 93, 129
  aesthetics, 121, 125–6
  ethnography perspectives, 13–14, 16, 17, 18, 21
  interviews as form of, 97
  places and spaces, 130
  representation, 153
social actors
  accounts and narratives, 92, 100, 105, 106
  aesthetics, 116, 117, 120
  analytic perspectives, 66, 68, 71
  and ethical issues, 174, 176, 183, 185
  ethnography perspectives, 16–17, 22, 29
  fieldwork, 35, 43, 46
  individual, 20–1, 28, 94, 105
    see also individuals, excessive research focused on
  interaction, 74, 76, 78, 88
  networks of, 88
  places and spaces, 129
  places and spaces, use of, 138, 139–40, 141, 142, 145
  Romantic view of, 100
social analysis, 4–5, 21, 93
  engagement with social world, 21–2, 34, 39
  everyday life as socially constructed, 14, 21, 28
  importance, 14, 16, 68, 70
  social action *see* social action
  social actors *see* social actors
  social institutions, 41, 57, 130
  social order, 17, 18, 22, 38, 46, 76

social analysis, *cont.*
  social organisation, 13–14, 38, 73, 92, 129, 153, 161
  see also interaction; social constructions; social life; social research; social sciences; social worlds
social anthropology, 12, 24, 47, 49–50
social constructions, 46, 106, 129
social encounters *see* encounters
social interaction *see* interaction
social justice, 186
social life, 41, 68, 93, 195
  ethnography perspectives, 13, 17–18, 19, 22
  places and spaces, 137, 151
  representations, 158
  temporal flow, 151
social phenomenology, 46
social research, 3, 5, 27, 58, 106, 170, 172, 191
  accounts and narratives, 97, 106
  conventional, flaws of, 174
  ethical issues, 174, 177, 183, 185, 186
    see also ethics of ethnography
  ethnography perspectives, 11, 12, 13, 15, 21, 22, 23, 24, 26, 27, 32
  fieldwork, 39, 46, 51
    see also qualitative research/inquiry; research; social sciences
social sciences, 44, 56, 58, 99, 182, 189, 192, 195
  ethnography perspectives, 13–14, 22, 26, 27
  see also natural science; research practice; social research
social worlds, 27–8, 38
  accounts and narratives, 99, 100, 108
  aesthetics, 110, 123, 126
  engagement with, 21–2, 34, 39
  ethical issues, 173, 182–3
  events in, 99
  general ethnographic accounts, 76
  places and spaces, 129
  representations *see* representations, textual
  science, 82–3
  sensory exploration, 40–1
socialisation, 39, 122, 124
sociology
  of art, 109, 110
  community studies, 133, 181
  constructivist approaches, 74–5
  discursive, 51
  grand themes of theory, 64

sociology *cont.*
  interactionist, 39, 45, 51, 66, 73, 74, 78
  'sonic,' 147
  theory, 51
'sonic' sociology, 147
Sorrows of an American, The (Hustvedt), 182
soundscapes, 40, 42, 70, 146–7, 149, 151
spaces *see* places and spaces
spatio-temporal order, 20
specialised knowledge, 53
speech acts, 65, 93, 94, 95, 105, 108
speech events, 60, 95, 100, 107
speech-exchange, 78, 79, 80, 81
spoiled identities, 117
Spooner, B., 114–15
Spradley, J. P., 92
sprezzatura (appearance of effortless competence), 117
stability, 14, 41, 161, 168
Stem Cell Bank, United Kingdom, 134
Stephens, N., 134
'stethoscopic listening,' 149
stories, 100–1, 102, 103, 104, 145
strangeness, 32–3
strategic interaction, 88, 89–90
strategy, 65
Stratford-upon-Avon, Shakespeare's house, 141
Strauss, Anselm L., 15, 56, 57–8, 63, 70, 88–9, 90, 91
'stream of consciousness' literary work, 159, 169
streets, 130, 135, 136, 150
structuralism/structuralist anthropology, 47–8
structuring forms *see* places and spaces
suspicion awareness, 89
symbolic interactionism, 24, 45–6, 50, 93, 168
symbolic nature of everyday life, 17
systematic approach, data analysis, 15

tacit knowledge, 116, 121
tact, 88, 89–90, 91
taken-for-granted categories, 32, 33, 35, 64
Tales of the Field (Van Maanen), 156
Taussig, M., 160
Tavory, I., 64
Taylor, S., 98
teachers, 77, 79, 112
techniques, 2, 17, 22
  aesthetics, 112, 121, 122, 123, 124, 125
technological reductionism, 53
technologies, multiple, 41–3, 52, 70
temporal and spatial systems, 20

temporal flows, 18
Tesch, R., 59
textbook knowledge, 8, 10, 16, 72
  grounded theory, 55, 57, 58
  methods textbooks, 2, 9, 12, 59, 62, 192
textual conventions, 153–4, 155
textual turn, 159, 160
The Ethnograph (software package), 59
theory of ethnography, 15, 16, 44–54
theory-building, 61–2, 70, 71
thick description/media, 28, 29, 67, 72, 76
Thomas, Julia, 74, 75, 141
Thrift, Nigel, 134
Tilly, C., 98
time/timescapes, 18, 20
  places and spaces, 129, 130, 136, 142, 144
Timmermans, S., 64, 173
tools, 119–20, 127
total institution, 68, 70, 91, 144
tourism, 132–3
tournaments of value, 69, 84, 122–3
'traditional' ethnographic strategy, 41
Traianou, A., 172, 173, 187, 188
transcription, 41, 52, 53, 63, 71, 82
Trobriand village, Omarakana, 136
trust, 172, 184
truth, in accounts of informants, 91, 96–7, 101
tuberculosis hospitals, ethnographic research at, 69
typologies, 70

United Kingdom, Stem Cell Bank, 134
unpredictability, 184, 188
urban and organisational settings *see* places and spaces
urban ethnographies, 129, 135
urban legends, 102
urban sociology, Chicago, 133, 138
urbanism, 150–1

Vail, D. A., 114
valuations, 123
value
  aesthetic values, 116
  exchange values, 116
  hierarchies of, 115–16
  kula ceremonial exchange of valued good, 122
  tournaments of, 69, 84, 122–3
value chains, 69
value-judgements, 115
Van Gennep, Arnold, 87
Van Maanen, J., 156

Vannini, P., 194–5
video-recordings, 42
vignettes, 154–5
Vincent, Norah, 181
visual culture, 44
visual materials, 38, 52–3
visual representation systems, 48
voice expression, 158, 159
voice of medicine, 80, 81
voice production, 111, 112
voice recorders, digital, 42
Voysey Paun, Margaret, 96

Wardle, H., 171
Weaver, A., 60, 193
Weber, Max, 24, 46
Welsh National Opera (WNO) company, 96, 103, 142–3, 176
West, C., 82
Weston, V., 91
Wetherell, M., 48
Whyton, T., 103
wine appreciation, 115
Wirth, Louis, 150

Wolf, M., 160
Woolf, Virginia, 169
work settings, 130, 135, 144
working knowledge, 119
working relationships with informants, 23
working the angles, in glassmaking, 126
writing, ethnographic, 153, 154
 confessions, 156–7
 emotions, expression of, 165–6
 evocative, 164, 165
 experimental, 157–8, 162, 163, 167
 literary forms, influence on, 156, 158, 160
 new forms, 157, 168
 realist forms, 155, 156, 164, 165, 167
 scientific, 157
 styles, 157, 161–2, 167
 see also autobiographical/biographical narratives; publishing considerations; representations, textual

Zenker, O., 161
Zerubavel, E., 144